POLITICAL HOLINESS

D0869124

Theology and Liberation Series

Editorial Committee

Leonardo Boff, Sergio Torres, Gustavo Gutiérrez, Jose Comblin, Ronaldo Muñoz, Enrique Dussel, José Oscar Beozzo, Pedro Trigo, Ivone Gebara, Jon Sobrino, Virgil Elizondo, Juan Luis Segundo

Ecumenical Consultant
Julio de Santa Ana

Books previously published in the series:

THEOLOGY AND LIBERATION SERIES

Pedro Casaldáliga
José María Vigil

POLITICAL HOLINESS

With a Foreword by
ERNESTO CARDENAL
and an Epilogue by
GUSTAVO GUTIÉRREZ

Translated from the Spanish by
Paul Burns and Francis McDonagh

ORBIS BOOKS

Maryknoll, New York 10545

The Catholic Foreign Mission Society of America (Maryknoll) recruits and trains people for overseas missionary service. Through Orbis Books, Maryknoll aims to foster the international dialogue that is essential to mission. The books published, however, reflect the opinions of their authors and are not meant to represent the official position of the society.

Published originally in Nicaragua by Editorial Envío, Managua, under the title *Espiritualidad de la Liberación*.

Original edition © CESEP—São Paulo and Ediciones Paulinas, 1993

English translation © Burns & Oates/Search Press Limited, 1994

First published in this translation in Great Britain in 1994 by Burns & Oates (under the title *The Spirituality of Liberation*) and in the United States of America by Orbis Books, Maryknoll, NY 10545-0308.

Typeset in Great Britain. Printed and bound in the United States of America

ORBIS/ISBN 0-88344-979-X

Theology and Liberation Series

In the years since its emergence in Latin America, liberation theology has challenged the church to a renewal of faith lived in solidarity with the poor and oppressed. The effects of this theology have spread throughout the world, inspiring in many Christians a deeper life of faith and commitment, but for others arousing fears and concerns.

Its proponents have insisted that liberation theology is not a subtopic of theology but really a new way of doing theology. The Theology and Liberation Series is an effort to test that claim by addressing the full spectrum of Christian faith from the perspective of the poor.

Thus, volumes in the Series are devoted to such topics as God, Christ, the church, revelation, Mary, the sacraments, and so forth. But the Series will also explore topics seldom addressed by traditional theology, though vital to Christian life — aspects of politics, culture, the role of women, the status of ethnic minorities. All these are examined in the light of faith lived in a context of oppression and liberation.

The work of over one hundred theologians, pastoral agents, and social scientists from Latin America, and supported by some one hundred and forty bishops, the Theology and Liberation Series is the most ambitious and creative theological project in the history of the Americas.

Addressed to the universal church, these volumes will be essential reading for all those interested in the challenge of faith in the modern world. They will be especially welcomed by all who are committed to the cause of the poor, by those engaged in the struggle for a new society, by all those seeking to establish a more solid link between faith and politics, prayer and action.

Contents

PART ONE
THE SPIRIT OF LIBERATION

PART TWO
THE LIBERATNG SPIRIT OF JESUS CHRIST

Abbreviations and Short Forms

AA   *Apostolicam Actuositatem.* Vatican II, Decree on the Apostolate of the Laity

AG   Ad Gentes. Vatican II, Decree on the Church's Missionary Activity

CD   *Christus Dominus.* Vatican II, Decree on the Bishops' Pastoral Office in the Church

DH   *Dignitatis Humanae.* Vatican II, Declaration on Religious Freedom

EN   *Evangelii Nuntiandi.* Apostolic Exhortation of Pope Paul VI

GS   *Gaudium et Spes.* Vatican II, Pastoral Constitution on the Church in the Modern World

LG   *Lumen Gentium.* Vatican II, Dogmatic Constitution on the Church

Medellín   Second General Conference of Latin American Bishops, held in Medellín, Colombia, in 1968. Translations of the final documents are in vol. 2 of *The Church in the Present-day Transformation of Latin America.* Washington, D.C.: USCC, 1970. Part also in A. T. Hennelly, ed., *Liberation Theology: A Documentary History.* Maryknoll, N.Y.: Orbis Books, 1990

NAe   *Nostra Aetate.* Vatican II, Declaration on the Relationship of the Church to Non-Christian Religions

OT   *Optatam Totius.* Vatican II, Decree on Priestly Formation

PL   *Patrologie Cursus Completus, Series Latina.* Ed. J. P. Migne. Paris, 1844–55

PO   *Presbyterorum Ordinis.* Vatican II, Decree on the Ministry and Life of Priests

Puebla   Third General Conference of Latin American

	Bishops, held in Puebla, Mexico, in 1979. Translation of the "Final Document" in J. Eagleson and P. Scharper, eds, *Puebla and Beyond.* Maryknoll, N.Y.: Orbis Books, 1980; also in *Puebla: Evangelization at Present and in the Future of Latin America.* Washington, D.C.: NCCB; Slough: St Paul Publications; London: CIIR, 1980.
RLT	*Revista Latinoamericana de Teología.* San Salvador
RM	*Redemptoris Missio.* Encyclical Letter of Pope John Paul II
Santo Domingo	Fourth General Conference of Latin American Bishops, held in Santo Domingo in October 1992. Translation of the final documents in *Santo Domingo: Conclusions.* Washington, D.C.: USCC; London: CAFOD and CIIR, 1993
SRS	*Sollicitudo Rei Socialis.* Encyclical Letter of Pope John Paul II
ST	St Thomas Aquinas, *Summa Theologiae*
UR	*Unitatis Redintegratio.* Vatican II, Decree on Ecumenism

Foreword

The theology of liberation had to produce a spirituality of liberation. In effect it has done so. This is the subject of this book.

This is, as one might have expected, a new spirituality, different from the traditional spirituality in which we older people were brought up. It is also a specifically Latin-American spirituality. Like the church itself, it is no less universal for being local. And it is a realist and not a theoretical spirituality.

This spirituality is radically different from that of those who close their eyes to society and politics: that is, to the poor, to the ever-widening abyss betwen rich and poor. This means that it is different from the bourgeois spirituality of the rich and the ruling classes—though these also contain poor, blind led by blind guides, poor people who also shut their eyes, to poverty, and to themselves.

This spirituality says radical things, and the reader will find them in this book: such as that the poor are the only sacrament for salvation. And that people are divided not into believers and unbelievers, but according to their attitude to the poor.

I maintain that theology of liberation means the same as theology of revolution. And therefore this is a spirituality of revolution—understanding revolution in a far more transcendent sense than the late October Revolution.

It is also—and why not say so?—a spirituality of socialism. Or, in other words, the spirituality of a universal utopia.

It is, too, a political spirituality. It was Gandhi who said that those who believe that religion has nothing to do with politics have no idea of what religion is.

This is a spirituality of consecration to the poor, conversion to the poor—a class option.

It is a practical spirituality, uniting contemplation and action. A militant spirituality, not in a party sense, but militant for the Reign of God. It is closely tied to Jesus, but to the authentic Jesus: historical and political, not the abstract, manipulated, betrayed Jesus, in whose name people have preached what he most opposed.

This new spirituality is also a rediscovery of God: of the true God, distinguished from all the false gods who have been preached to us over the past five hundred years in Latin America.

In reality, though, this is not a spirituality of Jesus, nor of God, but of the Reign—the Reign of God, which is love, justice, peace, brotherhood, sisterhood, freedom, forgiveness. Whether we believe or not in Jesus or in God, we must believe in this Reign.

This is an incarnated spirituality, but in the same way as the incarnation of God is not an abstract incarnation—simply God becoming man—but becoming poor, taking flesh among the outcast.

In our time and place, contemplation is different too: contemplation in liberative action, in reality and in the present, in the changing circumstances of our peoples. It is a contemplation, as this book rightly says, "with the Bible and the newspaper"—contemplation based on analysis of reality; and also a committed contemplation.

I believe this book covers all the subjects we might expect to find in a book entitled *The Spirituality of Liberation*, and also that many others readers might not expect to find in a book with this title.

As a final thought on the spirituality of liberation, I should say that Léon Bloy's words, "the only sadness is not being saints," are still valid. What has changed now is the type of sanctity.

Ernesto Cardenal

Preface

The structure of this book is very simple.

In the Prologue, Pedro Casaldáliga sets out the purpose, the why and the wherefore, of this volume.

In the Introduction, we establish the basic notions of "spirit" and "spirituality," while at the same time arguing for some general principles that need to be borne in mind, and that govern the framework of the two main parts.

Part One considers, under various headings, the spirituality of liberation according to the manner of Latin-American spirituality, the spiritual nature of the people, the current of spirituality that the Spirit, culture and history have poured out over the continent.

Then Part Two, under similar headings, describes the spirituality of liberation according to the manner of the Latin-American spirit empowered explicitly by the Spirit of Jesus, the Christian spirituality of liberation.

Classical treatises of spirituality were often ordered according to the different "virtues." The sections in these Parts One and Two in a way set out the "virtues" of the spirituality of liberation. We have treated each section differently, sometimes very differently, as the nature of the content and its particular requirements dictated.

The "Constants . . ." and "Seven Marks . . ." seek to provide a summary of the vision that has inspired the whole. The Bibliography has been limited to works dealing with the spirituality of liberation and to Latin-American authors or those associated with our spirituality.

The Epilogue, being written by Gustavo Gutiérrez, needs no further recommendation, and we express our heartfelt thanks for his contribution.

As this book has been conceived not as a thesis, but as an account springing from experience and as a "manual" of spirituality, it does not have to be read straight through; readers can start it and return to it at the sections that appeal to them most.

Prologue

Questions on the Ascent and Descent of Mount Carmel

John of the Cross, poet and mystic, companion of Teresa of Jesus in holiness and reform, a good teacher of Christian spirituality from being a good disciple of the Teacher, wrote his treatise on spirituality on the basis of the three great poems he composed, giving a divine meaning to the effusions of human love: "On a dark night," the "Spiritual Canticle" and "O living flame of love." Explaining them, as plainly as he could, even knowing how impossible the task was, and using the Bible, in his explanations, with the freedom typical of commentators of the good old days of allegorical interpretation, the saint from Fontiveros described the steps on the "ascent" to holiness, through the "nights" of the senses and the spirit, toward union with the Beloved, in the ineffable fusion of the "living flame."

Without betraying the untouchable beauty of true poetry, since "a rose is a rose is a rose" and it should not be touched, without claiming to describe in detail what could be lived only in the experience of faith, in response to requests from the "souls" he directed or with whom he shared the same arduous ascent, he revealed himself in honest autobiography.

As a Carmelite, it was natural for him to place this itinerary leading to God on Mount Carmel, so lavishly exalted by the Bible. If he had been a modern Latin American and had lived through the continental councils of Medellín, Puebla and Santo Domingo, John of the Cross might well—without betraying either holiness or poetry or orthodoxy—have written, as one possibility, the "Ascent of Machu-Pichu": the ascent and the descent. . . .

In the climate of Latin America and in the light of these councils, so much our own—in the light of and impelled by the demands of the gospel and its poor who fill the life and death of our peoples and the pastoral mission and martyrdom of our churches—we too dare to write poems and to "gloss" them freely. To our own air, to the Wind of the Living God and of the harsh Andes; with the freedom the Spirit gives us in the wide plurality and solidarity of this unique spirituality we have, which is the spirituality of Jesus of Nazareth.

Saving all distances between us, and with all due respect—mutual respect. . . .

I had for a time been concerned, involved, with the spirituality of liberation: wanting to see more books about it, more conferences, more theologizing—even knowing that spirituality is life and certainly not a technical process—when Gustavo Gutiérrez's now classic work on this spirituality, *We Drink from Our Own Wells*, appeared, and this book inspired me to write a poem of eight stanzas, "from Brazilian Amazonia," in times of trial and of "invincible *criollo* hope."

On the subject of trials, it is worth remembering that St John of the Cross lived buffeted by the daily misunderstanding of his own brethren in religion, was imprisoned and vilified, and had to defend himself, like so many other saints of the period, from the suspicions and tortures of the Inquisition. The spirituality, pastoral practice and theology of liberation were bound to be tried in these same fires. For their own good, since we know, in faith, that the sign of the cross is the best quality stamp on any Christian undertaking.

This poem is entitled "Questions on the Ascent and Descent of Mount Carmel" and I dedicate it: "To Gustavo Gutiérrez, spiritual teacher on the high plateau of Liberation, for his Latin American journey, *We Drink from Our Own Wells*." It goes like this:

"Por aquí ya no hay
    camino."
	"No through way here
	    now."

¿Hasta dónde no lo habrá?	To where is there no way?

Si no tenemos su vino
¿La chicha no servirá?

If we don't have their wine,
Will *chicha* not do?

¿Llegarán a ver el dia
cuantos con nostoros van?
¿Cómo haremos compañía
so no tenemos ni pan?

Will those who go with us
Live to see the day?
How can we have a party
If we haven't any bread?

¿Por dónde iréis hasta el
cielo
si por la tierra no vais?
¿Para quién vais al
Carmel,
si subís y no bajáis?

What path will you take
to heaven, other than earth?
For whom will you go to
Carmel
If you go up and don't come
down?

¿Sanarán viejas heridas
las alcuzas de la ley?
¿Son banderas o son vidas
las batallas de este Rey?

Will the balm of the law
Heal our old wounds?
Are this King's battles
Fought with flags or lives?

¿Es la curia o es la calle
donde grana la misión?
Si dejáis que el Viento calle
¿qué oréis en la oración?

Does mission find its harvest
In the curia or in the street?
If you let the Wind be still
What will you hear in prayer?

Si no oís la voz del Viento
¿qué palabras llevaréis?
¿Que daréis por
sacramento
so no os dais en lo que deis?

Without hearing the Voice
of the Wind
What words will you bear?
What will your offering be
If not yourselves in what
you give?

Si cedéis ante el Imperio
la Esperanza y la Verdad
¿quién proclamará el
misterio
de la entera Libertad?

If you let Hope and Truth
Yield to the Empire's sway,
Who will tell the mystery
Of the fullness of freedom?

Si el Señor es Pan y Vino	If the Lord is Bread and
y el camino por do andáis,	Wine
si "al andar se hace	And the Way that we walk,
camino"	And "paths are made by
¿qué camino esperáis?	walking,"
	What paths do you hope to
	find?

The title of this poem is "Questions . . ." because we ask questions on our quest: coming down and going up. Questioning ourselves, we move toward our inner selves; questioning God, we move toward God; questioning our brothers and sisters, we move to them. Questioning and answering.

These questions, furthermore, with their charge of insinuated reply, seek to point out the justifications we have—in these parts—for the variants in our spirituality compared to (sometimes in opposition to) other spiritualities: from other geographical and historical contexts; from other social milieux; from times now past, perhaps; colonizing, maybe, or depersonalizing and alienating—spiritualities, in any case, that are less our own.

"In Latin America, in the whole of the Third World," I once wrote when making personal notes for what was to become this book, "we have the right and the duty to be ourselves, here and now. And to live our 'hour' in a Christian way. And to make History and to make it Reign. To be here the universal church of Jesus, but with an indigenous face, Indio-Afro-Latino-American. (Woman's, young person's, peasant's, worker's, intellectual or artist's, militant or pastoral agent's . . ., I should add today.) We feel ourselves sensitized by the spirit of Jesus, in the midst of the poor (becoming steadily poorer and in greater numbers, in the last few years) and in the face of the History we have to live ("the end of history" for some complacent people; the beginning, at last, of the one, together, human History, for us, in the hands of the hungering masses). And we feel ourselves infected with the Freedom that is the Spirit. Therefore, we want to and must bear witness to the Crucified Risen Lord among these our peoples, oppressed and struggling for their liberation; therefore, we want to walk arm-in-arm with so many companions on the way and in hope." Christians and non-Christians, I should have to add today, who seek and struggle; still more now that certain utopias or their falsifications have been tumbled and we are being dragged back by the pretended victory of certain topias.

At that time, I also noted: "Liberation has its own sociology, its pedagogy, its theology. Great names, crucial books. Liberation also has, above all, its spirituality. It was just from the spirituality of liberation, lived out day by day, in poverty, in service, in struggle and in martyrdom, that the theology of liberation arose, which has systematically reflected on this life and its motivations in faith (the mystery of the God of Jesus in the mystery of this continental 'journey'). This is what our most qualified theologians bear witness to."

I even went on to state the obvious: "The features of this spirituality cannot be so 'original' that they bear no resemblance to the genuine Christian spirituality of all time. The Spirit is one alone at every moment and in every place. These features are different because they set the (only) Christian spirituality in a different time and place. In order to respond to the signs of a time of captivity and of liberation, (these features) will have to become (explicitly, effectively) liberative; and, in order to respond to the signs of the place called Latin America, they will have to become Latin American."

Dreaming already of a book of "Spirituality of Liberation," which has finally become a written reality thanks mainly to the head, heart and dogged Aragonese persistence of José María Vigil, I wanted the book to be "a shared brotherly spiritual reading; an introduction to other bigger books and other quests; a heartfelt echo of so much Latin American spirituality (and Caribbean, of course, because, well or badly christened, Latin America is the continent with its islands) lived, today above all, but in the past too, by our anonymous holy men and women, by our prophets and martyrs, by so many Christian communities struggling to re-experience in Latin American guise the evangelical beauty and crucified features (and Easter joy) of the Acts of the Apostles." Today—and this book is a good witness—I should also explicitly mention the holy indigenous and black patriarchs and matriarchs, the heroic village women—Indians, blacks, *mestizas, criollas*—those who work in fields, mines, industries, rivers, the crowds of holy innocents—prematurely martyrs—and that whole legion of sons and daughters of God, one but with many names, who go to make up the whole of Latin American spirituality, before and after 1492.

The book should be "a guide for travellers," I concluded, because "the path, in any case, would always be the Way of Truth and Life, Jesus Christ our Lord." More so today, we want this book to be a guide, no more: accessible and friendly; not to be studied but experienced, and not to be left on the shelves; a sort of *vademecum* for pilgrims of liberation, a manual to be used in the headquarters and trenches by the brothers and sisters fighting for the Reign. We hope this is not too much to claim for it. The purpose we designed it for, however, would not allow us to write a superficial book, or to leave out an adequate philosophical and theological grounding. So the book carries its weight of analysis and ordering, even though the two central parts are developed on more descriptive, experiential and everyday lines.

The "Questions . . ." poem can be understood without further commentary; however, we can "gloss" the stanzas—as St John of the Cross would say—and show that, in short, they mean that we have to "come down and go up," go to God and come to the world, contemplate and struggle at the same time; that there is no room for dichotomies in true Christian spirituality; that all those who are crucified with Christ are stretched out at once on the vertical and horizontal dimensions of the cross, in gratuitousness and effort, clinging, like roots, to the Time of History and spread, like wings, out to the Glory of the Eschaton.

Each of the stanzas, taken separately and given numbers, could be saying this:

1. "No through way here now."/To where is there no way?/ If we don't have their wine,/will *chicha* not do?

There is "no through way" ready made "here"; it is being made. Every spiritual journey is an adventure into the unknown, an unforeseeable joust and struggle between the spirit and evil, between our spirit and the Spirit, too. And the spirituality of liberation is a collective adventure into the unknown, even though freedom in the Spirit, the option for the poor, the justice of the Reign are as old as the gospel. Even though this joust and struggle, with their defeats and victories, are as old as human history.

And yet, responsible for one another, anxious for our time and place, we ask: "To where is there no way?" We could wait no longer to take advantage of the experience of so many who have gone before us and worked out their way, when so many brothers and sisters felt lost in the byways of spirituality; turning back, perhaps, from certain spiritualities that no longer met the needs and insights of the present, and without yet finding the new—legitimate and effective—way of living out their faith where they are.

If we don't have Europe's "wine"—its culture—which is neither better nor worse, a tradition worked out for "their" latitudes and in "their" processes (and, all too often, with pretensions to hegemony), can we not make do with the *chicha* (local spirit made from various grains and leaves) of our own very rich cultures and the wooden bowl of our own historical processes? Or can one drink to God only in the "wine" of the First World?

2. Will those who go with us/live to see the day?/How can we have a party/if we haven't any bread?

This is a most urgent question that is very much ours. A unique experience of companionship in everything, of eating together the same bread of exile and utopia, of struggle and death: "Will those who go with us live to see the day?"

The "day" of justice and freedom, the day of human rights respected at last, the day of life worthy to be called human life, when we emerge from this night of massacres and dependencies, of domination and alienation. How many of us must die "before their time," without living to see that "day"? How many must live, struggling, questioning, trying to see the Truth and the Good News, when the church is, perhaps, not appearing to them as a clear sacrament of this "day," when we Christians are not being a witness-community, an accessible evangelization, worthy of belief? How many men and women must go on living, struggling and dying, without seeing the day, excommunicated by a society that calls itself civilization, and by a religion that is incapable of seeing the treasure of Truth and Life they carry with them, a society that is perhaps condemning the living God of history in the name of a dead god of regulations? Why can the day of our God not be a human day, God's today our today?

How can we have the cynical cheek to claim that we are walking in companionship (*com-pan-ion, com-pañero, co-pain*: the word—at least in Latin languages—says "sharing bread" with those who walk with us, like, in the final instance, the greater Companion who walked on the road to Emmaus), if we do not have even the bread needed to share life, health, housing, education, participation, justice, freedom?

3. What path will you take/to heaven, other than earth?/ For whom will you go to Carmel/if you go up and don't come down?

There is no way to go to heaven except by the earth. Only in history can we welcome and hope for and make the Reign. If we do not take on the responsibilities of the age, in our daily lives of living and working together, struggling and celebrating, politics and faith—this Faith that is of the earth, like her sister Hope, since in heaven there is no more believing or hoping—what mission are we taking on? What call are we answering? How are we collaborating in God's work?

"What road will you take to heaven, other than earth?" We are persons of body and soul in indissoluble unity: we are not "pure" spirits. Christian spirituality is not a fleshless spiritualism. It is the following of the Word incarnate in Jesus of Nazareth; the most historical and "material" of spiritualities, in the biblical line of creation, exodus, prophecy, incarnation, crucifixion and resurrection of the flesh.

What road can we take, other than this "earth" of our Christian faith?

We do not travel alone, but in community, hand-in-hand in solidarity, as members of one single humankind—and, here, of one single continent—as members of the congregated church, but here, brought together in a Latin American form.

We cannot make spirituality an individualistic business, a *sauve qui peut*, a turning away from the suffering and struggle that surround us; because only disinterested, committed and freely-given love makes us holy, and in the evening of our life—St John of the Cross, once again, would say—we shall be judged on love. The "last"—and never was an adjective better chosen—judgment will be made on what we have or have not done for others: for their thirst, their health, their freedom. The Son of God and son of Mary, our brother in blood and inheritance, told us so in so many words.

Human Jacob's ladders, caught up in Jesus' own *kenosis*, we have to "go up" to God and "come down" to human beings, in an unending ebb and flow of contemplation and action, of self-giving and service, of spirit and matter. While we have time.

4. Will the balm of the law/heal our old wounds?/Are this King's battles/fought with flags or lives?

Maybe the commemoration, well or ill conceived, of five hundred years of Christianity in America, will have helped us to recognize, with no possible let-out, these "old wounds" of colonization, not only military and political colonization , but religious and cultural as well. A long cut, still not stanched, from five hundred years of violations and impositions—ecclesiastical ones too. In theology, in liturgy, in pastoral practice; in the training of priests and in religious life; in the autonomous and corresponding rights and duties of the churches of the continent; in the legitimate subsidiarity of our bishops' conferences and those of the religious orders; in the way men and women live and proclaim their faith; in the way all commit themselves to service to the Reign in history; in spirituality—understood as this book presents it: in its complex and harmonious totality, human-divine, contemplative-militant.

The "balm of the law," the rules and controls, the monopolistic centralization, the uniformity that ends by negating the universality of the "Catholic" Church, will not heal these wounds; it will merely inflame them still further, or leave them at the mortified stage of indifference, routine, fatalism.

The "battles" of the King of the Father's Reign are not fought with flags or codes, crusades or statistics, but lives, "life in abundance." Lives or deaths, perhaps; because the inescapable challenge facing the church in Latin America and the whole of the Third World—in the one Human World, rather— is to respond, as Jesus did, to those barred from life, to be good news to them of survival, of dignity, of liberation, and of hope. And to fight, as Jesus did, for all plundered lives and to proclaim, as he did, that human life is one, equal in value, stemming from the God of Life and born for ever.

In time and in eternity, the Reign is Life.

5. Does mission find its harvest/in the curia or in the street?/ If you let the Wind be still/what will you hear in prayer?

"Mission . . . finds its harvest" in the street, there where human beings work out their fate. Temples and curias must be at the service of the sons and daughters of God, perhaps outside the walls. . . . Religious worship and organization have no justification in themselves and are even blasphemous when, beside them or under them, through their indifference or interference, justice, charity and mission fail.

Mission happens in the risk and storms of human life, by the breath of the Spirit, obviously, and in the church, but definitely not in its closed sacristies and "curias."

"Do not deceive yourselves . . . repeating, 'Temple of Yahweh, Temple of Yahweh!,'" Jeremiah warned all casual worshippers. And Jesus, when the fullness of revelation had come, totally unmasked the insensitivity, casuistry, ritualism, and hypocrisy of the scribes and Pharisees.

The Wind of the Spirit is not tied down; it "blows where it will" and stirs up and refreshes hearts and structures. It goes on working, always. It creates, enlivens, sets free. If we allow the wind to fall still, if the power of legalism drowns the voice of the Spirit, we lay ourselves open to not hearing God, either in the Bible or in prayer, community or individual, liturgical or private. Or we lay ourselves open to hearing other gods.

No one can hear the God and Father of Jesus without simultaneously hearing the cry of God's poor, the groaning of God's creation.

6. Without hearing the voice of the Wind/what words will you bear?/What will your offering be/if not yourselves in what you give?

On the other hand, if we do not know how to welcome the Spirit, if we do not harken to its call, if we do not cultivate its gifts, if we are not receptive—also in silence and renunciation and self-giving—to this Wind that so often passes like "a gentle breeze," as in Elijah's Horeb, "what word" will we bear? What message will our life be? To what shall we bear witness? The mouth speaks out of the fullness of the heart. Empty of God, we cannot hand on God. We are not the Word, merely his echo, one of his voices, though an indispensable one, thanks to the co-responsibility he has entrusted to us.

In our pastoral work, in our celebration of the sacraments, it is not a question of "doing" pastoral work or "administering" the sacraments; it is not a question of "giving" catechism classes or instruction to those preparing for marriage or the host, like bureaucrats giving out cards. In pastoral work and in celebration—from mass and catechesis to working with peasants or politicians, or going on pilgrimages—we have to "give ourselves" to grace and our fellow human beings, experience what we proclaim, be what we preach, bear witness with our lives to the Mystery we celebrate.

Christian women and men are, above all, witnesses to life, and, perhaps, witnesses to death: martyrs, like so many sisters and brothers from this land that flows with milk and blood.

7. If you let Hope and Truth/yield to the Empire's sway,/who will tell the mystery/of the fullness of freedom?

Jesus was the "free man" in the face of the flesh and populism, in the face of the law and the empire; because of this total freedom, in obedience to the Father and his cause, which is the

Reign, he was borne to death on the cross and the victory of the resurrection.

The community of the followers of Jesus has to live this freedom "with which Christ has set us free" to its ultimate consequences—within our always limited field of play—this freedom that he, first, lived. For the glory of God the Father and for the life of the world; without giving in to any power and challenging all the idols that dominate people and all the empires that hold sway over peoples.

If the church, daughter of freedom, mighty wind of Pentecost, gives way to any empire—as it so often has—who will proclaim the mystery? Who will speak the truth to Pilate, Annas or Herod and uphold the battered hope of the people?

The spirituality of liberation is the spirituality of freedom; because only the free can liberate. And it is the spirituality of poverty, set free from egoisms, consumerisms and vain possessions. The civilization of love proclaimed by the bishops of Latin America at Puebla simultaneously demands the civilization of poverty, which the martyr Ignacio Ellacuría defended in El Salvador.

8. If the Lord is Bread and Wine/and the Way that we walk,/ and if "paths are made by walking,"/what paths do you hope to find?

There is no ready-made path in spirituality, even when we follow masters and schools, ancient or modern, and even if we feel ourselves clothed in the multitude of brothers and sisters who have gone before us or come with us on our travels. There is no ready-made path, but Jesus is the way. And he himself is the bread and wine we need for the journey. There is no need to wait for maps to replace our spirituality or to stop us from creatively exploring new heights or greater depths. Walking in him, according to his Spirit, we make a safe path by walking.

Everything and everyone may let us down; we shall spend "nights of the spirit" or spells of isolation from the institution, but we shall have Company. And we are communion. We come from the Trinity-community, we live through and in it, we are going to it.

And yet our spirituality, like the spirituality of any human being, in any church circumstance or any religious or cultural situation, is an adventure into the unknown, a struggle with all risks, the greatest throw of our freedom; it is both the meaning of and the quest for our being.

There is no path. There is a Way. And we make the path by walking.

This is what the stanzas, with their questions, mean. And they mean more, if stirred, since poetry has the advantage of meaning more than the words say.

And this book means the same, in greater detail. Going into the minutiae of life, always with a view to tackling, at one and the same time, basic human spirituality—in our case, Latin American—and specifically Christian spirituality—in our case, the spirituality of liberation.

A lot of ink has flowed over this "of." Whether there is a theology "of" work," a theology "of" liberation. . . . In my view, an adequate reply has repeatedly been given. The theology of work limits itself to a theological study of the human phenomenon of work. The theology of liberation systematically covers the whole field of Christian theology, but always from the standpoint and in the dynamic of integral liberation. So I believe this book has the right to call itself, without arousing doubts or polemic, *The Spirituality of Liberation.* Because it does not deal just with the spiritual experience of liberative processes or actions—personal and social—but with the whole of human spirituality, its most intimate and personal side as well as its more communitarian and social implications—but always in the light of that liberation with which the Spirit sets us free, and in the service of the total liberation of the Reign.

Let me make clear from the start that we are not writing a *Theology of Spirituality,* but a book *of spirituality,* and, specifically, of spirituality of liberation, from Latin America and for Latin America, even though we believe that the spirituality of liberation, as such, is "opportune, useful and necessary" for the whole Third World, and even for the whole world, with the necessary changes of emphasis and references. What John

Paul II has said on more than one occasion of the theology of liberation and its universal validity, can, we believe, be said even more truly of the spirituality of liberation. What individual, community, or people has no need of liberation from sin, from various captivities, and from the "fear of death"?

We also have to recognize in all honesty that giving the title "Latin American" to this spirituality is conventional and even debatable, since other spiritualities—including some contrary to this in some respects—are also present in America, and could claim the title "Latin American" from their geographical spread and the time they have been present on the continent. As Pablo Richard says, not everything that comes out of Latin America is Latin American. The culture and theology still dominant in Latin America are largely European (and the bold authors of this book were both born European, though they tried, a long time ago, to be reborn Latin American). The theology, and the spirituality, of liberation *are Latin American*, not only because they originate in Latin America, but above all because they take up the conflictive identity of this continent of "captivity and liberation" as their deepest personal and historical challenge, and as their most human and Christian utopia.

Neither would we want to fall into the chauvinism of claiming as specifically Latin American contributions to the spirituality of liberation what belongs to the spirit and Spirit of liberation in any part of the world and at any time, without nationality or frontiers.

This book tries to be ecumenical, and even "macro-ecumenical," as we make clear throughout. Nevertheless, because it is written by two Catholics, it will be obviously Catholic in its terminology. It also seeks to be for everyone, lay people and clerics, women and men. But as it has been written by two male clerics, it quite possibly has less to say to the demands of lay and feminine spirituality.

What matters is life. And what has impelled us to write this book, with many hesitations and with no greater pretensions, is the same impulse of the liberator Jesus: that on this continent of death, "all may have life, and life in abundance."

P.C.

Introduction

Spirit and Spirituality

1. The Problem of Terminology

"Spirituality" is, decidedly, an unfortunate word. We have to say this at the start, so as to tackle the problem head on, because many people will find the first difficulty with this book in the title itself. For them, spirituality may mean something removed from real life, useless and perhaps even hateful. These are people who, legitimately, shun old and new spiritualisms, unreal abstractions, and see no reason to waste their time.

The word "spirituality" derives from "spirit." And for most people, spirit is opposed to matter. "Spirits" are immaterial beings, without a body, very different from ourselves. In this sense, what is not material, what does not have a body, would be spiritual. And one would say that people are "spiritual" or "very spiritual" if they live without worrying much about material things, even about their own body, trying to live only off spiritual realites.

These concepts of spirit and spirituality as realities opposed to material and bodily reality come from Greek culture. From that, they moved to Spanish, Portuguese, French, Italian, even English and German.... So that whatever might be labelled "Western culture" is, in effect, as it were infected with this Greek concept of what is spiritual. The same is not true, for example, of the Quechua, Guaraní or Aymara languages.

Neither did the ancestral tongue of the Bible, the Hebrew language, the Semitic cultural world, understand "spiritual" in

1

this way. For the Bible, spirit is not opposed to matter, or to body, but to evil (destruction); it is opposed to flesh, to death (the fragility of what is destined to die), and it is opposed to the law (imposition, fear, punishment).[1] In this semantic context, spirit means life, building, power, action, freedom. The spirit is not something that is outside matter, outside the body and outside tangible reality, but something that is within, that inhabits matter, the body, actuality, and gives them life, makes them be what they are; it fills them with power, moves them, impels them; it propels them into growth and creativity in an impulse of freedom.

In Hebrew, the word for spirit, *ruah*, means wind, breath, exhalation. The spirit is, like the wind, light, strong, flattening, unpredictable. It is, like breath, the bodily wind that makes us breathe and take in oxygen, lets us go on living. It is like the exhalation of our breathing: while we breathe, we live; if we don't breathe, we die.

The spirit is not another life but the best of life, what makes life be what it is, giving it love and strength, looking after it and moving it forward.

We can say that something is spiritual in that it has the presence of the spirit in it. So, from now on, we abandon the Greek sense of the word "spirit" and will take care to use it in its biblical, indigenous, African, not its split "Western," sense.

2. First Definitions of Spirit/spirit and Spirituality

On the basis of the above, and to get us under way, we can now set out some provisional definitions.

—The spirit of persons is what is deepest in their being (leaving aside the question of the "psyche," which, like Xavier Zubiri, we would not call "soul," "since the word is overloaded with a special, highly debatable, meaning: a substantial entity living 'inside' the body"[2]): their ultimate "motivations": "Spirituality is the motivation that impregnates our life projects and decisions..., the motivation and mysticism that steeps and inspires commitment..., the motivation of the Spirit. So to speak of motivations is to speak of sprituality."[3] It is their ideal, their utopia, their passion, the mystique by which they live and with which they infect others. We would say, for example, that people "have a good spirit" to mean that they are of "good heart," well-intentioned, well-motivated, truthful. We say they "have a bad spirit" when they are ill-intentioned, dominated by low passions, or give an impression of being false and untrustworthy. We say they "have a lot of spirit" when we sense they are motivated by deep impulses, by compulsive desires, by an inner fire that makes them bubble, by inner riches that make them overflow. And we say, on the contrary, that they "have no spirit" when we see them uninspired, without passions or ideals, when they are caught up in a coarse and rudderless life.

On occasions, instead of spirit and spirituality, we shall use relative synonyms—meaning, conscience, deep will, self-control, guiding values, utopia or cause for which one fights, life direction—in order to keep away from the restricted Greek concept which unfortunately comes to our minds from time to time.

—"Spirit" is the concrete noun and "spirituality" is the abstract noun. Just as "friend" is the concrete noun and "friendship" the abstract. Friends are those who have the quality of friendship; the form or way in which they live it makes them have one or another sort of friendship—more or less intense, more or less sincere. The same happens with the spirit and spirituality: we can understand the spirituality of persons or particular realities as their way or form of being spiritual, as the fact of being stamped with this character, as the fact of living or happening with spirit, whatever this spirit may be.

Spirituality is a dimension susceptible to a certain "measure" or evaluation. That is, there can be a greater or lesser, better or worse spirituality in a person or a reality, to the extent to which the presence of a spirit in them is greater or lesser, better or worse. Persons will be truly spiritual when there is a clear presence and marked activity of spirit in them, when they really live with spirit. And depending on what this spirit is, so will their spirituality be.

Although there is, strictly speaking, the difference between concrete and abstract in the meanings of "spirit" and "spirituality," in fact we normally, in everyday speech, interchange the two without making the due distinction between them. So, often when we say "spirituality," we could or should be saying, more concretely, "spirit." So when we ask what spirituality we have, we could be asking what spirit moves us; or when we say that someone is a very spiritual person, we could mean the same by saying that he or she shows a lot of spirit (or a very strong spirit, since spirit cannot be quantified).

—This last example leads us to mention a habitual confusion. The concept of people having "a lot of spirituality" or "a lot of spirit" would not be applied to ambitious people who make it their aim in life to acquire money and power at any price. We should not apply it to them because, mistakenly, we tend to think of spirit and spirituality in positive terms only, as if only good spirits and spiritualities, those that fit in with our ethical values, were worthy of the names. So, for example, we speak of "committed Christians" thinking of those committed to justice, as though there were no Christians equally committed to injustice![4]

But no: there are very different and even contradictory spirits and spiritualities. There are good spirits and not so good ones. There are persons of much and persons of little spirituality. There are those of better spirituality and those of worse. An ambitious and exploitative person who tries to dominate others has a lot of spirituality, but one of egoism, of ambition, an idolatrous spirituality: the spirit that moves him is a bad one.

In some Christian circles it is said that "spirituality means living with spirit," but this affirmation is understood as "in our image and likeness," meaning: we take as spirituality only our own, the one we value, the Christian one; by spirit, by the same token, we mean only the one that serves us as a reference point: the spirit of Christian faith, hope and charity. We unconsciously take for granted that those who do not live with this spirit have no spirit at all, possess no spirituality.

The reality is much broader. The spirit (spirituality) of a person, community or people is—in the "macroecumenic" sense we are giving the term[5]—their life motivation, their disposition, what inspires their actions, their utopia, their causes, regardless of whether these are better or worse, good or evil, in accordance with our own or not. Because those who do not have our spirit also have spirit; those who do not have a Christian spirituality and even those who claim to reject spiritualities also have spirituality....[6]

3. Spirituality, the Patrimony of all Human Beings

Every human person is animated by one or another spirit, marked by one or another spirituality, because human beings are basically also spiritual beings. This statement can be understood and explained in a thousand different ways, according to distinct anthropological, philosophical and religious currents. We are not proposing to enter into this debate in this book; the overall statement can stand. We have to make the assumption that readers of a book on spirituality will share the conviction that human beings are not "exclusively material" beings.

The classic statement that human beings are spiritual beings means that men and women are something more than biological life, that there is something in them that gives them a quality of life superior to the life of mere animals. This plus, this something more that distinguishes them, that makes them what they are by giving them their human specificity, is that mysterious, but very real, entity which so many religions and philosophies, throughout history, have called "spirit." Under this or another name, spirit is the dimension of the deepest quality we have, without which we would not be human persons. This personal depth[7]—profundity, in the language of the classic mystics—is forged by the motivations that make us vibrate, by the utopia that moves and inspires us, by the understanding of life we build up laboriously through personal experience, in living together with our fellows and other beings, the mysticism we lay down as the basis for our individual definition and our historical orientation.

The most conscientiously we live and act, the more we cultivate our values, our ideal, our mysticism, our basic choices, our utopia ... the more spirituality we have, the deeper and richer our profundity. Our spirituality will be the measure of our very humanity. (In Christian terms, spirituality, as what is most profoundly human, would be what makes people be most "in the image and likeness of God," what best reflects their sharing in the nature of God.)

Spirituality is not the exclusive patrimony of special people, professionally religious, or holy; it is not even exclusive to believers.[8] Spirituality is the patrimony of all human beings. And more: spirituality is also a community reality; it is as it were the conscience and motivation of a group, of a people. Every community has its culture and every culture has its spirituality.

4. Is Spirituality Something Religious?

So, what has spirituality to do with religion? Has not spirituality always been thought of as a religious affair? To answer these questions, we need first to make a diversion.

Being a person is something deeper than being simply a member of this particular animal species called the human race. It means taking up one's own freedom in the face of mystery, fate, the future; it is asking history for a meaning, giving a personal answer to the ultimate questions of existence. At one moment or other in our lives, we all break through the superficial level on which we normally live, like leaves carried on the current, and formulate basic questions: "What is being human? What is the meaning and purpose of our life? Why is there suffering? How do we achieve happiness? What is death? What can we hope for?"—the questions that Vatican II says all people ask of the different religions (NAe 1c).[9] These are not "formally religious" but "deeply human" questions, or, more precisely, the deepest human questions—though, in our view, asking oneself these questions is in itself formulating the religious question.

We all have to face up to the mystery of our own existence. We inescapably have to choose values to give backbone and consistency to our life. In one way or another we have to select a point on which to build and define the structure of our conscience, the position we take up in relation to reality, within history.[10] This is our basic option. And what is genuinely religious is this deep basic option, this human depth, rather than any dogma or rite, any belonging to a particular denomination. Because in this basic option we are defining what value we place at the centre of our life, what is our absolute aim, what is our God, or god. The great master Origen said that "God is that which one places above everything else."

We cannot cease being "religious"—in this basic sense—without abdicating from the very depth of our own humanity. Not even if we abjure a particular religion will we stop being religious in our human depth.[11] God, said the unquiet Augustine of Hippo, is for me "more intimate than my own intimacy."[12]

This deep religiosity is the same as what we have called spirit or spirituality.[13] Spirituality—this deep religiosity—is what ultimately delineates us as persons, what defines us—saves or condemns us—before God, not the religious practices which, derivatively, we may perform, perhaps sometimes without involving this depth.

The maximun value these religious practices can acquire is being the personal expression and community vehicle of that spirituality, of that deep religiosity. If for any reason, with sincere honesty, anyone should in conscience reject religious practices or membership of a conventional religion but continue to live in truth the deep convictions of existential truthfulness, he or she will not be lost, nor will God be worried.

5. What, then, is Christian Spirituality?

All we have said above might well worry some readers: can it be that in this book on the spirituality of liberation they are not going to discuss explicitly Christian spirituality, such as that of the cross and of baptism, that of prayer and the following of Jesus? Of course we are going to discuss it, and all its basic demands. Furthermore, we have to say that we are already discussing it, even without calling it such, since all that we have said so far of spirituality in general is also applicable to explicitly Christian spirituality. That is, if the spirituality of following Jesus deserves to be called spirituality, this is because it fulfills the requirements of the definition of spirituality given above; in other words, because it is motivation, impulse, utopia, a cause to live and struggle for.... Following Jesus will be the definition of its specificity. Christian spirituality, as spirituality, is, on principle, one more example of the many spiritualities to be found in the world of human beings: Islamic, Maya, Hebrew, Guaranf, Buddhist, Kuna, Shintoist....

It is quite possible that this answer will leave some readers still unsatisfied, asking: Is there not "something more" in Christian spirituality, something lacking in the spiritualities of other religions?

On principle, looking at things in a normal light, Christian spirituality is no more than "one more example" of religious spiritualities. We repeat: looking at things "in a normal light." Now, if we look at things in the light of Christian faith, we do find a new and particular "something more." What is this?

To answer this, we need to turn on the light of Christian faith, moving on to this other plane of knowledge, beyond, or deeper within, gratuitous, undeserved, which in itself, before our response in faith, makes us neither better nor worse, but which is a "different" light from the "normal light."

6. Looking at Things from Christian Faith

Christian faith is a particular light: it is not the only religious light that exists—Islamic or Quechua faiths are, for example, also religious lights, and they all come from the One who is the Light; but we are here confining ourselves to the Christian viewpoint. Like any religious view or view from faith, it gives us a contemplative outlook on reality; that is, it makes us discover, in admiration, a dimension of reality that is accessible only in the light of that same faith. This is the dimension of salvation that God is carrying forward in human history. And within this dimension, we see two views, inseparable from one another but clearly distinguishable: *the order of salvation* itself and *the order of understanding of it.*

With regard to the order of salvation, faith teaches us that the presence of salvation is beyond our capabilities and that it has no limits of time and space, nor of race or language, nor even of religion. We all have a direct relationship with salvation, because "God desires everyone to be saved" (1 Tim. 2:4). We are all potential bearers of salvation and we are all called to collaborate in its construction. All, then, are incorporated into the order of the bringing about of salvation. God makes use of everything and everyone to go on weaving salvation into every life and the whole of history. God communicates with women and men and addresses the word to them through the Book of Life, which is creation and history, in daily happenings and under the signs of the times and of places. So, God acts in "many and various ways," often unknown to us, but as old as the history of humankind (Heb. 1:1). We, for our part, feel both challenged and stimulated by this work of God's in the midst of this world and ourselves. And as the spirit we are, and to the extent that we go on filling ourselves with it, we collaborate more fully with salvation itself—often without knowing it. In the spirit that moves everyone, every group, every people, there is a sure presence of salvation. By the light of faith, we discover that the spirit, the spirituality of each of us, of each spiritual family, of each people, are salvific realities, belong indisputably to the order of salvation and are called to collaborate in it. Christian faith thus gives us a highly ecumenical, "macroecumenic" vision.

Christian faith, however, also providesd us with a particular meaning and new significance of explicitly Christian saving realities. God has not only created the world and made it the scenario of salvation; not only created human beings and made them one of the principal protagonists of salvation, but has willed to communicate more fully with them in order to make salvation more accessible and comprehensible to them. God has not only revealed himself through the mediation of creation and history, but has decided to make a direct, personal revelation. Christians believe that in Jesus God has spoken the word in flesh, in blood, in history, in death and resurrection. In Jesus of Nazareth, born of a woman (Gal. 4:4), the fullness of God dwells personally and historically (Col. 1:15-20). In him, God is revealed as love. God has revealed in him the meaning and end of existence: the utopia of the Reign. And God's own self is revealed in the course taken by Jesus as the anticipated realization of the fullness of the New Humanity.

With this full revelation, God moves human beings, draws

them to God, shows them the dynamic and meaning of history and of each life and gives them the cause and motives for living, for sharing and for laying down their own life.... In other words, God becomes present to them with the Spirit, in their spirit, sending them strengthened on the road to salvation. Realities such as the incarnation of God, the church community and the sacramental life provide more examples of an explicitly Christian spirituality. Access to this manifest revelation of salvation—which is an inexplicably gratuitous gift, on principle—clearly makes the experience of salvation easier to grasp.

Furthermore: we should say that God, through all the means of this revelation—the history of Israel, the word of God in the Bible, the church and sacraments—not only guides and strengthens the spirit of God's daughters and sons, but that in a new way God sends them God's own Spirit as the Holy Spirit of the Father and the Son, as the Spirit of the risen Jesus.

These specifically Christian realities, which belong to the order of the manifestation and resultant understanding of salvation, are not absolutely necessary manifestations for salvation itself, but are necessary for understanding its revelation and for experiencing it as Christians. We Christians believe that their finality derives from their being a mediation in the mediator Jesus, and that on this account we should be deeply grateful for them.

This distinction, which is very important, between the order of the reality of salvation and the order of its manifestation or understanding on our part, does not coincide with the division between sacred and profane, or between what is directly ethical and explicitly religious.

7. Non-Christian and Christian Spirituality

In the light of faith, then, how do we value, by comparison, the spirituality of those men and women who have not had access to the Christian revelation and that of those who have had this access?

A first—hasty but very common—answer has been to say that those who have not known the Christian revelation live with a "spirit" (lower case), whereas those who have known God through this revelation live by "the Spirit" (capital). God would certainly help both categories, but in a very unequal way. Furthermore, in this view, it has often been thought that those who have not known the Christian revelation or not become members of a Christian church have no "supernatural divine life" in them, but only a "natural human spirituality." On the other hand, those who, with their knowledge of revelation, share in the life of the church, are living not with mere "spirit" but in the life of the "Spirit" itself.

That this answer is so common is probably due to its being that given by "spiritual theology" or the classical study of spirituality. This, in effect, was conceived as study of "the supernatural life," of "Christian perfection" or "asceticism and mysticism," which from the outset left the possibility of a "spirituality of non-believers" out of consideration. The fact that they cannot exercise the "virtues" that Christians do is a commonly upheld view in classical spiritual theology.[14]

It is, though, as we said, a very hasty answer. It embodies a very widespread way of thinking, but one that shows scant respect for the data revealed by faith. It creates a real abyss between those who have known revelation and those who have not, for which there is no justification. The word of God tells us otherwise. If we are to be faithful to this word, we need to answer the initial question with the two following statements:

(a) All human beings have spirit and spirituality, not only those who know the Christian revelation, not only those who lead an explicitly religious life. Spirit and spirituality—in the meaning we have given these concepts—are an essential dimension of us all and the patrimony of any personal life.

(b) The Spirit of God is present and active in all of us, not only in those who have become members of a church through explicit acceptance of the Christian revelation. And this Spirit of God is the Spirit of the Blessed Trinity, the Spirit of Jesus, which is at work too in those who do not know the Christian revelation. (Let it be clear, however, that this double assertion we Christians make in the light of our faith is not shared by non-Christians, nor can we, in a spirit of proselytism, claim that they should share it.)

8. "Spirit" and "spirit"

Up to now we have generally been talking of "spirit" with a lower-case "s," but we have just introduced the "Spirit" with a capital "S," the Spirit of God, the Holy Spirit, the Spirit of Jesus. We are not going to attempt to define this Spirit, because God is indefinable and because we know basically what we are talking about.[15] But we are going to examine what relationship there is between the spirit and the Spirit.

The spirit is the essential dimension of human persons in which the Spirit of God finds the special ground for its activity in each person. The Spirit of God works on our spirit. It gives us spirit, meaning depth, energy, freedom, fullness of life. It gives us Itself. The very name "Spirit" is related to the human experience that gave rise to what we call "spirit."

Let us make some distinctions:

(a) *In men and women who have not known the Christian revelation* the Spirit of Jesus is present and active in their spirit "in the ways He knows," (see AG 7, 9; LG 16; UR 3). Some of these men and women are not even believers, but the Spirit of God is at work in them too, and even interceding in them too "with sighs too deep for words" (Rom. 8:26), in the common cries of humankind. "In him we live and move and have our being" (Acts 17:28). The Spirit "enlightens everyone" (John 1:9) so that they may have life (John 10:10). Others of these men and women have not had access to the biblical word of God, do not know the God of Jesus, but invoke the living God in their own religions under another name and through their own myths and rites. And the "God of all names" (as the *Missa dos Quilombos*[16] puts it) sends them God's Spirit, hears them and welcomes them. And saves them: they are not second-class daughters and sons of God.[17]

(b) *In peoples that have not known the Christian revelation,* the main setting for God's action in them and their access to God is their spirituality, their mysticism, their culture. God, who walks with every person and every culture, is present in the culture, wisdom, spirituality of every people. (It is worth recalling here what Vatican II states about the "secret presence of God," "the Word sown" and the "preparation for the gospel" in peoples who do not know the gospel: see AG 9; GS 57; LG

16; also Puebla 401. This means that the gospel does not reach anywhere as a "purely pagan" place, but rather as somewhere where it meets the Word already present: "The first missionary is the Holy Trinity, which, through the Logos and the Spirit, becomes present in every cultural fabric."[18]) And this action of God's in every people is a facet of God's self-revelation to this people and to all peoples on earth, including Christian ones. This shows that all peoples have a spark of the light of God in their cultures, in their wisdom, in their religious cosmovision, in their spirituality. They all have spiritual riches to share. And God's action in them is action for the whole of humankind, as universal as in the sacred history of Israel.

(c) *In men and women who have known and accepted the Christian revelation* the Spirit of Jesus is known and invoked by its revealed name. This does not necessarily imply that its action is reinforced by them better than by those who do not know it explicitly and do not form part of the church: the Gospels are very clear in stating that explicit belonging to the People of God does not always go with greater faithfulness to the Spirit (see Matt. 25:31ff; Luke 19:25ff; Matt. 21: 28-32). It means that they have at their disposition a new source of knowledge to enable them to know the Spirit and to walk the paths of salvation—which is precisely one of the aims of revelation. For Christians, the revelation of salvation, with its mysteries and gifts: the Word of God, the incarnation of God in Christ, the communion of the church... are so many more sources of spirit and spirituality. Christians, besides sharing a common spirituality with men and women who have spirit even though they do not explicitly know the Spirit of Jesus, can live a characteristically Christian spirituality, one, that is, consciously based on the salvation brought by God in Christ Jesus. We could say that the Spirit has endowed itself, in the mystery of Jesus, with a specific mediation: to act, through living faith, on those who accept this mystery.

9. Two Types of Spirituality

From the above it will be clear that we are distinguishing between two types of spirituality. The first is the "basic human," ethical-political spirituality that exists in all of us, whether we know the Christian revelation or not. This level of spirituality, though it comes in the final analysis from the source of the Spirit of God, drinks from the sources of life: history, social conditions, praxis, reflection, wisdom, contemplation—all that feeds the heart and mind. This spirituality is the subject of Part One, "The Spirit of Liberation."

Christians have an additional level of spirituality deriving from the explicitly Christian categories which provide their faith. This is the subject of Part Two, "The Liberating Spirit of Jesus Christ."

The first, then, is that basic, ethical-political spirituality we all have. The second is the religious, evangelical-ecclesial spirituality, that of Christians in this case.[18]

Just as classical treatises on spirituality divided their treatment into sections according to the "virtues," so we have divided the following two parts into sections dealing with the "virtues" proper to the spirituality of liberation.

Let us state once more that by dealing with Christian spirituality in Part Two, we are not forgetting that there are many other non-Christian religious spiritualities, each corresponding, in its own way, to the basic needs of heart and mind. And in calling the spirituality dealt with in Part One "non-religious," we are using "non-religious" in its generally accepted sense, which is not to deny our acceptance that all personal "depth" has an anthropologically religious character.

We trust that this approach—theologically correct and just in human terms—will take us beyond all dichotomy in spirituality, so that we Christians (or those we can influence) will never again treat non-Christians as if they were people "without spirituality," or feel in any way superior to them. Or assume that there can be a religious spirituality without a basic human spirituality. We write from our background, and we know that if we are not spiritually Latin Americans first, we cannot be spiritual as Christians.

PART ONE

THE SPIRIT OF LIBERATION

A Passion for Reality

Reality as Basic Reference: "Feet on the Ground"

Latin American spirituality is clearly characterized by constant basic reference to actual conditions. A passion for reality, an elemental "realism"—even if at times it also seems "magic"—is perhaps the first characteristic of its general approach.

The reference is a double one: to origin and end. To origin: because every action, every analysis, every theory, every study, every experience, every project . . . has to start from the actual situation. To end: because the process is always one definitely aimed at a central objective: to get back to the actual situation. "Starting from" and "returning to" the reality: this is the very un-magic "realism" of our spirituality.

It also means starting from within to move outward; that is, through a process of concientization, seeking the self-propelled development of persons and the community, not an authoritarian, imposed, coercive development from outside.

The approach is always one of respect for and honesty with the situation:[1] respecting the truth of reality, being faithful to it, letting oneself be guided by the real aspects, never ignoring, distorting, let alone falsifying reality.

This realism can be seen graphically illustrated in the famous "see-judge-act" method. Originating with Pierre Cardijn's Young Christian Workers movement, referred to by Vatican II (AA 29), this was first used on an official church level in Latin America at the Tenth Annual Meeting of CELAM, held in October 1966, which prepared the organization of the Medellín Conference of 1968. It decided the structure of what became the conference documents, under the tripartite scheme: "Facts/Reflection/Recommendations."[2] The technique has been widely used in pastoral work and generally used throughout the church, either under that name or not, from the early 1960s to the present. It has spread beyond the religious spheres of theology and pastoral work to education, politics and the trade union movement. Its most striking achievements have been in theology (the theology of liberation) and education (Popular Education, "conscientization"). In both fields, Latin America has produced writers and practitioners of world stature. The whole movement can be seen as an imprint of the Latin American spirit that has become a contribution to the world community.

In Latin America, this method has moved beyond being a simple accidental or peripheral "methodological question" to become a structure of our minds, our work, our thought: "If we associate theological reflection with historical tasks through the mediation of the social sciences, this is because we want to avoid the danger of a 'pure' theology, which would inevitably end up as gratuitous overproduction of definitions, in other words a 'hemorrhage of meaning' owing to the 'infinity of the words' of its incontinence."[3] It has become a salient feature of our spirituality: starting from the situation, shedding light on it and changing it, to go back to it and change it again and start again from this changed situation in a new cyclical process that revolves endlessly round the situation, taking turns with it.

This passion for reality has become a guarantee of authenticity for Latin American spirituality, a touchstone for avoiding sterile abstraction and getting to grips with actual reality, for moving quickly from theory to practice, for moving beyond mere interpretation to transformation, for abandoning all idealism and spiritualism and putting our feet on the ground in commitment and organized action.

Analysis of the Situation

Analyzing a situation means moving beyond uncritical acceptance of it, beyond passivity, resignation, political ingenousness. The new approach is that of ongoing "analysis," understood as a still closer relationship to the situation: the quest for the deepest possible understanding of it.

"Analysis" is understood as the search for historical and structural causes: historical causes, because the innermost and deepest roots stem from the past, coming from farthest back and deepest within; structural causes, because we are concerned with permanent and basic causes, beyond the merely accidental. This attitude makes us people with "radical" views, because we go to the "roots" (*radices*) of problems and solutions, not content with staying on the surface and accepting the first empirical explanation put forward.

This stance of realism and ongoing analysis imposes a high degree of discipline, sobriety and rational discourse on us; we need to find a way of combining this with festivity and openness, administered and laced with an intelligent dose of pedagogy, and never to lose sight of the fact that we wait in hope, if our "realism" is not to become harsh and overbearing.

We try to tackle everything in a spirit of "critical realism." Our permanent analytical attitude has become part of our way of life. In many church circles it has become customary to begin meetings by analyzing the national and international situation. The preparatory document for the fourth CELAM conference (Santo Domingo, 1992), drawn up in February 1990, stated: "Analysis of reality, as a means of carrying out pastoral work incarnated in our continent, has been growing in importance. Its influence in Latin America stems from the Pastoral Constitution *Gaudium et Spes*. The Medellín and Puebla conferences empowered and matured this approach. It is a major field for dialogue between the social sciences and pastoral work" (no. 769).

Analysis, hermeneutics, interpretation, have become the obligatory first step in all planning, study, or practice. "An attitude of 'total' critique of supposed values, communications media, consumption, structures, agreements, laws, codes, conformism, routine. . . . An attitude of uncorruptible alert. Passion for the truth"[4]—leads us to ask ourselves what the "social setting" of anything is, what it is for, how it fits into the geo-political scene, and, finally, "How does it affect the poor?" And this leads us to take hold of the analytical tools at our disposal. This is why liberation theology and spirituality, with an overtly missionary purpose, have no hesitation in taking the risks implicit in using—not slavishly, to be sure—analytical tools forged outside the Christian current, just as St Thomas Aquinas did in his time with the pagan Aristotle, and just as the popes' social encyclicals have done in our time by using Marxist and psychoanalytical theories.

The approach of using ongoing analysis of the social situation, and the particular features of this analysis, constitute an aspect of the Latin American liberation movement that has excited most attention and aroused most polemic. It is certainly a novelty, and an original Latin American contribution.

Ethical Indignation

Every great synthesis of thought, of values, of meaning, every spirituality, crystallizes around a basic human experience that serves as its catalyst. In the spirituality of liberation, too, there is a basic human experience that unifies and gives cohesion to the overall synthesis of meaning now shared by so many persons, groups, communities, organizations, and peoples who feel themselves inspired by this same spirit on this continent.

This basic spiritual experience is something that marks us at every stage of our lives.[1] It sits at the foundation of our spiritual formation, defines us, constitutes us. It founds empathies and antipathies. Those who have this experience in common feel a spiritual affinity among themselves reaching beyond the frontiers of faith.[2] Sometimes, indeed, Christians feel that the distance between them and their brothers and sisters in faith who do not share this experience is greater than the distance separating them from non-Christians who do share this experience. (And God seems to do the same, in making distinctions not so much between believers and atheists, as between those who allow themselves to be challenged by the "basic reality" of the poor and those who do not, as suggested by Luke 10 [the good Samaritan], Matthew 25:31ff ["I was hungry..."] and 21:28-32 [the two sons]).

This basic human experience is what we call "ethical indignation." To make this concept more understandable, let us try to break it down into component parts. We can distinguish several elements in it: 1. perception of "basic reality"; 2. ethical indignation at this reality; 3. perception of an inescapable demand; and 4. our basic stance or option.

1. In the first place, then, comes perception of "basic reality," what the situation is in its crudest form, what lies at its root. This means our coming to appreciate in the situation something that seems to touch us at our most sensitive point. Just as we might not be able to touch an open wound because it has laid bare a nerve that would make our whole system jangle if touched, so there are realities and situations that reveal highly sensitive, essential dimensions to us, that commit the absolute values we need to integrate if we are to realize the meaning of life. In these realities and situations we seem to "touch" the most sensitive points of life, the "absolute," what concerns us beyond all possibility of denial and provokes an uncontainable reaction in us.

The "basic reality" that in Latin America today has become the matrix that reveals absolute values, which demand an unavoidable response, is the experience of massive, engineered poverty on the continent. By this we mean poverty in its multi-dimensional overall sense: not only the growing destitution in which the masses are sunk, but also the historical panorama of this poverty, its structural causes, the atavistic aggression of outside powers against the native peoples, the permanent conflict between the right to force and the forces of the Right. . . .

2. Through a series of historical and cultural factors that have come together in recent years, this reality can be grasped and interpreted in a new way by a growing number of men and women throughout the continent, who see it as involving basic values they cannot ignore in forming the framework of their consciences and understanding themselves, the world, and history. On perceiving this basic reality we feel an "ethical indignation."

This is a "radical" ethical indignation that comes from very deep down, from the deepest roots of our being. It is not an indignation that stems from any particular circumstance or ideology, but an indignation we know we feel by the mere fact of being human, so that if we did not feel it, we would not feel ourselves to be human. It is such an irresistible indignation that we cannot understand how other human beings can fail to feel it.

It is a fact that over the last few decades, this ethical indignation has grown into a massive phenomenon in Latin America—we are thinking of the processes of conscientization, secularization, politicization, cultural transformation: these are not strictly Latin American in themselves but have come about here with special characteristics. A generalized consciousness of the ruling injustice has spread over the whole continent, bringing with it, to an extent not found in other parts of the world, methods of consciousness-raising among the people, sensitivity to injustices—especially to unjust social structures: colonialism, dependence, underdevelopment, imperialism, "social sin" and the like—perception of the urgent need for social change, the boom in social sciences, and the extension of studies and techniques of social analysis with the resultant politicization. One can say that after these decades the consciousness of the people of Latin Ameica is different, has been transformed, and has lost the socio-political ingenuousness in which it was previously sunk. This massive phenomenon of consciousness is one of the factors that has formed the New Latin American People.

3. This indignation is not something that stays where it is, like a sterile feeling that does not engender any dynamism. It is a radical indignation that brings with it an inescapable demand. It affects us, shakes us and moves us, imperatively. We feel questioned by it, in the depths of our being. We see it bringing an inescapable challenge: we know we cannot compromise with, tolerate, live with or agree to injustice, because to do so would be to betray what is innermost and deepest in ourselves.

4. Now comes, unavoidably, the time to take a stance, to make a choice. Choice is inevitable, since when faced with an inescapable demand, to ignore it or turn one's back on it is also a form of choosing. It is also a basic choice, since it is made by

virtue of those basic values in life that have been seen to be definitively involved in the actual situation perceived. It is therefore the most fundamental choice a person can make.

The stance taken might be a negative one: the opposite attitude to ethical indignation is hardness of heart, lack of sensitivity, indifference.

In this "basic experience"—which can be dissected into these four elements only in methodology, not in life—we take our stance in relation to the reality of the poor. And in doing so we define ourselves. We define what our attitude is going to be in relation to absolute values. We establish what our cause is going to be, what meaning our lives are to have.

This basic human experience is, then, what determines the meaning of our own lives, and determines it "on the basis of reality," on the basis of the actual reality of a situation, the real situation in which the poor find themselves, the major fact of our times, the most basic "anthropological" setting. From this we deduce:

—There are people who spend their lives without facing up to this "major fact," people who remain on the level of little private or group situations, without coming to know anything of the greatest conflict of our age: "Men are divided into those who declare their presence in the face of the misery of the world of today and those who do not."[3]

—The poor play a crucial role in the world. They are the ones who really tell us what the world is.[4] Any assessment of the state of the world outside the world of the poor is an essentially limited, distorted assessment.

—"The poor evangelize us," we say as Christians.

—Today we cannot define the meaning of life without facing up to the poor, or without declaring ourselves in relation to the crucial conflict of our age: the peoples against the great powers.[5]

—We have to find the meaning of life from the meaning of history, from the oppressed peoples.

—The point of view of the poor and oppressed is more fruitful, through being more real, for enabling us to see the meaning of history than that of the powerful.

All these are reasons why contact with the situation of the poor is necessary for all those who were not born into and are not experiencing that situation. It is contact with the poor, in effect, that makes reality real for us. (In some parts of the First World, there are "exposure programs" to provide experience of contact with the situation of the marginalized. Here we do not need anything like that; we need only to keep our eyes open to what is happening all around us.)

The poor are the only absolutely universal "sacrament" and the only sacrament absolutely necessary for salvation.[6]

This basic experience and the basic choice it implies are also a religious act, even if carried out with no consciousness of belief. In the basic choice made in this basic experience, we define ourselves before God. By defining ourselves as people by making a "basic" choice in relation to ultimate reality, we define ourselves in relation to God. In this experience, it is God whom we meet. (Thomas Aquinas states that all human beings, by performing a first rational act, define themselves in some way as being for or against God, even if God has not been explicitly proclaimed to them.)

This is because:

—we are brought up against the most serious questions about our lives, about reality: the meaning of reality, of history, of humanity, of our own being;

—in the reality of poverty we are confronted by the One who said: "just as you did it to one of the least of these who are members of my family, you did it to me" (Matt. 25:40);

—in this encounter we are defining the meaning of our lives, and in doing so are recognizing certain particular values as absolute, as our "god"—as Origen said: "God is that which a person places above all else";

—we are defining what stance we take before God, what inspires us, our disposition, our ultimate motivation, our "spirit."

Ethical indignation is also compassion. It is feeling the world's pain as our own, suffering with it. The origin of this spirituality, the passion at the source of this spirit, is what stands behind the theology and spirituality of liberation.[7] It is also what underlies all revolutionary utopias: "one does not become revolutionary from science, but from indignation."[8]

In ethical indignation, we are imitating the indignation of God. This indignation, first described in Exodus 3, is the model for ours. God listened to the cry of his people and took a stance in relation to it; God decided to enter the struggle for historical liberation.

Jesus, too, had compassion for the crowd left hungry (see Mark 6:34).[9] The starting-point of his vocation, as of that of so many prophets before and after him, had to be the ethical indignation he felt at the suffering of his people.

There is another type of religious experience, more commonly recognized as "religious"—that of inward-looking religious feeling, which makes no reference to this "major world situation," that of certain charismatics, of spiritists and others. This other type of religious experience produces another type of religion.[10] It is another type of basic foundational experience. It produces a different type of "spirit," a spiritual disposition different from the one those of us who start from ethical indignation as a basic experience feel.

Joy and Festival

The people of Latin America live in festival, in dance and song. All their lives are shot through with festivity.[1] Neither hunger nor struggle nor natural disasters prevent them from organizing a dance at the first opportunity; all their mourning and all their striving is done to singing. They move from tears to laughter as the most natural thing in the world. The originally indigenous or black dances, spread throughout the continent, have cross-fertilized with dances that came directly from Spain, Portugal and other European countries, creating a rich multi-coloured tapestry like the shawls of the women of Guatemala. Every Latin American country of course has its own native dances. And in the areas with a high black proportion of population, they are famous for creating and assimilating new dances. Among the indigenous peoples, religion, old wars, harvesting and fishing, love and birth, longings and death, have always been and still are accompanied by typical dances and songs, often prolonged till well into the night—sometimes, indeed, going on for days.

Whole populations, living in the most precarious conditions, are joyful, laugh, sing and dance. The anthropologist Sylvanus Morley described the modern Mayas, after living among them for several decades, as "jovial, joking people, fond of amusing themselves, and their cheerful and friendly character impresses all foreigners who come into contact with them. The competitive spirit is not strongly developed . . .".[2] People laugh at themselves most naturally. They often make joy a barricade against misfortune or humiliation, even against death, which is so often premature, inevitable, widespread, and which ends up as a familiar presence. Indians, blacks and *mestizos*, accustomed for centuries to having to live alongside lords and ladies and bosses—or the less community-minded sort of priest—have made passive resistance into a real art form.[3] They will say "Yes" or meekly accept an order or charge, faced with the impossibility of saying "No" in view of the results of the "No's" of the past. This attitude, as indeed their innate festivity itself, can turn into a vice. In Brazil, for example, "festivity" often means irresponsible outbursts of joy.

International observers visiting Central America, for example, have been struck by seeing crowds dancing, singing, laughing, in times of repression and war, while being wounded and dying.

We are not a Cartesian people, governed by thought. We start from natural phenomena and are not ruled by the clock: night, day, the sun, the moon, the land and its cycles of fruitfulness strike the hours for us. We are a people of events, of places, of dates, of symbols . . . very concrete, very material. We are deeply attached to "sacramentals": things that can be kissed, carried, touched. Nature itself is quasi-sacramental for us, as can be seen typically in our religious observances, and the indigenous ones that survive—and in the syncretism we adopt as a form of resistance.

Official formalities, in business, in politics, in religion, in industry and commerce, are easily ridiculed. Latin American popular and serious literature, cinema and cartoons are full of this mocking.

Theatre and the ability to stage things are virtually spontaneous. "Socio-drama" is a normal expression, fitting naturally into any festival, into popular education, the liturgy and even manifestations of political party, trade union and even guerrilla militancy.

It is often said, and the statistics prove it, that Latin America is a young continent. This, however, applies not only to the age of most of its inhabitants, but to the spirit that animates us. St Antonio María Claret, Archbishop of Santiago de Cuba, knifed in Holguín by supporters of black supremacy, precursor of so many efforts at promoting human rights, accurately grasped the significance of this characteristic of our America, for evangelization too, by calling it "the young vine."

It could also be called the musical continent. The Andean *quena*, the Mexican *marimba*, the *atabaque* of black Brazil and a thousand other instruments and rhythms translate and give cadence to the cultural and historical progress of this continent.

Festivals have no set hours. A sort of "state of *fiesta*" can be interwoven, in a logic that defies rules and prejudices, with work, suffering, prayer. Here, being responsible, in the true sense, has never meant being strait-laced or harsh.

In mountains and fields, on the banks of great rivers, in the smaller towns and cities, life is still lived largely in the open air, without undue prudery. Living-space is shared in a way envied by those who live in the huge "de-natured" urban sprawls, or by visitors from other more introverted or sophisticated cultures.

Festivals are also pluriform expressions of meeting and communicating, of myths and memories, of eating and drinking, of faith and sensuality, of utopia and satire. Who could systematically analyze what is really happening in the Rio carnival or the huge gatherings of Mexicans at Guadalupe? The candles lit for the dead, in nearly all our countries, produce a culture-shock for those unable to understand the amalgam of mourning and laughing, drinking and believing, death and vitality, that these celebrations involve.

We believe all these charisms of joy and festivity are a real gift from the household gods of these lands, many and one, and that it would be a real betrayal of the legacy of our elders and a denial of our own spirit not to go on cultivating this characteristic. We need to be just as alert to cultural invasion, the mechanization of life, commercial consumerism, and "Macdonaldizing" homogenization, as to armed and political imperialism. The transnational macro-empire uses culture on a more basic level than money and arms. The indigenous peoples, violated by the first conquistadors and compulsive missionaries, have expressed this with dramatic truthfulness. They have said it of the imposed Bible: when Pope John Paul II visited Peru in 1985, a delegation from various Indian movements presented him with a Bible and asked him to take it back, as it had caused so much suffering to the native peoples. How right we should be to say it also of the huge mass media invasion we suffer: 71 percent of all television shown in the cities and towns of the 122 countries of the Third World is produced in the U.S.A., Japan and, to a lesser extent, Russia and Brazil. 65 percent of all news bulletins originate in the U.S.A.. Four news agencies (two U.S., one British and one French) were responsible for 86 percent of news broadcast in 1986. "By day they murder the body, by night—through the unconscious—they kill the soul."[3] Joy, like utopia, is an essential feature of the Latin American spirit, and not to be taken away.

Hospitality and Openness

To an ever-increasing extent, the First World is generally characterized, and sometimes defined, as a cold world, locked into its own concerns, its own interests. (Never, perhaps has this been better expressed than by Henry Kissinger's words to Gabriel Valdés, Foreign Secretary of Chile: "You come here talking about Latin America, but we are not interested in that. Nothing important comes from the South. History has never been made in the South. The axis of history starts in Moscow, goes through Bonn, reaches Washington and goes on to Tokyo. Anything that might happen in the South has no importance.") Part of this attitude may be explained by its older, growing and sophisticated urban culture. Large parts of the Third World, on the other hand, particularly Latin America, are and are seen as, hospitable, cordial, effusive.

One has to distinguish, needless to say, between one part and another. The Indians of the Altiplano, for example, are, in many ways, people of silence. But in general, openness and hospitality are characteristic of our people: we have a great capacity for welcoming new arrivals, travellers; the doors of our houses are soon opened. In rural areas above all, it would be inconceivable to refuse a visitor food and lodging: the common adoptive fatherhood and motherhood, "fostered" sons and daughters, are ample evidence of this. This makes the recent phenomenon of abandoned and ill-treated "street kids" in urban conglomerates, the product of modernity and poverty, all the more striking.

31

In the remoter areas of the interior in particular, it is also striking how even "marked" persons or those who involve some risk for their host, are welcomed: murderers in flight from the law, political suspects, guerrilla fighters, prostitutes. . . . This cultural legacy has been totally overthrown in the cities, where people have to lock their doors and windows, build walls and put up shutters. Normal practice used to be: "Open hearts, open doors and windows." It is still usual to greet strangers, to talk loudly in public places—squares, markets, offices, buses, halls. . . . Inner life and family secrets are soon targets of words, laughter, song. Secrets do not suit us very well.

Families are extended, the result of tribal, indigenous or black, culture. And godparenthood is not only formally important, but exercised as something real, even to its furthest consequences. In many places, being a godfather or godmother is at least as important a relationship as being a blood brother or sister.

As a people, we are not over-concerned with profit or efficiency. The indigenous culture has left us a still-living legacy of barter as opposed to buying and selling. We believe in the "economy of giving"—even if the tactics used by those responsible for contacting Indians in the so-called "pacification" or "quietening" programmmes have made some aboriginal tribes somewhat excessively ready to ask for gifts.

Gratitude is a basic characteristic of the Latin American spirit: "*Gracias a la vida, que me ha dado tanto*, Thanks be to life, which has given me so much," sang Violeta Parra. And "*Gracis a Dios*, Thanks be to God," say our people constantly.

We have been superficially accused of being lazy, and so condemned to inefficiency and poverty on account of this. Many explanations can be found for this supposed laziness: genetic and climatic, caused by socio-economic precariousness, by malnutrition, by endemic diseases, by inherited physical defects. And one has to recognize that this attitude of not counting the cost, not saving up, of giving and receiving, living for the day without anxiety, and knowing how to make a fresh start every day, how to believe in the future and even dream about it, has much that is spiritual, aware and deliberate about it.

Hugs, kisses, effusive confidences, warmth of welcome, exchanged invitations, are typical of much of society. Friendships are liable to be passionate; a friend is one of the family.

The objections the people and many theorists have to a rigorously planned economy or a mathematically ordered life stem from this wish to live freely and spontaneously, to go on creating and to try out what is new and different. Migration in Latin America is often an evil and has become a veritable social epidemic, with incalculable consequences in terms of social uprooting. Paulo Evaristo Arns, who as Cardinal Archbishop of São Paulo, one of the main targets, knows the subject well, has called migration and its consequences the biggest pastoral challenge facing the church in Brazil. And yet coming and going from one State to another, living in a wide variety of places, also has the virtue of being the means of getting up and out of a disastrous situation in one place. Being a pilgrim and changing places are very much part of our nature.

Feminine influence stamps not only what we might call the nuclear family life, but all family life, even if family members are all adult and scattered. In Latin America the mother is the spiritual, affective, confidential boss in the home. The proverbial Latin American *machismo*—in fact neither worse nor better than that in other parts of the world—has not been able to cover up this beneficent, heart-warming presence of the mother.

Relations in the workplace, when they have not yet been subjected to the iron rules of big firms, completely imported or controlled from outside, tend to operate on a "mates" basis, despite the efforts of the traditional overseers in sugar mills and the like, and managers and directors of modern enterprises, who eventually find themselves forced to adapt to Latin American ways. The clock has a certain "cosmic" quality—we tend to give time a non-Cartesian flexibility, indicated by specifying "Nica," "Paraguayan," "Brazilian" . . . time—and events, *fiestas*, personal circumstances, all naturally and acceptably modify timetables, schedules and plans. Everything, in the end, combines to encourage us to be open, in a way the super-technological First World so disdainfully rejects, or longs for.

Many Europeans, or people from the First World in general, find it impossible to re-adapt to the cold schedules of life and work in the industrial nations after spending time living and working in Latin America. The churches too have had to adapt; those that do not find an innate resistance to their petrified codes and practices.

We must not let the "rising culture" rob us of these charisms of our native spirituality. Any political or social development, if it is to be truly ours, even when it seeks legitimate modernization, economic change, and business efficiency, must at all costs keep our openness and hospitality, without sacrificing them to the idols of individualism, efficacy, and profit. They will have to learn how to make these Latin American charisms part of their modernization, economy, and business. A touchstone for politicians and other leaders of the people; a touchstone, equally, for all Latin American men and women who want to develop as themselves.

An Option for the People

The "Irruption" of the Poor

The most important phenomenon registered in Latin America over the last decades, and the one that has left the deepest mark on its spiritual climate, has, without doubt, been the emergence of the poor. Of course the existence of the poor as a massive and basic fact has been an age-old phenomenon on the continent. Their recent emergence, their new self-awareness, their becoming a new subject of history, form the most significant element in the spiritual make-up of Latin America.

The word generally coined to describe this phenomenon was "irruption": an incursion, invasion, breakthrough, by the poor. It sought to express a nascent, uncontainable energy, something advancing inexorably, gradually but firmly imposing itself. In 1968 the Medellín Conference spoke of "a muted cry pour[ing] from the throats of millions of men and women asking their pastors for a liberation that reaches them from nowhere else." Eleven years later, the Puebla Conference noted: "The cry might well have seemed muted back then. Today it is loud and clear, increasing in volumne and intensity, and at times full of menace."[1] The poor were irrupting on to the continent, in all aspects of society: the economy, politics, culture, communications media, religion. No aspect of life escaped their challenge.[2]

Since then there has been increasing recognition that the "option for the poor," if it is not be discriminatory or reductively "preferential," has to be an option for the masses of the people.

35

The "logic of the majorities" has to be maintained as criterion and judgment in any political or social agenda, as in all projects aimed at solidarity and transformation. This is not because the masses are inert, but because they have their own needs and move at their own pace; because we do not seek to devalue the calling of the active and organized poor themselves, the "poor with spirit" as Ignacio Ellacuría called them, since "when the poor embody their poverty spiritually, when they become aware of the injustice of their situation and of the possibilities and even the real obligation they have in the face of structural poverty and injustice, they change from being passive subjects into active ones, thereby multiplying and strengthening the salvific-historical value that is theirs by right."[3] What the philospher and theologian-martyr Ellacuría wrote of the evangelical prophetic value of the poor is equally true of their socio-political dynamism.

The situation has, though, changed a lot over the last ten years. The apparently uncontainable "irruption" has been checked by the regrouping of conservative forces, by the advance of free market economics, by the "avalanche of capital versus labour" of the North against the South. In 1968 Medellín spoke of the misery in which the continent lived as "an injustice which cries to the heavens" (Justice, 1). In 1979 Puebla noted the growing deterioration in the living conditions of the people: "It is not just that we feel obliged to remind people of individual and social sinfulness. The further reason lies in the fact that since the Medellín Conference the situation has grown worse and more acute for the vast majority of our population" (487); "Recent years have seen a growing deterioration in the socio-political life of our countries" (507). The decade of the 1980s is generally known as "the lost decade" and the events of 1989 and 1990, bringing "the end of history," have not helped us.

If in the past it was the powerful, alone and unrivalled as a class, who determined the course of Latin American society, over the past few decades the poor have taken stock of their existence and reclaimed the right to share in the making of history, forming themselves into a new historical agent. The amorphous masses of the poor are taking stock, organizing and forming a people, a new force in history.[4] In doing so they are following a great tradition: perhaps no other continent has such a history of rebellion: native uprisings, runaway slaves, resistance movements (five hundred years!), revolutions.

The present situation of the people as an entity is complex. In some areas the popular movement as an expression of consciousness and organization of needs, claims, and hopes seems to be gathering strength. In others the people are still subjected and exploited, or anaesthetized, inert. In others they are regrouping their forces, readjusting to changing situations, forming new fronts, and adopting new strategies, along a most creative "alternative" line. There has undoubtedly been discouragement and they have suffered reverses, but the emergence of the people as a historical agent is now an irreversible step taken into the future of Latin America.

The emergence of this new historical agent has become a central reference point in Latin American thinking. The people have become a new social entity, both in the area of understanding and in that of practical action for change.

The Option for the People as Hermeneutic

The option for the people leads us to a new manner of understanding and confronting our situation (an epistemological break). We are abandoning the cultural naivety implied in not being aware of the varied make-up of society. In doing so we are ceasing to think and feel with the patterns of the ruling culture, which caused us to internalize the points of view and interests of those with power. The viewpoint of the poor has become the determinant of our way of thinking.

This spirituality has thus become a very "located" spirituality, located specifically in the "social setting" of the poor. Every element of life, culture, politics, society, religion, moves from being an abstraction—or a pretended neutral sphere—to a location in the social setting of the poor. This is the answer to the question of "where from," of the place we choose to view the world from, to interpret history and to situate our transforming actions. The social setting of the poor is taken up like an option, implying: "First, the social setting opted for; sec-

ond, the setting from which and for which theoretical interpretations and practical plans are made; third, the setting that
configures the actions undertaken and to which actions themselves are bent or subordinated."[5] Now we judge everything
from the social setting of the poor: "If the state of domination
and dependence in which two-thirds of humanity live, with an
annual toll of thirty million dead from starvation and malnutrition, does not become the starting-point for *any* Christian
theology today, even in the affluent and powerful countries,
then theology cannot begin to relate meaningfully to the real
situation. Its questions will lack reality and not relate to real
men and women . . . 'We have to save theology from its
cynicism.'"[6]

We take on the viewpoint of the oppressed, not as such
(though we must also always take on the needs and "denied
rights" of the inert oppressed, of the masses), since as such, as
inert oppressed, their point of view coincides with the interests
of their oppressors, but as rebels:[7] that is, insofar as they have
taken stock of their situation, overcome their traditional alienation and become historical agents, "poor with spirit." In
any event, the option for the people seeks to include the
marginalized poor, to make them take stock, become mobi-
lized and struggle.

Behind this taking on of a social setting lies the ethical
indignation we feel at the situation: the feeling that the reality
of the injustice unleashed on the oppressed is so serious that it
merits our unavoidable attention, our perception that life itself
would lose its meaning if we were to live with our backs turned
on the poor, the irreversible decision to consecrate our own
lives in one way or another to the service of the people, in order
to eradicate the injustice of which they are the victims.

As we discover that the causes of the situation of the poor lie
basically at the level of the structures of society, so we discover
the inescapable political dimension of the situation. By broad-
ening our outlook, we find that there is also a geopolitical
dimension, in the shape of the international conflicts that
hinder the emergence of the people as an agent on the international scene also.

Those who work with the people, such as militant politicians and social workers who have made this option for the people, have realized that this new spirit implies a pedagogical break in their work: accepting the poor as agents of their own destiny, going along with them as protagonists, ceasing to treat them as beneficiaries of aid, no longer living "for" the poor, but "with" them, in communion of struggle and hope, always helping them become the makers of their own future.

This spirituality is convinced that the outlook of the poor is the only genuine point of view from which to study the meaning of life and of history. The outlook of those with power inevitably involves glossing over the real situation in order to justify themselves. The overall state of the world cannot be seen adequately from the point of view of those who hold the power, from the standpoint of the First World: "The metropolises are prevented from having hope: they are threatened by the 'establishments,' which fear any future that excludes them. Their tendency is to work out pessimistic philosophies and theologies, denying people as beings of transformation. This is why in order to think—and there are those who think— outside this scheme of things in the metropolises, one has first to 'become' a Third World person."⁹ Or, in Pedro Casaldáliga's words: "If you don't become Third-Worlders/you will not enter into the Kingdom of Heaven./If you don't make the Third World yours/ you will not even be a human World./And you will not enter into the Kingdom/if you do not enter into the World." The poor, therefore, are called to play the role of educating the consciousness of the world,¹⁰ above all the consciousness of those nations that have for centuries been and still are the oppressors of the Third World.

Conversion to the People

The option for the people is a conversion to the people. It is a class option. And so in many cases it involves moving away from one's own class, though this is not the whole story. And as such it is also a political option, since it places a person at a particular juncture of the correlation of forces in society; it incorporates him or her as an active member of society.

The option for the people forces many who make it to act

consciously as members of their own social class, to become part of it as aware and active militants. Others find that this option makes them leave their own class, while others, without abandoning it, start fighting for the interests of the people (acting against their own class from within it). Where one is does not matter as much as whose side one is on.

Conversion to the people also has its temptations: "vanguardism" and "basism." Through vanguardism we fall into the error of supplanting the people, directing them as a leader who has to be obeyed blindly; in the name of an option for the people, we subject them to passivity and obedience; the historical agent is then forced back to being an object. Through basism, on the other hand, we fall into blind following of any opinion held by the masses, any view taken without due care and discernment, and without us helping the masses to be self-critical.

Many Latin Americans, believers and non-believers, have found and are finding the emergence of the poor to be the basic reality of our time on the stage of history, and opting for their cause has been the fundamental choice they have made in life and the way they plan their lives. This "spirit" has therefore been and is for them a true "religious" experience, in the sense we have indicated. "I want to throw in my lot with the poor of the earth," we sing with José Martí.

Purposive Action

"There are times when the best way of saying is doing," to quote José Martí once more. We believe that there are situations in which the only way of saying liberation—for example—is to make it happen. And we have to believe that, in one way or another, at all times and in all situations, the only way of saying is doing. This amounts to saying that ideology means militancy. Being true to our beliefs means orthopraxis, and faith means love: "Deeds are loves."

Not being Cartesian, this continent is not theoretically inclined. The "economy of gift" is an indigenous legacy. It is not enough to speak friendship or greet one another; we have to give and give ourselves. Latin American hospitality (as presented above) as a characteristic of the basic spirituality of the continent means offering one's whole household, sharing one's living space, without appealing to more or less legitimate privacies.

This disposition has had a decisive influence on Latin American philosophy and religion. It was natural for the pedagogy and theology of liberation to originate here. Even Latin American Marxism has been notably critical of Marxist political orthodoxies when these have proved ineffective. We don't produce revolutionary theories here; we make revolutions. Plans are agendas. This practical immediacy has given rise to both admiration and alarm on the part of outside observers. The creative spirit of the continent lends itself to experimentation, and even improvization, but in deeds, in purposive action.

In political, trade union, or pastoral action, whether or not the terminology is used, the triplet "see, judge, act" has over the last few decades come to signify the overall struggle for liberation. Many men and women have left their professions, academic posts and even families, parishes or convents, because they felt frustrated in a way of life and service that "did not perform" the actual deeds demanded by the times. "Fulfilling oneself" has come to mean doing so in action, in carrying out specific and transforming works. "Personal fulfillment" demands social fulfillment. For this reason, subjectivist personalisms, as well as class, state or status barriers upset us spiritually and make us call out for the interpersonal, practical, neighbourhood, national, or world-scale contexture that our interrelatedness and our inclinations to action demand.

The "pedagogy of the oppressed" first worked out by Paulo Freire, and the whole process of conscientization of peoples, communities, groups, and leaders that followed from this, are worked out in an alternation of theory and practice, action and evaluation, which finally always leads again to action.

Tell me if you "do" and I will tell you if you "are."

In this light and with this spirit we need to review the course of our personal life and the projects of the association or bodies to which we belong. If we plan much and carry out little, we are betraying this dynamic of the soul of the continent, above all today, when frustration grips so many and when the gods of the *aeon* seek to convince us of the ridiculous uselessness or the more or less "alternative" practices and processes upheld by the best of Latin America. History comes to its "end" only where there is no more utopia to chase, or love to bear.

All this shows that Latin America is not on the margins of the dominant note of modern thought, which is everywhere so strongly marked by the primacy of action. Marxism, in particular, has made its contribution here: the point is not to "interpret" the world, but to change it.

Modern philosophy is, undoubtedly, a philosophy of putting things into practice. Technology is its experimental aspect. And "the bottom line" has become its central dogma. From this flow all the dangers and sins of a short-term pragmatism with regard for neither others nor the future: dangers and sins that we must avoid in our Latin American spirituality if we are not to fall into activism or worship of efficiency. The challenge is to combine action with contemplation, openness with efficacy.

In Contemplation

The people of Latin America are universally, deeply, effusively religious. Religion flows from every pore. In this the indigenous and black legacies are as evident as the—welcome or unwelcome—Iberian one.

Throughout whole regions of Latin America it would be impossible to find a single atheist. Secularism is clearly an extraneous and spurious phenomenon for us, which is not to say that it does not exist in some quarters, among certain sections of the population. Even atheistic communism has had to bend in the face of this universal religiosity.

This religiosity stems from a sort of natural inclination to discover mystery, live in it, and appeal to it. The Spirit and "spirits" form part of the cosmovision of mythology and daily life: birth and death, husbandry and harvest, travels . . . all have their palpable blessings and curses. The most immediate and spontaneous explanation is always "supernatural," mythical.

Ecology is not a fashion or a need or a tactic for survival. The earth is our mother; she is holy, the goddess, "Pacha Mama." Nature is the great natural "home" of the human family. Here ecology is what the word means etymologically: *oikos*, "house," even if there is less of the *logia*, less of reasoned study than of immediate experience. The Indians accuse the whites of hunting for hunting's sake—as in the famous letter from Chief Seattle to President Franklin Pierce in reponse to his offer to buy a large tract of Indian territory.

Our people live in a "magic realism." The great novels of

Latin America, universally valid but at the same time different and special, recapture this magic realism in figures, families, or places, that have come to stand for the whole of reality: the patriarch, Macondo, the Maddalena river. . . .

The natural forces of the earth are like the blood, the breath, the soul of Mother Earth. Water is drunk as though kissing it, and is a constant element in rituals, as is fire. Animals, birds, and fish, with their cries, flight, presence, blood, are elements of sacrality, of worship. We live within our geological environment as if it formed the walls, ceilings and rooves of our great house, nature. The huge rivers, towering mountains, impenetrable jungle, endless variety of our flora and fauna, and great diversity of climate, make the geo-cultural body of the continent a being of exuberant vitality.

The images of Indian or African divinities or Christian saints, including photographs of ancestors and typical family groups, that adorn people's houses, are not simply images or photos made of wood, plaster or card. As in the Christian East, they are "inhabited icons." They have embodied the presence of these gods, these saints, these relatives.

There is no doubt that the macro-urbanization and super-technification of modern life is weakening this capacity for contemplation and close identification with nature in Latin America, as elsewhere. But we think we can stop this process in time. The First World has made a U-turn and is desperately crying out for the presence of nature with its still-guarded secrets and its primal purity of water, air, and vegetation. We still have a lot of pure nature. As the indigenous peoples themselves keep telling successive conquistadors and exploiters, they, the natives, are saving nature, not only for themselves, but for the whites as well. Indigenist, anthropological, and pastoral bodies have been able to say, quite rightly, that the native peoples are the specialists in and natural guardians of the environment of this continent, just as the Indians, blacks, and *mestizos* are of its religion and mystery.

Solidarity

Solidarity, in its current acceptation, embracing all faiths, flowering in a multiplicity of creative, concrete, lasting actions, is a typically Latin American, and up to now more specifically Central American product. In Central America, Nicaragua, El Salvador, and Guatemala, in particular, have raised solidarity to the order of the day for history and for the church.

The different names given to love over the centuries flow together today in this one word with such a suggestive richness of content: solidarity.[1] It means reognition, respect, collaboration, alliance, friendship, help. And more. It is tenderness on the effective and at the same time collective level—"the tenderness of peoples," in the words of the poet Gioconda Belli. It is a way for different groups of people to help one another, but in a way that makes them all grow at the same time, because solidarity recognizes the identity of "the other." It supposes stimulation of the independence and otherness of the communities that come together. You can only be in solidarity with those you recognize as other and free, and equal. This is why autonomy, liberation and solidarity have grown together in Latin America. And the processes of liberation have given rise to a lot of spontaneous, daily and often heroic solidarity.

An empire, a transnational company, the middle classes . . . can give alms; they can never make solidarity, unless they are converted, become unfaithful to themselves.

Solidarity in Latin America, with this specific name, written, sung, shouted, often heroically, by poor to poor, persecuted to persecuted, risking or even giving their own life—because there have been many martyrs of solidarity, from the continent or on the continent, and solidarity in Latin America has involved and often still involves a vocation to persecution, prison, and death—is the disinterested tapestry of common objectives, innate affinities, correlation of blood, culture, utopia, the need to fulfil oneself and face up to common struggles together, effective adhesion to the cause of the other, which becomes one's own. Solidarity here means struggling together for the liberation of all.

Among us, only those who make the rights of brother and sister their duty, co-working liberation with them, can be said to act in solidarity.

Etymologically too, deriving from *in solidum*, solidarity means going together into challenge and hope, or submerging oneself collectively in one and the other.

Solidarity is political charity.

As John Paul II has said: "Peace is the fruit of solidarity" (SRS 39), because solidarity is the complementation of justice. Where justice fails to reach, solidarity makes a point of reaching.

The word solidarity has the advantage of not yet being devalued by frivolous usage, as "charity" has been, nor has it been reduced to confessional interests or invoked for short-term aid projects. This is why we say it reaches across credal boundaries, it is "macroecumenic," pointing out common causes and seeking continuity.

Solidarity has not yet been devalued, but there is always the danger that an insufficiently politicized solidarity can cover for the inadequate exercise of justice and human rights for individuals, groups, nations or systems. Just as charity should never have taken and should never take the place of justice, so solidarity should never take the place of true international law, the rights of peoples or the duties of a real international "order."

In recent years, it seems that personal, group and institutional examples of solidarity have multiplied to such an extent in Latin America that there is no statute, demonstration or celebration, in the cultural, political or religious sphere, that does not explicitly proclaim solidarity and appeal to actual cases of solidarity in action. Being a conscious, militant Latin American has come to mean acting in solidarity.

We should not forget that solidarity is a two-way process, something "given and received." Latin America has given itself and has aroused and received from the rest of the world a great deal of solidarity. It has had and still has dramatic occasions for making and receiving solidarity: under military dictatorships and pseudo-democratic governments; in the drama of political persecutions and their resultant refugees; through mounting campaigns against torture and "disappearance," in support of human rights and against continuing domination by the imperial, free-market North; by supporting liberation processes in other continents too; by generating the creation of innumerable solidarity committees in countries of the First World. In 1989, according to Ana Patricia Elvir, general secretary of the Nicaraguan Committee for Solidarity with Peoples, there were "2500 local committees of solidarity with Nicaragua, most of them in the U.S.A., Europe, Canada and Latin America, but also in Africa, Asia and Oceania." In 1992, when the peace agreement between the FMLN and the government of El Salvador was signed, a huge poster proclaimed emotionally: "Thank you, International Solidarity!."

Just as there is a death-dealing internationalism of power, profit and the arms trade, so there is also the life-bringing internationalism of solidarity. A Sandinista militant and delegate of the word testified truly: "Solidarity internationalizes love." It upholds the hope of those who give it and those who receive it, as the Chilean worker-priest Juan Alsina wrote, twenty-four hours before being shot after the military coup of 1973: "If we go down, something of your hope goes down with us. If we rise to new life from the ashes, this is something newly born in you."[2]

Solidarity, which is now our legacy, sealed with the blood of thousands of brothers and sisters, will have to go on being a life commitment, an ultimate horizon, and a daily task for all the sons and daughters of the continent.

Solidarity is now a legacy sealed in blood throughout Latin

America: the common martyrdom of the continent has led us into solidarity with one another. Each martyr has become a banner proclaiming solidarity. On the day following the emblematic martyrdom of "St Romero of the Americas," Mgr Méndez Arceo founded the "Mgr O. A. Romero International Secretariat of Solidarity," which declared: "A church (or an organization) acting in solidarity bears the 'mark' that identifies its authenticity: persecution."

Solidarity is not compassion—unless we give "com-passion" back its original meaning of suffering with—but communion in commitment. Neither is it almsgiving, but a communion of goods.

Latin America is much more than a song to be sung when we feel nostalgic: it is a family drama, a burning mission we carry in our hands, an inheritance we cannot hand over to outsiders, a memory of innumerable martyrdoms, our one and indivisible future. Either we are saved as a continent or we sink as a continent. Many nations and many ethnic groups, but one family home. Until now they have succeeded in dividing us to conquer us: with Spanish and Portuguese, with their various crosses and different swords, with national securities and North-v-South geopolitics.

In our Latin America, any church, any political party, any trade union, any club, any cultural association, that does not live out continent-wide solidarity as something endemic to its very being and its purpose, denies itself the future and prostitutes itself.

We are all Nicaragua. We are all Chile and Paraguay. We are all Haiti. We are all the root Amerindia or Afroamerica—the thousands of abandoned children or the women or workers and peasants who are prevented from being themselves in free aboriginal dignity, by the system, the States, by the Empire, by de-naturizing imported culture.

In our Latin America . . . solidarity is the being of a whole continent taken up as a common liberating challenge. For each of us here, to be in solidarity with the other is to struggle together for the liberation of all.[3]

Radical Faithfulness

Militancy, like constancy, cannot be kept for the "peak times." It must require a continuity in militancy, a continuity we can call faithfulness.

"Faithfulness" means virtually the same as constancy in taking up a cause, beginning on a process, defending the oppressed. Here, in effect, the committed sectors, those groups we should call militant, have given proof, are giving proof, and have done so more than ever in recent decades, of this radical faithfulness.

The various campaigns undertaken—such as, for example, the Mothers of the Plaza de Mayo, the various organizations set up to trace the "disappeared," campaigns for indigenous rights, for land reform, for release of political prisoners, for amnesties, for legal processes to counter the barbarities committed by armed forces, by death squadrons—all these campaigns have demonstrated, come hell or high water, in the most adverse political and even juridical circumstances, a doggedness worthy of these causes, which are truly the most worthy. Those who have taken part in them—militants, lawyers, leaders, natives, peasants, sociologists, pastoral agents—have persisted in this constancy to the death. In this sense, they have proved constant to the end.

In addition, as we progress further in all these campaigns, and especially as the continent becomes more conscious of itself, looks beyond explicitly or exclusively socio-economic concerns, and increasingly vitally and openly discovers the ethno-cultural dimension, so we grow in faithfulness to the roots of our own cultures, our origins. It can be said without exaggerating that in overall, public and organized terms, never have the indigenous cause and the black cause been so much the order of the day, so widely recognized as such, with pleasure or pain, by friends and enemies. At least the causes are plain to see, the laws are in place.

This radical faithfulness, which retrieves the roots, brings them out into the light of day and demands conversion to them, which defends the outcasts, those who are banned and silenced, and which dares to the point of death, has probably been the greatest factor in moving beyond (so far beyond as to renounce) excessively ideologized approaches that ignored all these categories of people. It has forced those who operated in this way to a broader faithfulness. Those who trusted in committees, paramilitary organizations, and other bodies, have had to look out beyond these.

It has also led to people overcoming their previous fatigue. We know that it is easy to ask a few, a very few, born as though predestined to it, to be heroes; it is very difficult to ask whole groups or masses of people to be heroes. And yet throughout the continent we have all felt ourselves, under the dictatorships, in movements for land, for housing, and the like, shaking off our traditional inertia to a very significant degree. Official policies and even immediate results were very much against us, and yet we showed an exemplary perseverance.

We have also moved beyond our usual "prudence" in many ways. Family traditions in some cases, religious upbringing in others, the weight of the ruling groups, or of legal, political and juridical frameworks, all helped to keep the people discreet, in the background, quiet. The past few years have seen them moving away from this "prudence," because of their radical faithfulness. In Brazil, for example, there has been explicit recognition, even openly proclaimed in words and writing, by jurists, bishops and others, that what matters above all is not whether something is "legal," but whether it is "legitimate." This is an example of what we mean by moving beyond prudence.

Then, increasingly, this faithfulness to the roots has led us out of ghetto, group, private concerns. The banners are now raised for the great causes, and these are becoming wider. So, for example, the indigenous groups who initiated the "alternative" campaign to the commemoration of 1492-1992 originally called it an "indigenous campaign," but gradually came to the conclusion that it had to be an "indigenous, black, and popular campaign." And trade unions and political parties have also had to come together in search of an understanding: the union is not everything; neither is the party: they complement one another. And both unions and parties have had to open discussions with the "popular movement," which is something broader, sometimes more diffuse, but reaching out to sectors unaffected by unions and political parties.

This process leads more and more to concentration on causes. Political parties have always been tempted to make themselves their own objective, their goal, as have trade unions (though the same can be said of popular movements). It seems that, increasingly, in both theory and practice, there is a quest for causes, for great causes.

All these campaigns, this resistance that has sometimes taken place over long years in prison, in silence, in clandestinity, on the margins, have stamped a mark on civil society, in the fields of education, agrarian reform, inner city rebuilding, on the life of the churches, too; they have built up an attitude of rebellious faithfulness: faithfulness to causes, to faiths also, and at the same time a capacity for rebellion, required at root by the alternative, complementary solution when faced with more official, more conservative plans and attitudes.

Another characteristic of this radical faithfulness in militancy has been what is called in Brazil "*dar a volta por cima*," leapfrogging. After reverses such as the UNO victory in the 1990 elections in Nicaragua, the failure of "Lula" to capture the Brazilian presidency in 1989, or a number of lesser setbacks, the people regroup and continue the struggle for land, for housing, for health, for education. In contrast to the fatigue, nihilism or neo-nihilism so evident in parts of the First World, Latin America seems to have a great capacity for healing its wounds. We return to life and the struggle with great ease.

If one looks at the documents produced as protests, manifestos, declarations of solidarity and the like, the last word, the final order, is always one of hope. In particular, the experience of our martyrs has proved supremely positive: "The blood of the martyrs bears fruit...." Archbishop Romero's phrase sums up the hopes of one and all, Christian and non-Christian alike: "I will rise again in the people of El Salvador."[1]

The expression, "the fatigue of the good" was used by Pius XII. Jesus said that the children of darkness are wiser, perhaps more persevering, than the children of light. And in the past few years, we have experienced a sort of fatigue, a self-confessed foreseen defeat, as utopias and ideologies have fallen. And yet the bulletins and manifestos continue to appear, meetings and congresses are still held. There is a great concern to take hold of our utopia once more. There is a phrase much used in pastoral work with indigenous peoples, and repeated in many documents: "reorganizing hope." In the face of so much hesitation, discouragement, renunciation of utopias, we are reorganizing hope, being, in an old expression, "defeated soldiers of an invincible cause."

In this process, we are discovering that we have to be faithful in all areas of life. People were often faithful, even fanatically so, to the aims of the party, to the orders of the resistance movement, and yet fell down in faithfulness within their own families, in control of their own passions. Somehow they fell into the bourgeois pattern of a double standard.

Total faithfulness places the cause above personal life. Being faithful is more important than staying alive: "We have to sail; we don't have to live," was the motto of the Naval College of Sagres in Portugal; it became a resistance song against the military dictatorship in Brazil. Slogans such as "Victory or death," or "Freedom or death," have been translated into a thousand varieties, not usually so trenchant. And tens of thousands—men, women and even children—have given their lives for causes, for the cause.

Martyrdom has become virtually endemic. No militant rules out laying down his or her own life; some proclaim their own death. "Deaths foretold" have been multiplied by the thousand. Most adult militants—guerrilla fighters of course, but also lawyers, trade unionists, politicans, human rights activists, pastoral agents, even artists—know that singing to a guitar, witnessing at a tribunal or signing a manifesto, have for years involved risking death.

In Brazil they speak of those "marked for death." Death in Latin America has become a widespread mark. The "marks" of Revelation have become the mark of a whole people. All the people of Latin America who have the understanding and will to defend the cause of liberation, the very roots of their identity, their otherness, who struggle for human rights, are, at least to some extent, people marked by a death foretold.

These martyrs then become a new motive for remaining faithful. Many streets, *barrios*, institutions and the like bear a martyr's name. Their anniversaries are celebrated, to the point where the calendar has scarcely a day not marked in red. Every day has its one or several martyrs.

So faithfulness has to be to death, and to the dead. Obviously any union, any organization, any people, that forgets those who gave their lives for the causes it is supposed to be defending, does not deserve to survive. If it loses its memory, it loses its rights. Jesus told the scribes and Pharisees that their ancestors murdered the prophets and now they build tombs for them (Matt. 23:29ff par.). Here it would be: you built tombs for them, but when less advantageous times came, you forgot them, or even destroyed their tombs. Sometimes, for the sake of a quiet life, we are tempted to put what reminds us of them out of our sight. And as the proverb says: "What the eye doesn't see, the heart doesn't grieve for." Or, "Out of sight, out of mind." And once out of mind, wiped from memory, the dead soon leave our life.

Everyday Faithfulness

A revolutionary spirit will always find, one way or another, a tension between utopia and reality. Utopia is always so *u-topic*, so "without a place here," so "in another place," that it is also resistant to lodging in our lives. Paradoxically, it is easier to lay down one's life on the altars of utopia than to hand it over in everyday faithfulness, in the obscurity of anonymity and the minutiae of everyday living. It is easier to love great causes from a distance than to make them a living part of our everyday commitment. It is easier to make expansive gestures to the gallery than to be faithful in the little details that make up the dim pattern of anonymous daily life.

"It is easier to win freedom than to administer it every day," said Bolívar. It is easier to win a revolution than to carry it on with a sustained mystique over the following years, as the Sandinista experience showed. A heroic insurrection is easier than the "daily revolution" needed in society and our own individual lives.

The liberating spirit is not a spirit of libertinage, of anarchy. This would be a false liberation. Ours is a disciplined spirituality, even in the cause of the revolution it seeks to serve. We live day-by-day, to a disciplined schedule, giving our work, rest, socializing, prayer, each its allotted time. The more utopic we are, the stronger and more impulsive our mystique is, the more direction and limits we need, so as not to spread ourselves too thinly.

Authenticity is impossible without discipline and self-control to order our lives and activities. The best revolutionaries have always been models of discipline and self-control. Liberty and celebration can easily be misunderstood, exaggerated, pushed to undue excess. Discipline, order, method, planning, feedback, faithfulness in little things, perseverance, tenacity . . . are the marks of our spirit. This is the "realism" of those who are "genuinely and consistently utopic."

"Utopia has its calendar." Facing up to each day as it comes means living in the actual situation where the struggle for utopias takes place; it means having the capacity to surmount the misery and failure implicit in all human striving seen close-to in the ring of reality, with no idealization. They alone have true hope who are not scandalized or discouraged by everyday experience.

Being faithful day-by-day, on the individual level, is also what is involved in personal wholeness, in the unity of personal life, in overcoming the split personality implied by being "two-faced" or operating a double standard. Increasingly today, the requirements for personal wholeness and Christian holiness are seen to lie in the ascesis of self-control—ensuring that it is our "adult" rather than "child" or any other of our many selves that increasingly controls our situation—of psychic maturity, of harmonious relationships with others on all levels: family, workplace, pastoral care, union or political party, ecumenical work, leisure, idleness. This is not easy: "*Mea maxima poetitentia, vita communis,*" said St John Berchmans: "My greatest penance is life in community"; "*Dos son los problemas, dos:/los demás/y yo,*" says Pedro Casaldáliga: "There are two problems, two:/other people/and myself."

Being open to criticism and growing in this true ascesis of communal criticism, as well as forcing oneself to be truly democratic at work, in dealing with people in general and with one's own team, are real spiritual experiences.[1] We also need the ascesis of harmony, of balance: through not knowing how to live harmoniously day-by-day, many militants have destroyed their families, their feelings, their personal balance, their political utopia . . . and some Christian militants have also destroyed their own chance of holiness.

Being truly faithful day-by-day implies surmounting the self-deceit characteristic of those who feel great ethical indignation at national or world injustices, those who feel deep "compassion" for the oppressed of distant lands and even contribute generously to their aid, but at the same time have no compassionate sensitivity to the needs of those closest to them, and fail to see where their immediate duties lie: to family—wife or husband, children, parents, grandparents—to community—care of common property, responsible participation in communal works, not being a burden on others, neighbourhood projects, the local environment—to the rest of society—paying taxes, fair business dealings, obeying traffic laws. . . .

Certain classic forms of monastic life, of strict enclosure, valid in earlier ages, are today not necessarily the best ways of responding to the demands of human solidarity and social responsibility. It is not enough to retire to the desert alone to live with God and wrestle with the Devil. The challenge of good and evil also has to be faced in solidarity with others. (This is not to deny the validity of specific vocations to deep contemplation, always in solidarity, as vocations to prayer, to witness to transcendence; these are more needed than ever in the midst of a dark, "short-termist" world.)

Day-to-day living is where it is hardest to overcome personal contradictions: the gap between utopia, ideals, generosity, noble and heroic gestures on one side, and the egoisms of shared living (with spouse, at home, in the community, at work), corruption, failure in little tasks, weakness in such human things as gluttony, sexual immaturity, alcohol, on the other. How we behave day-by-day is where those around us perceive the basic vices that we usually fail to see in ourselves: bossiness, self-importance, pride, making use of others, irresponsibility. . . .

Personal harmony requires an inner structural coherence: this means a deep harmony and cohesion between our basic attitude and our specific actions.[2] Only when there is coherence between these can we achieve harmony, authenticity and veracity, and do so on all levels: inner life, individual, family, locality, economic, public. Witness would be the chief sign of veracity, and martyrdom its supreme form.

Those who struggle for utopia, for radical change, saints marked by the liberating spirit, are all of a piece; they carry faithfulness from the root of their being on to the smallest details that others overlook: attention to the littlest, respect for subordinates, eradication of egoism and pride, care for common property, generous dedication to voluntary work, honesty in dealings with the state, punctuality in correspondence, not being impressed by rank, being impervious to bribes. . . . Detailed everyday faithfulness is the best guarantee of the veracity of our utopias. The more utopic we are, the more down-to-earth!

There is a saying that "Every man has his price," that for one reward or another (money, power, distinction, honours, comfort, sex, fame, adulation ...), everyone, one day or another, will end up giving in, selling conscience, dignity, honesty. Corruption is a major plague at all levels of most societies; denunciations of it and impotence in the face of it are a common refrain. The new man and new woman, filled with spirit, really cannot be bought, even in little things and on bad days.

How we act day-by-day is the most reliable test for demonstrating the quality of our lives and the spirit that inspires them. This is where we have to put these counsels into practice: "Be what you are. Speak what you believe. Believe what you preach. Live what you proclaim. To the final consequences and in the smallest everyday matters."[3]

This "day-by-day" has become one of the main forms of "ascesis" in our spirituality: the heroism of the everyday, the domestic, the routine, of faithfulness even in the smallest details. Everyday faithfulness has become one of the chief criteria of authenticity—because "those who have the message of liberation and those who really liberate are not the same."[4]

Tell me how you live out an ordinary day, any day, and I will tell you if your dream of tomorrow is worth anything.

Utopia is not a chimera. It has to tackle the "incredible inertia of the actual" (Romano Guardini) and the "unbearable lightness of being" (Milan Kundera).

The *Kairos* can come only in the *kronos*. It breaks out in the *kronos*, and has to be accepted there today, every day.

PART TWO

THE LIBERATING
SPIRIT OF
JESUS CHRIST

Going Back to the Historical Jesus

The Question of the Historical Jesus

The spirituality of liberation, like the theology of liberation itself, is characterized by its strong concentration on the historical Jesus. Our spirituality is not only christocentric: it puts the historical Christ-Jesus at its core.

The theme of the historical Jesus as opposed to the Christ of faith acquired its credentials in modern theology at the end of the eighteenth century, in the context of liberal Protestant theology, concerned as it was to discover biographical data about the "true Jesus," both as a reaction against the dogmatic tradition of the Catholic Church, and as a response to the criticism arising from the rationalism of the Enlightenment.

The problem, however, goes back to the New Testament itself, where tension can be found between the historical Jesus and the Christ of faith. This tension has resurfaced periodically throughout the history of the Christian churches,[1] particularly at times of major crisis and renewal.[2] In the last two centuries it has affected European theology in a special way. In our day, many theologies and spiritualities are attempting to see Christ in historical terms.[3] Among these, the theology and spirituality of liberation have perhaps made the deepest and most serious efforts in this direction.

This might be seen as due to two main causes. The first is that Latin America has discovered a very strong parallelism between the historical situation of the continent now and that of Jesus of Nazareth in his time.[4] The second is the "circular-

61

ity" existing between the social situation and the most accessible image of Jesus. "A particular (social and/or ecclesial)
setting leads more clearly to emphasizing and understanding
the historical Jesus, and the historical Jesus refers back to a
particular setting. . . . Being faithful to the situation of Latin
America—and to the whole Third World in general—and to its
needs sends us back more clearly to the historical Jesus; and
understanding of the historical Jesus has led to a clearer and
deeper understanding of the Latin American situation and its
demands. This is really a single movement with two distinct
and complementary phases, leading to historicization (according to the historical Jesus) and to Latin-Americanization of
faith in Christ."[5]

In Latin American spirituality and theology, "historical
Jesus" is used without direct reference to the debate about
retrieving the biographical elements of his life. Its use does not
refer to a marginal or circumstantial aspect, but to something
deeper. It is a challenge to the veracity of faith and its capacity
to preserve the whole of the mystery hidden and revealed in
Jesus Christ. For us, the "historical Jesus":

— evokes recuperation of the theological import of the
history of Jesus of Nazareth for our life as Christians, within
the specific history of the continent of Latin America;[6]

— explains the deep link that exists between the church's
faith in Jesus Christ and the commitment this faith forces it to
make with the suffering history of the Latin American people;[7]

— responds to a core question around which all others
revolve: maintaining the dialectic between the way Jesus acted
out his obedience to the Father and how this challenges the way
Christians here and now act out their faithfulness to Jesus. If
Jesus was the making-present of God and the Reign of God,
then there is no way to live as children of God except the way
he lived.[8]

What we are reacting against

As can be seen, this particular christology specifically "focused on the historical Jesus" is a characteristic and very
marked feature of our spirituality. This is no ingenuous,

improvized or inconsequential feature. It is not a matter of just "going back to Jesus," but one of genuinely "getting Jesus back." It starts from the suspicion that "in the name of Christ it has been possible to ignore and even contradict basic values in the preaching and activity of Jesus of Nazareth."[9]

We suspect that "Christ has not infrequently been reduced to a sublime abstraction . . . an abstraction that makes it possible to ignore or deny the very truth of Christ," as evidenced in those charismatic and pentecostalist groups "which invoke the Spirit of Christ but without enquiring into the specific Spirit of Jesus."

We suspect, too, that many discourses on Jesus as universal reconciliation "seek to exclude Jesus from the conflictivity of history and find in Christianity a support for any ideology of peace and order and a condemnation of any type of conflict and subversion."

A suspicion also arises in regard to the frequent tendency to unbridled absolutization of Christ, which is accepted unquestioningly in the spontaneous understanding of many Christians. Effectively, if Christ is made into an absolute from all points of view, then any "personalist reduction of Christian faith," making contact with the "Thou" of Christ the ultimate and correct correlation to the "I" of the Christian, can theoretically be justified. The total absolutization of Christ internalizes an a-historical concept in Christian understanding, since "if Christians already possess the absolute, it is quite understandable that their interest in what is historically non-absolute should be reduced."

Writing out of the context of South Africa, Albert Nolan has given vigorous expression to these same suspicions:

> Over the centuries, many millions of people have venerated the name of Jesus; but a very small number have understood him, and a still smaller number have tried to put what he wanted done into practice. Their words have been distorted to the point where they mean everything, something or nothing. His name has been used and abused to justify crimes, to frighten children and to inspire heroic folly in men and women. Jesus has been

honoured and worshipped more often for what he did not mean than for what he really meant. The supreme irony consists in some of the things he most energetically opposed in his time becoming what has been most preached and spread through the length and breadth of the world . . . in his name![10]

The question for us is not how to demythologize the figure of Jesus, but how to de-manipulate it:

> The demythologization of Christ is important; but in Latin America it is more important to de-manipulate Christ and rescue him from connivance with idols. Demythologizing Christ in Latin America does not primarily mean establishing his historical existence against the rationalist critique, although this has to be done too, but not letting reality be abandoned to its misery through abstracting him from history. What we are trying to do in Latin America in going back to Jesus is prevent Christ from being presented in connivance with idols. Graphically, one might say that what is in crisis is not simply "the name" of Christ, which may have lost meaning, but what really happens "in the name of Christ." If a post-Enlightenment culture casts doubt on Christ, the actual situation in Latin America makes us indignant at what happens in the name of Christ.[11]

The question is not, then, theoretical or academic. Decidedly, we have to rescue Jesus, "and one cannot find a better, more effective and more obvious way of doing this than going back to Jesus."[12] So for us, "going back to Jesus," insistently revindicating the "historical Jesus," is not an intellectual exercise, nor an archeologist's or catacomb-specialist's mania, but passionate concern for being faithful, anxiety to recover the true face of Jesus, the authentic and normative revelation of God, the genuinely Christian character of God and the church.

What does appealing to the "Historical Jesus" actually mean?

Latin American spirituality "understands the historical Jesus to mean the whole of the history of Jesus." And,

> What is most historical about Jesus is what he did: that is, what he did in order to operate actively on the conditions of the time and to transform them in a particular direction, in the direction of the Kingdom of God. It is what he did that unleashed history in his day and that has come down to us as unleashed history. What is historical here is what unleashes history. . . . The historical aspect of Jesus is not, therefore, in the first place, simply what can be dated in space and time, nor the doctrinal aspect. . . . What is historical about Jesus is, for us, in the first place, an invitation (and a requirement) to do what he did, to follow his example for a purpose. . . . What we have to ensure when we speak about the historical Jesus is, above all, that we do what he did.[13]

So going back to the historical Jesus does not mean wanting to know more about him, but wanting to know him better. Knowing Christ—and not just knowing more about him—is something we achieve not intellectually, but in doing. We know him to the extent that we understand what he did through experience, and by assimilating this and making it ours, we come to be more fully in tune with his cause and his person, which complement one another.

We believe that what Jesus did is what provides access to the whole of him, what enables us to shed light on, understand better, and judge the importance of other aspects that go to make up the whole: isolated incidents from his life, his teaching, his inner disposition, his fate and what we might call his personality.[14] The best setting for really knowing Jesus is simply carrying out what he did, following him.

Following the historical Jesus is at the same time the best way of accepting the Christ of faith. "By the mere fact of reproducing what Jesus did and was to the fullest extent, by being of Jesus, we are accepting Jesus as ultimately normative, and in doing so declaring him to be something truly ultimate; we are now declaring him, implicitly but effectively, as the Christ, even though this confession needs to be explicitated later."[15]

Appealing to the historical Jesus means that we do not wish to fall into the idealist trap of believing in a Christ without Jesus, a Christ without flesh. The historical Jesus is the historical flesh of God. If we are to avoid any form of gnosticism, ancient and modern, our criterion must always consist in going back to the historical flesh of Christ. The historical Jesus is the normative criterion of revelation.

The Christ of faith, the risen Christ, is the same historical Jesus of Nazareth, totally transfigured and raised to the right hand of God.[16] Our spirituality always insists on this identity between the risen Christ and the historical Jesus: liberation theology, for example, declares that, "the risen one is the crucified one," and not just someone raised, who could be anyone.[17] On this point it is following the line taken by John in the New Testament: the Messiah who came in the flesh is the criterion for testing all spirits (1 John 4:1-3).

This going back to the historical Jesus—to the historical face of Jesus Christ—has made us discover the faces of Christ as described by Puebla; "young children, struck down by poverty before they are born . . . young people, disoriented . . . the indigenous peoples, . . . Afro-Americans, . . . the peasants . . . deprived of land, . . . labourers . . . ill-paid, the underemployed and the unemployed, . . . marginalized and over-crowded city dwellers, . . . old people. . . ." (Puebla, 30ff). We have discovered this collective face of the Suffering Servant in Latin America, described in liberation theology and spirituality, according to the most appropriate biblical reading of the Servant of Yahweh.

The Christian God

Latin American spirituality is characterized by a special approach to the subject of God.[1] While in Europe and North America the subject has been approached from the dialogue with atheism, here on a "Christian continent," with the great majority of the population "oppressed and believing," the question is urgent and challenging as part of our struggle against inhuman idolatry. The problem relating to God is not so much atheism as idolatry.[2]

So we do not ask whether we are believers or atheists, but rather what God we are believers in or atheists of. Our problem is not whether or not God exists, but which is the true God; the question is to discern between the true God and the multitude of idols.

This approach stems from the conditions on this continent, where most of the people are Christian, where everything seems to be done in the name of God, and where even destitution and exploitation are covered over with a veneer of religious legitimation. Five hundred years ago, when the Christian faith was first brought here, many things were done in the name of the Christian God that contradicted God's most obvious will. The cross legitimized the sword. In the name of Jesus, the baptism of slaves deported from Africa was carried out at gunpoint. In the name of God, obedience to the monarchs of the empire overseas was demanded, even after the various wars for national independence. Even in the last decade we have seen conflicts in which the cross was carried by both sides. And still today, the oppressed majorities are Christian and those who oppress them call themselves Christians. The name of Jesus is spoken by oppressed and oppressors with totally contradictory meanings. It is clear that the idols of power and money are active and devouring many victims, but doing so in a Christian disguise.

This context of the struggle of the gods is where the Spirit has given us an instinctive spiritual sense for revindicating the genuine Christian God, a passionate quest for the "God of Jesus," a constant desire to discern the Christian quality of our God, and a continuing undertaking of unmasking idols. We declare ourselves atheists of the idols, even if they have Christian names. We join with the atheism of all those who deny the idols.

In this discernment of the true God as opposed to the idols, our spirituality lets itself be guided by the same criterion we use in other fields: Jesus of Nazareth. We seek the "Christian" God, that is the God of Christ, the God Jesus showed us. Here too, this means going back to the historical Jesus. In rediscovering Jesus, the church in Latin America has had to come to terms with many aspects of its image of God; these were not, in effect, reconcilable with the God of Jesus. This is a basic crisis, because it concerns the roots of belief; it is also a purifying crisis, particularly when it succeeds in overcoming resistance to conversion to the God of Jesus.

We should not have an idea of what God is before knowing Jesus and then, later, in faith, discover that this God we thought we knew (derived perhaps from Aristotle, from cultural religious traditions or from our own basic instincts) is present in Jesus. This is how our affirmation of the divinity of Jesus has often actually worked: in stating that Jesus is God, we have not modified our previous idea of God, but "corrected" the understanding we may have had of Jesus in the light of our previous idea of God. So we were not letting ourselves be evangelized by Jesus, but encasing Jesus' evangelization in the straitjacket of our previous mental constructs, which were alien to Jesus. So many Christians, who call themselves such, worship other gods, other idols, confusing them with the Christian God.

But it should not be like this. The Christian God has nothing to do with any idea we might have of God before knowing Jesus. "No one has ever seen God. It is the Father's only Son ... who has made him known" (John 1:18). In order to know the truly "Christian" God, we have to renounce our previous ideas of God and learn what, who and how God is, starting from Jesus.

"The New Testament does not tell us so much that Jesus is God as that God is Jesus." To clarify: this means that we have to learn in Jesus everything we can know about God. It means that we cannot manipulate the revelation God makes in Jesus by correcting it—consciously or unconsciously—in accordance with what we thought or believed we knew before about God; we must, on the contrary, correct our idea of God in the light of what Jesus shows us about God.

Believing in Jesus means believing in his God the Father, in the biblical God.

The quest for the Christian God is the most radical quest the church itself can undertake. It is a question of knowing whether the God we worship is really the God of Jesus or a masked idol. And this quest also involves analyzing the role Christian faith plays in society and in history. While ours may appear to be a Christian God in the restricted circles of biblical reference and our personal lives, it may nevertheless be performing social functions (legitimizing courses of action and institutions) that run entirely counter to God's plan. So the question ranges beyond the good will of individuals, the community, or the institutional church:

> We cannot take for granted that our God is the God of Life made manifest in Jesus. It is possible to say mass every day, to spend our time in perpetual adoration of the Blessed Sacrament, or to carry out our functions as a parish priest, religious superior or bishop, and still put across the image of a God who is not the Father of Jesus. It can very well be the God of an institution, of a culture, or the projection of infantile wishes. We have to exercise constant discernment to make sure that our God is not the God of sacralized human attributes.[3]

So, what is this God revealed in Jesus like? What is the Christian God we believe in like? The spirituality of liberation gives a clear account of, and a passionate witness to, its God in each and every one of its chapters. Here we propose simply to bring together a few broad brush strokes:

— We believe in the *God of Jesus*, the God Jesus specifically revealed in his flesh, in his works and also in his words, in his living history.

— We believe in the *God of the Reign*, the God of Jesus, who has revealed his plan for history to us and charged us with the task of putting it into effect—of building his Reign.

— We believe in the *incarnate God*, universal but specific, in *kenosis*, who took flesh, culture, sex, dialect, regionalism....

— We believe in the *God of history*, made manifest in history, making history, accompanying it and handing it over to human beings as our responsibility.

— We believe in the *God of life*, who engenders life and glories in life ("*Gloria Dei homo vivens*": St Irenaeus),[4] who desires that all should be saved, that they should have life and have it abundantly (John 10:10).

— We believe in the *God of the poor*, universal but partial.

— We believe in *God the liberator*, shown in power liberating the people, raising the lowly out of the dust and pulling the mighty down from their thrones.

— We believe in the *God of all names*, active and present in all peoples and religions, who listens to all who sincerely call on God under any other name, who does not require people to abandon their own culture for God's sake.

— We believe in *God the Father and Mother*, who created men and women in his/her image, equal in dignity, complementary in achievement.

— We believe in *God the Trinity*, original communion, ultimate community.

— We believe in *God struggling against idols*, who counters the principalities and powers of the age, the gods of death.

> The God whom the missionaries preached was a God who blessed the powerful, the conquerors, the colonizers. This God demanded resignation in the face of oppression

and condemned rebelliousness and insubordination. All that was offered to us by this God was an interior and other-worldly liberation. It was a God who dwelt in heaven and in the Temple but not in the world.

The Jesus who was preached to us was barely human. He seemed to float above history, above all human problems and conflicts. He was pictured as a high and mighty emperor who ruled over us, even during his earthly life, from the heights of his majestic throne. His approach to the poor was therefore thought of as condescending. He condescended to make the the poor the objects of his mercy and compassion without sharing their oppression and their struggles. His death had nothing to do with historical conflicts, but was a human sacrifice to placate an angry God. What was preached to us was a completely other-worldly Jesus who had no relevance to this life.

These were the images of God and Jesus that we inherited from our conquerors and the missionaries who accompanied them. . . .

[We] began to read the Bible with new eyes. We were no longer dependent upon the interpretations of our oppressors.

What we discoverd was that Jesus was one of us. He was born in poverty. He did not become incarnate as a king or nobleman but as one of the poor and oppressed. He took sides with the poor, supported their cause and blessed them. On the other hand, he condemned the rich. "Blessed are you who are poor" (Luke 6:20), "Woe to you who are rich" (6:24). He even described his mission as the liberation of the downtrodden (Luke 4:18). That was the very opposite of what we had been taught.

At the heart of Jesus' message was the coming of the Reign of God. We discovered that Jesus had promised the Reign of God to the poor: "Yours is the Reign of God" (Luke 6:20) and that the good news about the coming of God's Reign was supposed to be good news for the poor (4:18). . . .

Jesus was and still is . . . the true image of God. The

poor and oppressed Christians of today, together with those who have taken an option for the poor, can now see the true face of God in the poor Jesus—persecuted and oppressed like them. God is not an almighty oppressor. The God we see in the face of Jesus is the God who hears the cries of the poor and who leads them across the sea and the desert to the promised land (Exod. 3:17). The true God is the God of the poor who is angry about injustice in the world, vindicates the poor (Ps. 103:6), pulls down the mighty from their thrones and lifts up the lowly (Luke 1:52). This is the God who will judge all human beings according to what they have done or not done for the hungry, the thirsty, the naked, the sick and those in prison (Matt. 25:31-46).

We are grateful to God for the grace that has enabled us to rediscover God in Jesus Christ. "I bless you Father for hiding these things from the learned and the clever and revealing them to mere children" (Luke 19:21). It is by the Spirit of God that we have been able to see what the learned and the clever were not able to see. We no longer believe in the God of the powerful and we want no gods except the God who was in Jesus. "I am Yahweh your God who brought you out of the land of Egypt, out of the house of slavery. You shall have no gods except me" (Exod. 20:2-3).[5]

The Trinity

Believing in the biblical God, as taught by Jesus, necessarily means believing in the Blessed Trinity. The God of Jesus, the Christian God, is Father, Son and Spirit, the Blessed Trinity.[1]

In Jesus the Son of the eternal Father exists as a person. He is the only begotten Son of God in history. And in the mystery of Jesus the eternal Spirit of the Father and the Son lives and acts in history.

The union of the three divine persons in community flows together, is expressed, loves, and saves in the taut historical union of these two natures that make up the one Jesus, Christ the Lord. The God that Jesus is, lives, and reveals to us is neither solitary nor distant; this God is both transcendent and immanent. Both "the history of the Trinity and the Trinity in history" belong to Christian faith.[2] This is the God-in-three-persons who becomes the God-for-us, the One-community and the Eternity-history.

"The Blessed Trinity is the best community," as the base communities declare (and as Leonardo Boff entitled his more popular work on the Trinity). It is the source, requirement and end of all true community. The church of Jesus has to be trinitarian or it will not be Christian. Christian spirituality is necessarily trinitarian. Christian spirituality in the church and in the world is called to make the mystery of the Trinity present within the ups and downs and hopes of human history.

The Trinity is, in itself, the beginning and end of the Reign. The Reign, on earth and in heaven, is the gift of the Trinity, poured out in a process running through and beyond history: in fulfilling the lives of its sons and daughters and in the integrity and beauty of its creation.

The Glory of the Trinity is the accomplishment of the Reign.

"Trinitarian-ness" has to be the essential mark of any true evangelization, of the authentic church of Jesus and of any spirituality with claims to be Christian.

The community and historical nature of the Trinity revealed by the gospel have to be proclaimed in evangelization, celebrated and "institutionalized" in the church, and internalized—in faith, hope and charity—by all Christians and by the whole church community.

The *personal attributes* of Father, Son and Spirit also have to be explicitly internalized, as such, by any true Christian spirituality and with their own special characteristics in the spirituality of liberation.

Like the Father
who is the mother-source of life, inexhaustible creativity, absolute acceptance, origin and return of all that exists,

we Christians must develop within ourselves and in all the spheres in which we act:

— a passion for life and its advancement;

— the integral promotion of ecology;

— an attitude of understanding, welcome, fatherhood and motherhood of biology and spirituality, of politics and the arts;

— the memory of our origins and the meaning of life and history.

Like the Son
who is human being and divine being,

Son of God and son of woman,

Word and service,

The Chosen One and the faceless one,

the poor baby in the manger and the proclaimer of the beatitudes,

put to death and the Name-above-all-names,

God's compassion and anger,

death and resurrection,
we Christians must harmoniously integrate, surmounting
all dichotomy:

— divine sonship and universal brother- and sisterhood
(as Brother Charles de Foucauld, the Litttle Brothers and Little
Sisters of Jesus, and thousands of priests, religious and lay
people have wonderfully coupled this supremely humanitar-
ian and evangelical aspiration to be "universal brothers and
sisters" to the spirituality of liberation);

— contemplation and action, receptivity and planned
activity, the proclamation and building of the Reign;

— the dignity of the children of God and the "opprobium
of Christ";

— spiritual infancy and "perfect joy";

— the folly of the cross and the security of knowing in
whom we place our trust;

— mercy and prophecy, peace and revolution;

— failure and the paschal victory.

Like the Spirit

who is the love between Father and Son and the "love that
is in all loves,"

the bottomless inner depth of the very God and of all who
contemplate God, and at the same time the dynamization of
everything that is created, that lives, grows, changes,

Pater pauperum, Consoler of the afflicted, *go'el* of the
marginalized, initiator of liberty and of all liberation, advocate
for the justice of the Reign,

oil of mission, Easter jubilee and mighty wind of Pentecost,

witness in the mouths and blood of the martyrs, the one
who raises up, clothes and reassembles dry bones and stran-
gled utopias,

we Christians,

— in militant contemplation and evangelical liberation,

— in ongoing conversion and daily prophecy,

— in tenderness, in creativity, in *parresia*,

— borne along by this Spirit that is for ever the Spirit of

the Risen Christ,

will take up:

— all the causes of truth, justice and peace;

— individual human rights and the right of peoples to be different, autonomous and equal;

— the aspirations of the "alternative society" and the fruitful tensions in a church continually called to be converted (*"ecclesia semper reformanda"*: UR 6; GS 43; LG 7, 9, 35);

— the legacy of our martyrs;

— the daily dawning of utopia, over all its twilights, and the consummation of history, against the wicked "end of history."

In Latin America, the spirituality of liberation has adopted "the motto of the Russian Orthodox socialist reformers of the late nineteenth century: 'The Blessed Trinity is our social agenda,'"[5] while also keeping it as the whole agenda of our faith. Because the Trinity is not only mystery; it is "agenda," at once home and destiny: we come from it, we live in it, we are going to it.

A Latin American painter might well transpose the famous Andrej Rublev icon of the Trinity into local figures and symbols. In it, there are three persons equal in communion of love; the three are setting out on a journey, with staves in their hands; the three are seated at a table sharing the bread of life; the three have left a space at the table to welcome any traveller willing to share their meal.

"Reign-Focus"

The theme of the Reign of God is a key one in our spirituality. It is the theme that we focus on above all others.[1]

Reign-focus implies various things. In the first place, that the sum total of spirituality is not uniform and homogenous, that it has different dimensions, values, themes, requirements, all susceptible to grading; that this grading implies a hierarchy (Vatican II reminds us that "there exists an order or 'hierarchy' of truths, since they vary in their relationship to the foundation of the Christian faith" [UR 11]) and allows a core around which the other elements revolve. Every generation of Christians has sought, one way or another, to discover "the essence of Christianity," its core, the absolute in terms of which Christian identity is defined. Every generation, every theology, every spirituality, has given its own reply.

When asked to give its reply to this question of the essence or core of Christianity, the spirituality of liberation here too brandishes its criterion of "going back to the historical Jesus" (see the section with this heading above). It does not seek to philosophize or theologize on the essence of Christianity; it seeks to understand what Jesus' objective, core, absolute, cause, was. (This element of the spirituality of liberation is essentially christological, though its very centrality implies all the other dimensions: ecclesiology, eschatology, Christian identity, commitment to history.) Here too, by referring back to the historical Jesus, the spirituality of liberation puts forward a vision of the essence of Christianity that clashes with

77

other replies that in its view depart from following the Jesus of
history and imply distortions and even deformations of Christianity.

This section, then, answers the questions: What is most
important for Christians? What is the core, the absolute priority, what becomes the ultimate source of meaning and hope for
our lives and struggles? We look for the reply not in a
theological theory, but starting from what the Jesus of history
actually did. What was most important, the core, the cause, the
absolute for Jesus?

What was not Absolute for Jesus

Jesus was not the absolute for himself. Jesus did not preach
himself as the core. This has become clear today for exegesis
and christology. Jesus himself stood "in relation" to something
outside himself: "The first thing that strikes one in beginning
to analyze the reality of Jesus of Nazareth is that he did not
make himself the center of his preaching and mission. Jesus
knew himself, lived and worked from and for something
distinct from himself."[2]

This means that our spirituality does not allow us to absolutize
Jesus and fall into a personalist reduction of the Christian faith.
Although the Jesus of history whom we accept as the Christ of
faith occupies such a central place—indeed, just because of
this—Jesus is never an absolute, shutting us into a personalist
intimacy isolated from history and eschatology, and so removed from the Reign. Following Jesus in this personalist
reductionism (very easy to do when we absolutize Jesus) is, in
our spirituality, a way of doing what Jesus wanted us not to do.

By the same token we have to discount all personalist, or
intimate reductionisms based not on Jesus but on the Holy
Spirit, the Trinity, or the "life of grace," or religious experience itself. A-historical charismatic movements, the cultivation of religious experiences for their own sake, of religion for
the sake of religion, take no account of the core of Christianity.

The core, for Jesus, is not simply "God." Jesus did not speak
of "God" *tout court*. We have already developed this in the
section "The Christian God" above. Jesus was not a Greek and

could never conceive of speaking of God without reference to history, without relating to God's children. Jesus did not speak simply of "God," but of the Reign of God and the God of the Reign: "the final reality for him was not simply 'God' but the 'Kingdom of God'.... For Jesus, God is not a reality that could be not linked to history, or history to God, but the relationship of God to history is essential to God.... Jesus too understands final reality as a dual unity, a God who gives himself to history or a history that comes to be according to God."[3]

Our spirituality is not based "in God alone," or in a "God alone": the *solus Deus,* or St Teresa of Avila's *"Sólo Dios basta"*—"God alone suffices," needs to be reformulated in the light of the absolute of the Reign. We cannot be content with calling on the unadorned name of God: we need to discern whether behind the God we invoke stands Jupiter, Moloch, Mammon, or the Father of our Lord Jesus Christ. Simple reference to "God" is no guarantee of Christian quality.

Jesus' purpose was not to found a church. This is something that theology has long quietly accepted. Jesus did not set out to found a church, in the conventional sense of the word, though this does not prevent the church from being founded on Jesus.

Our Christian attitude reacts against all forms of church-focus, that is, all forms of making the church the core, the absolute, to which everything else must take second place. Church-focus is one the heresies most casually and with the greatest impunity introduced into the history of faith, in the most unabashed and also the most subtle forms, both in the past and in the present.

Jesus did not absolutize the kingdom "of heaven." The Gospels do not make heaven, "in its absolutely transcendent version, distinct from and opposed to its realization in human history," a core issue for Jesus. Jesus does not seem to imbue us with an obsession for "personal eternal salvation," as has so often happened throughout the history of Christianity. Jesus does not make "heaven" the core of his life and message. We are well aware that "kingdom of heaven" in Matthew is a circumlocution meaning the same as "Reign of God," but it still seems necessary to say what we have just said with regard to a distant "heaven," existing only in the other world.

Our spirituality is not given over to transcendentalist perspectives alone, to a heaven that is in no way (without, logically, denying a proper understanding of it as gratuitous and transcendent gift of God) here and now, to a salvation that is of an entirely different order ("heterosalvation"), to the alienation that would have us live hanging on apocalyptic dates for "Jesus to come again."

What was Absolute for Jesus

What was absolute for Jesus was the "Reign of God." This, long agreed in exegesis, is now no longer a debating point in theology.[4] Jesus expressed this clearly in the core petition of his prayer: "Your kingdom come" (Matt. 6:10).

It is not enough, however, to state that the Reign of God is the core issue for Christianity; we must also be clear about its basic meaning. Attempts have been made to interpret it as "the other world," as grace, or as the church, but, as Leonardo Boff has written: "the Kingdom can also be proclaimed as a utopia of a fully reconciled world anticipated, prepared and begun already in history through the commitment of men of good will. I believe this last interpretation translates, on the historical and theological levels, the *'ipsissima intentio Jesu.'*"[5] So what was the Reign of God for Jesus?

The Reign of God was a real obsession for Jesus, his only cause, since it was an all-enveloping cause. The phrase "Kingdom of God" appears 122 times in the Gospels, ninety of these in the words of Jesus himself. The Reign is the effective kingship (reign) of the Father over everyone and everything. When God reigns, all is changed. "Justice, freedom, brother- and sisterhood, mercy, reconciliation, peace, forgiveness, closeness to God; all these make up the cause for which Jesus fought, for which he was persecuted, arrested, tortured and condemned to death."[6] All this is the Reign. The Reign of God is the total overturning and transfiguring of the present condition of ourselves and the cosmos, purified from all evils and filled with the condition of God.

The Reign of God does not claim to be another world, but

this old world changed into a new one, for human beings and for God: the "new heavens and new earth."[7] "The Kingdom is the destiny of the human race."[8] It is the utopia that all peoples have lived dreaming of and that the very God—in the serving, crucified and glorious flesh of Jesus—sets out for the human race so that we can go on building it and hoping for it.

To look at things with Jesus' eyes, we have to look at everything *sub specie Regni*, from the standpoint of the Reign, from its interests; to feel things with Jesus' heart, we have to feel everything out of passion for the Reign, lying in wait for the Reign.

The Reign and Christian Identity

Being Christians means being followers of Jesus, by definition. So being Christian means nothing other than living and struggling for Jesus' cause.[9] If the Reign was the core, the absolute, the cause, for Jesus, it has to be these for his followers as well. The Reign is Christians' "mission," the "basic mission" of every Christian; all other specific missions and particular charisms are then simply embodiments of this one "great Christian mission."

This means that whenever men and women, wherever and under whatever flag, struggle in support of Jesus' cause (justice, peace, brother- and sisterhood, reconciliation, the closeness of God, forgiveness . . . the Reign), they are being Christians, even without knowing it. (They are doing so at least in some sense, in the chief sense. This is not to put forward the thesis of "anonymous Christians," though, since we do not see them as "anonymous members of the church." We shall return to this aspect more explicitly later.) On the other hand, when people speak of themselves as Christians or followers of Jesus they do not always bring about love and justice, Jesus' cause. Sometimes, even, in the name of Jesus, they oppose his cause (love, equality, freedom). The criterion for measuring the Christian identity of persons, values, or any other reality, is their relationship to the Reign of God, their relationship to Jesus' cause.

Although the theme of the Reign of God is as central as we

have just indicated, we all know that in fact it has been pushed to the sidelines in the actual life of many churches. Many present-day Christians never heard any mention of the Reign of God in their basic Christian education. Many of us have discovered the Reign of God in the course of our involvement in the spirituality of liberation. And in the course of this involvement we have also had to re-image and rediscover the whole of our Christianity. We have discovered that all Christian themes, elements, virtues, values, find their true meaning and importance only in correct relation to the Reign of God. So true Christian prayer is "prayer for the Reign"; Christian chastity is only "chastity for the Reign"; penitence has a proper Christian meaning only if it is "penitence for the Reign."

The Reign of God in History

To discover the theme of the Reign of God is to discover the full dimension of the inevitable historical character of Christianity. Our God is a God of history, has entered into history, has a purpose and a plan for history, and has shown these to us in Jesus. God's plan is the Reign of God. The Reign of God is the dream, the utopia God cherishes for history, God's overall design for the world, the arcane mystery hidden for centuries and now revealed fully in Jesus. God has shown it to us in order to hand it over more explicitly to our responsibility. So being Christian implies a task in, and a responsibility for, history. In this sense, taking on the viewpoint of the Reign of God places us in the situation of having to read Christianity historically. And we are not saying that this reading is "one among many," "one of many possible interpretations," but the one that is closest to Jesus' own vision, the one that shows least "interpretation," so the one that "translates, on the historical and theological levels, the *'ipsissima intentio Jesu'*."

The meaning of the life of human beings is the Reign of God. Persons are fulfilled to the degree that they are capable of devoting their lives to the utopia that constitutes the goal, "the destiny of the human race." In their hearts all human beings feel the call of the absolute, of values summoning them to unconditional, unreserved self-giving. And all peoples, in their religion, culture, deepest values, possess a collective intuition of the utopia of the Reign, whatever name they may give it.[10] So to the extent that persons, communities, and peoples respond to this call, they are carrying out the will of God, fulfilling the meaning of their lives, even if they are not conscious of doing so.

Christians—as individuals, communities, or peoples—are no more than human beings like others, who feel the same call as others in their conscience, but who have had the luck (the gift, the grace) to hear the message of revelation, God's plan for history and for human beings, this plan that all individuals, communities, and peoples can intuit without revelation. Having, by the grace of God, full knowledge of God's plan—the Reign—does no more than imbue us with a new spirit and increase our responsibility.

The Reign of God is in history and beyond history. It has its own development, growth, and history. It is the history of salvation, because salvation is the Reign coming into being. And it is also beyond history because it will reach its fullness beyond history. The fullness of history is not another history ("heterosalvation"); it is this same history ("homosalvation"), but brought to its fullness, introduced into the order of the will of God (GS 39). The Reign of God and its history (the history of salvation) are not outside the human condition, as though on another level, another plane. They belong to our condition, to the one and only history. They are not another reality, but another dimension of the only reality, of the one history. There is only one history. Faith helps us to discover, decode and contemplate the dimension of the Reign that exists in our condition and in "secular" history and its processes.

The Reign is already present, but is not yet fully so. Our task is to go on building it, with the grace of God, and to try to hasten its coming. We know that we cannot "identify it *with*" any situation in this world, but faith allows us to "identify it *in*" situations in this world and our history.

To be faithful to our task of building the Reign, we are bound to act in ways that bring it closer. These actions are limited and always ambiguous. None of them can be "identified *with*" the Reign of God (as the concept of the "eschatological reserve" indicates), but this does not make it any less urgent for us to put our hand to them, since it is only through such actions that we can "identify the Reign *in*" our history.

"The Kingdom alone is absolute. Everything else is relative" (EN 8). This means that all our Christian actions have to be purposive action for the Reign, "living and struggling for Jesus' cause," militancy for the Reign. This is the objective, the cause. Everything else is means and actions in the service of the Reign. These actions do not have value in themselves or for themselves, but only insofar as they serve the Reign.

For us, the driving force, the engine, the objective, the cause, the reason and meaning of our life, of what we do, of our purposeful Christian action, is the Reign of God. All things take on meaning precisely through their service to the Reign. Our spirituality is one of service to the Reign as an absolute. Everything else remains subordinate to the Reign, however sacred and untouchable it may seem to us. The core is the Reign. Our spirituality is "Reign-focused."

This core dimension of "Reign-focus" in the spirituality of liberation gathers all its main characteristics together in a garland: it is a historical, utopic spirituality, ecumenical, from the poor, liberative, not church-focused.

Incarnation

The spirituality of liberation has made incarnation one of its main themes, within the framework of following Jesus. Incarnation takes place in Jesus; he is the model. All the necessary consequences can be derived from this.

In Jesus, God *became flesh*. God became an actual human being; that is, took on flesh and blood, sex, race, country and social situation, culture, biology, and psychology. Jesus was all these, entirely a person, fully human. He was not only God (Monophysitism), nor apparently man (Docetism), nor simply man (Arianism). He was fully human, and in him dwelt all the fullness of God (Col. 1:19).

Unlike the Monophysitism latent in so many spiritualities, the spirituality of liberation believes firmly in the full humanity of Jesus. In him, God loved our flesh, took it on, made it God's, made it holy. This fact invites us to attach supreme value to humanity, our being human, human beings: God was not content to love us from a distance. God asks us not to flee from the flesh of history toward the fleshless spirit of spiritualisms. Only by entering into the flesh can we be witness to and witnesses of the incarnate God. There is no other way. Only what is taken up can be saved, according to the classic adage of the Fathers. Incarnation is for salvation. Liberation comes by way of incarnation.

In Jesus, God *became history*. God did not move into the Olympus of changeless and a-historical essences in which the

Greeks thought the gods lived, but into history. God was revealed in history by taking it on.[1] God thereby made dichotomies impossible: "The gospel is the point/to which all roads lead./The presence of God in the march of man!/The gospel is the fate/of the whole of history./The history of God in the history of man!," as the *Alleluia* of the "Mass of the Land without Evils" declares. There are not two histories.

The incarnation is itself history. It is not just a moment, the moment of metaphysical contact between two natures, the human and the divine, as Greek thought would have it. Without denying the undeniably ontological dimension of the incarnation, worked out by the Council of Chalcedon,[2] we have to say that the incarnation is not a moment, but a process, history.[3] It is the whole of Jesus' life that is a "process" of incarnation, not just the moment of the annunciation to Mary: "And Jesus increased in wisdom and in years, and in divine and human favor" (Luke 2:52). In Joseph's workshop, in the desert, in temptation, in prayer, in the Galilean crisis, in the darkness of faith. . . . In Jesus, God became process, evolution, history.

The spirituality of liberation takes up the process-character of human life, its evolution, its growth, its ups and downs, its temptations, its crises, its confusions, routine and monotony. And it also takes up the historical processes of peoples, their anguishes and hopes, their struggles for liberation. The "historicity" of Jesus and the very form in which he took it on become our model and source of inspiration.

Our spirituality leads us to try to draw close to God by imitating God, following God, entering into history as God did, in the same way as God did, precisely not turning aside or evading history, not seeking God outside history. We try to meet God by taking flesh in the day-to-day processes of history. God's way is the way of incarnation in history. So the more we seek God, the more we come face-to-face with history. The more eschatological we are, the more historical we become.

In Jesus, God *emptied himself*, in *kenosis*. God did not become generically human, but specifically poor, "taking the form of a slave" (Phil. 2:7). He "lived among us" (John 1:14), among the poor.[4] He did not come into the world in general—which would in itself have been an "emptying"—but into the world of outcasts. He chose that social level: on the margins, among the oppressed, with the poor. The *kenosis* of the "in-carnation" did not consist simply in taking on "flesh" (the metaphysical union of two natures, the aspect on which classical theology and popular Christian belief both concentrate, under the influence of Greek philosophy), but also in taking on "poverty," the poverty of humankind. (This shows the limitations of the word "incarnation" itself. Others would make just as much sense: humanization, inculturation, historification, emptying, or, perhaps best of all, "impoverishment," or even "option for the poor," in the sense of taking on poverty and the cause of the poor.)

Following Jesus in this spirit has led a whole host of Latin Americans to make a physical and mental exodus toward the poor, to find a place in their world and culture, moving to the periphery, the margins, the desert. . . . The idea of "inserting oneself" in this way has become an outstanding feature of religious life in Latin America. Back in 1979 the Conference of Latin American Religious (CLAR) stated: "One can speak of an exodus of religious moving to the marginal zones of cities and out among the peasants to attend to the most needy and in search of a simpler and more evangelical religious life."[5] At the same date Puebla confirmed this: "religious increasingly find themselves in difficult, marginalized areas; in missions to the indigenous peoples; and in silent, humble labours" (733). For some, this phenomenon of "insertion" marks the beginning of a "new cycle" of religious life in history.

The church, as a whole, if it wishes to be increasingly evangelical and more effectively evangelizing, will have to go through this exodus and into this emptying process. It will have to insert itself—with its human and material resources and all its institutional weight—into the social situation of the poor majorities, among the greatest needs of the poor, on the periphery of this human world divided into rich and poor. The mystical body of Christ has to be where the historical body of Christ was.

In Jesus, God *took on a culture*, became "inculturated." The eternal divine word expressed itself in temporal human language: "God, revealing himself to his people . . . has spoken according to the culture proper to different ages" (GS 58); "The gospel is the word/of every culture./The word of God in human language!" (*Alleluia* of the "Mass of the Land without Evils"). And God took on this human language with all its limitations. The universal Word muttered in dialect. He took on the context, became contextual, sank his roots entirely into his actual situation. He was born into a dependent colony, was known as "the Galilean," and spoke with a regional, Galilean accent.

The incarnation asks us to live immersed in our own context, to take on contextuality, to be what we are and to be it where we are; to love our own flesh—land, ethnic group, culture, language, idiosyncracy, physical form, local peculiarity. A truly incarnate love requires us to defend ourselves against the "rising culture" of science and technology, with its levelling, homogenizing tendencies, rolling over the riches and peculiarities of indigenous peoples—though without depriving ourselves of the benefits of scientific and technological advances.

Having experienced a Christianity coming from a corner of the Mediterranean European land mass, the mystery of the incarnation also reminds us of the need for inculturation, for taking on the culture of each people to live its faith and build the church in it.[7] The spirit of the "incarnate Word" forbids the preaching of a "foreign culture" as though it were the content of faith, as well as the canonization of any culture as Christian, as opposed to others.[8] No culture is inherently better than another in God's sight. God is "the light of all cultures," as the Entrance Song of the "Mass of the Land without Evils" puts it. God loves them all equally because they are all special sparks of God's original light. Just as each person is the unique, unrepeatable image of God, so each people, each culture, is also the collective and different image of the God of all names, of all cultures.

The incarnation requires the church not to be foreign, not to be Eurocentric or ethnocentric, to decentralize itself, to make itself indigenous, to make space for local leaders and the whole local community to participate meaningfully, and above all to respect the culture and religious identity of peoples through inculturation and inter-faith dialogue. As Pope John Paul II has said: "Conversion to the Christian faith does not mean a destruction of the cultural and religious identity of those being evangelized, but its full development with the gospel" (RM 52).

In Jesus, God *entered into the course of peoples' history*. God became a citizen of a colony of the Roman Empire, with the social consequences this entailed. God took a place in the balance of social forces, spoke out, took an unequivocal stance on the side of the people, the poor.

In Latin America, the Spirit of Jesus makes us enter into the course of our peoples' history, taking up their concerns, immersing ourselves in them, sharing in their advances and retreats, defining ourselves unequivocally on the side of their cause, against whatever empire.

If we believe in the God of Jesus, in the incarnate God, it is not possible not to become involved in politics. We cannot follow our God along a different path from the one Jesus trod, that of the present, actual course of our peoples' history, a history today made up of underdevelopment, poverty, dictatorships, national security regimes, paper democracies, masked imperialism, the foreign debt, the politics of accommodation, market forces, public and private profit, free-market ideology, lack of opportunity for the poor to better themselves, lack of care for the masses. . . .

In Jesus, God went alongside the people, the poor and outcast, even though they semed to lack any historical importance. In Jesus, God showed the world, those who thought they were making history, that God's history takes place on the underside, is made by the little ones. Following Jesus today implies going on weaving the fabric of history with its true historical agents, even though it seems they have been deprived of any share in history, even though it is proposed to impose the "end of history" on them. Jesus also came into history at a time when the empire had triumphed, but he did not believe in the "end of history" in the shape of the *pax romana*; he believed in the Reign.

In Jesus, God *took on conflict*. History is an ongoing conflict, and God got his hands dirty in it. There was nothing antiseptic about the incarnation. God took on "the likeness of sinful flesh" (Rom. 8:3) without repugnance, without turning aside or "washing his hands" like Pilate. Jesus did not avoid conflict; he was afraid, but moved forward. He foresaw that the conflict would prove mortal, but did not pull back. He did not "die"; they took his life. He knew it was at stake and freely laid it down (see John 10:18). He was shut out by the priests, judged to be out of his mind (John 10:20; Mark 3:21), persecuted, arrested, excommunicated by the religious authorities, threatened with lynching (Luke 4:28-9; John 8:59), captured, executed.

Conflictivity taken on—not sought but not avoided either when the interests of the Reign are at stake—is a characteristic feature of the spirituality of liberation (see the sections on "Cross/Conflict/Martyrdom" and "Political Holiness" below). This does not claim to be neutral, a-political or abstract. Unlike the passivity and indifference with which human society of the past few centuries has viewed various Christian theologies and spiritualities, liberation theology and spirituality have aroused a lively polemic. They have annoyed the imperial powers and the Sanhedrin, just as Jesus did. This can be a sign—not a guarantee in itself—that they are following in the steps of their Master. The spirituality of liberation is incarnate in history, takes part in conflict, in ambiguity; it does not require angelic purity on the part of the protagonists of conflict to become involved in actual conditions of people on this earth.

The incarnation is revelation of God. It tells us a lot about God. It is our main source of information (John 1:18). It tells us what God is like. The God of the incarnation is the utterly human God:

> Our God is a humanized, incarnate God. His Son, the Word, Jesus Christ, Jesus of Nazareth, born of woman,

son of Mary, a man in history bound by a culture, at a certain period, under an empire. . . . The mystery of the incarnation, for us Christians, is the greatest expression of the human solidarity of God. Jesus Christ is God's human solidarity with human beings. With every human person, with every people, with the course of their history. Our God is a humanized, most human, historically utterly human God. For our faith, human rights are the historical concerns of God. . . .

For us, there are not two human histories: one secular history aside from God and another supernatural history that God looks after, makes his own. Without denying what theologians have called the "natural order" and the "supernatural order," "nature" and "grace," we confess a single human history, because the God who saves is the same creator God. . . .

This human-ness of God, of Jesus Christ, who is the humanized God, goes through an actual, specific historical course, one full of tensions, temptations, conflicts with the great ones of the age: of the Roman Empire, of the Temple, of Jerusalem, of the Jewish absentee landowners, of the legalism that kept the people in a real spiritual captivity. . . .

And if we believe in this God, if we accept this Jesus Christ, God made flesh, a man of conflict, accused and condemned to death, hung on a cross, eliminated by the imperial, religious and economic powers of his age . . . , then we must, as a church, as the community of those who follow Jesus, necessarily revise and change our own theology (the way we systematize our Christian faith), the celebration of this same Christian faith in the liturgy, the administration of the experience of faith in pastoral work, and the way every Christian experiences this faith in spirituality. . . .[9]

For all these reasons, the spirituality of liberation is a spirituality of incarnation, passionately concerned with real conditions (see the sections "Passion for Reality" above and "Contemplatives in Liberation" below), always attentive to the signs of the times in order to scrutinize them, analyzing conditions, anxious to incarnate faith in them, to inculturate and adapt the message to every situation. As Vatican II says: "This accomodated preaching of the revealed Word ought to remain the law of all evangelization" (GS 44); "Preaching must not present God's word in a general and abstract fashion only, but it must apply the perenial truth of the gospel to the concrete circumstances of life" (PO 4; see also GS 43, 76; CD 13; OT 16; AA 24).

This characteristic—this one too—of the spirituality of liberation does not come from the influence of any new philosophical theory, but from going back to the historical Jesus, to the God-with-us.

Following Jesus

Being Christian is not a matter of belonging to a school, not even to Jesus' school. He himself could apply both to himself—despite his complete and resultant credibility—and to us the warning he gave the people with regard to the teachers of Israel: do not seek to try and do what I say; do above all what I do. Jesus' great concern was not to create a school of doctrine or a religious institution, but to encourage a living following. (The Gospels themselves reflect this in the number of times the verb *akoulouzein*, "to follow," appears: seventy-nine, of which seventy-three apply directly to Jesus.)

Being a Christian means being a follower of Jesus, and the church is the community of those who follow Jesus. We are now his body in history. He is a teacher-prophet, a teacher-way. He not only proclaims truth; he is the Truth, because he does it. He not only announces life; he is Life, because he gives it. He is the Way of the Truth for the fullness of Life. The first Christians and the Christians of the communities in Latin America today well knew and know how to synthesize this greatest requirement in following Jesus: being Christian means starting on the *odos*, on the way, on the "journey."

It is true, as the exegetes remind us, that we are concerned not so much with the *ipsissima verba* or the *ipsissima facta*, the exact words Jesus used and the precise deeds he perfomed, as far as historical knowledge can give us access to them, but with the *ipsissima intentio Jesu*, the basic motive he had for saying these words and carrying out these actions. Nevertheless, we can divine his motive only from his words and his actions.

A very typically "magisterial" culture, such as existed in the Hebrew, but above all in the Greek world, perhaps could not, or was not prepared to, immediately grasp the renewing approach of this new Teacher, who came first to do, and only after that to teach. It could not appreciate someone who "wasted" thirty years as a simple local worker, who went about, as traveller and way, doing good, who summed up all his teachings in the practice of love and the extreme practice of loving to the point of giving his life. No one has taught, in the way he did, with words, with his life, with his death, that "deeds are love."

Jesus' disciples are invited to follow him, from the first moment (see John 1:39), and genuine discipleship, throughout Christian history, has been synonymous with following. At the same time, throughout this same history, this following has been distorted or obfuscated by a double temptation: that of codifying the very mystery of the historical Jesus in doctrinal dogmas and the spiritual "revolution" this brought with it, and that of reducing to a mimicry of following—imitation—what should have been, down the centuries, substantially the same and yet always changing, a responsible, creative, prophetic following.

If we believe that Jesus of Nazareth embodies the full revelation of God in person and in history, it is logical that those who "worship the Father in spirit and truth" (John 4:23) should try to follow this Jesus in spirit and truth. No one has seen God (John 1:18), except the Son, who is Jesus. No one has fully "carried out" God in history except this the Son in history. Following Jesus is, then, in the final analysis, "carrying out the God of Jesus," which is done through following the actual Jesus of Nazareth.

Living Tradition (the first apostolic or post-apostolic communities, the Fathers, the *sensus fidei*, the magisterium and the saints) has always sought to reactivate this following of Jesus as the authentic form of belonging to the church of Jesus. Every geographical, cultural, historical or social conjuncture has both made possible and required a way of following Jesus, or has shown a preference for certain approaches and practices—always, at least intentionally, faithful to the same and only Jesus—that would better serve living and proclaiming the gospel in a particular time and place, and show a suitable face of this unique and yet plural Jesus. So Latin America, with its different cultural and social setting, and its time of need and commitment, has to find its own local and prophetic way of following Jesus here and now.

With the breakthrough of the poor, and thanks to the searching and successes of recent biblical studies, the Spirit is bringing a new face of Jesus to the fore in our spiritual experience, and asking us to follow certain approaches that are specifically our own. So to the classic European "lives of Jesus," we respond with "The Practice of Jesus" (Hugo Echegaray) or "Jesus, Man in Conflict" (Miguel Bravo); the paintings of Jesus by Velázquez or Rouault have their counterpart here in the drawings and murals of Cerezo Barredo or Pérez Esquivel.

When the image of Jesus changes, the understanding the church has of its mission, of evangelization, of following Jesus, also changes—without Jesus ceasing to be Jesus or the church ceasing to be the church of Jesus. So for those of us who seek to follow Jesus, making him present today and inculturating him here, it matters greatly for us to be attentive to this new face of his that is appearing in Latin America and profoundly affecting our accustomed modes of following, of being church, of evangelizing.

Clearly, in no cultural or historical conjuncture can essential aspects not subject to variation be cast aside. We honestly believe that in certain historical conjunctures fundamental aspects of the real historical Jesus have in fact been pushed too far into the shadows. Our purpose in this section is to enquire into the main *features of this new face of Jesus* that is emerging at this spiritual juncture in Latin America, and to ask what *attitudes of his* we should make more firmly ours. (So as not to overburden this list with biblical references, we simply refer readers to the four Gospels. The features and attitudes are given in summary form here; many of them are given more detailed treatment in other sections.)

The features would be these:

— *A historical Jesus, revealing God.* God is revealed to us in history, and, in a special way, in the history of Jesus. Today we know Jesus better than ever and feel very close to the Jesus of history. And we have come to realize that the historicity of Jesus forms a constituent part of the incarnation of God. What the historical Jesus said and did, all the aspects of his person, are glimpses of God's revelation for us, and paths along which to follow Jesus. The New Testament does not so much say that Jesus is God, as that God "is" Jesus; that is, we do not know previously or aside from Jesus who "his" God is, and then apply this idea to Jesus, but, on the contrary, we know the God of Jesus through the historical Jesus. The God of Christians is revealed to us in the overall history of Jesus.

— *A deeply human Jesus.* As opposed to a Christ understood almost exclusively as God, we have rediscovered the Christ of our faith—true God—in the historical Jesus, a true human being, who grows, discerns, evaluates, doubts, decides, prays, is angry, weeps, does not know, has faith, goes through crises. . . . Everything in his life is an example of achieved humanity for us; only God could be so deeply human.

— *A Jesus devoted to the cause of the Reign.* The most definite historical fact we know about the life of Jesus is that the central theme of his preaching, the reality that gave meaning to all his actions, was the Reign of God. Jesus did not preach simply "God," nor the church, nor himself, but the "Reign of God." This is the cause for which he lived, of which he spoke, for which he risked all, for which he was tortured, condemned and executed. He was a man devoted to a cause. The Reign was his radical and absolute option.

— *A Jesus who proclaimed the God of the Reign.* Jesus did not speak simply of God. God is not a metaphysical being who can be thought of in himself, set aside from human beings and human history. The God of Jesus is the God of the Reign. Jesus gathers together and refines the Old Testament traditions about God: a God of history, a God who listens to the cries of his people, who intervenes in history to set them free, who suffers with them, who takes on their progress to the Promised Land. . . . Jesus did not preach an abstract, spiritualist, a-historical, impassive God, unmoved by historical conflicts.

— *A poor Jesus, incarnate among the poor.* Jesus was really poor, lived among the poor, saw things from their point of view and in accordance with their interests. He continually took up their cause, against those who held power. He made the sufferings and aspirations of the poor his own. His poverty and his social position among the poor are a basic fact running through the whole of Jesus' life and message.

— *A subversive Jesus.* Jesus did not preach a message with no social relevance; indeed, not only was his message relevant, but he acted and rebelled as a real subversive. He put forward an order of values that subverted the established order, a new set of human relations, and a new type of human-divine relations. He accepted neither social conventions nor religious legalisms. He defined power and authority as service. He put forward a new image of God. He was a nonconformist. He proclaimed and ushered in a Reign of God that implied the restructuring and transformation of the world of his time.

— *A Jesus who put the Reign into effect.* Jesus' relationship to the Reign was not just a verbal one, but a matter of doing. He revealed the Reign "in deeds and words." Jesus' mission did not consist solely in giving out information about the Reign, but in bringing it about, a task to which he devoted his whole life, to the extent that one of the Fathers called him "the King and the Kingdom" in person. Jesus' actions were designed to put the will of God—the Reign—into effect in history itself, in his actual situation. His words and proclamation formed part of this effort.

— *A Jesus who denounced the anti-Reign.* Jesus not only proclaimed the good news, but denounced all that was opposed to it. He denounced social groups—not only individuals—that exploited the people in the social and/or religious sphere. He raised an impressive social protest against all forms of oppression, including those of the Temple and its religion.

— *A free Jesus.* Jesus took a free attitude to family, society, money, the powerful and the powers, the law, the Roman Empire, the Temple, persecution and death. He was even free toward the people, when they behaved selfishly or irresponsibly. "People" in the midst of the people, Jesus was neither "basist" (as we call those who absolutize the views from the grassroots, without taking a properly critical approach to them), nor paternalistic; he neither infantilized nor canonized the people.

— *A Jesus for the life of the people*. Jesus appeared as a witness to the God of life, who wants the people to have life and have it in abundance. And he demonstrated this to be his mission by referring it always very practically to the basic stuff of human life: bread, health, clothing, freedom, well-being, personal relationships. . . .

— *A compassionate Jesus*. Jesus had compassion on the crowds, on the sick, on human suffering. He was moved to his depths. He took a line of scandalous solidarity with those who were officially deprived of all solidarity: lepers, prostitutes, publicans.

— *An ecumenical Jesus*. He, son of a people that held itself to be exclusively chosen, had no sectarian mentality; he came to knock down barriers of separation. His view fitted into the macro-ecumenical approach of the Reign. He declared that all who were on the side of the Reign were with him. He set out the conduct of the schismatic Samaritan who made a neighbor of his Jewish enemy as a model for all. He showed love of the poor as the eschatological criterion of salvation that will judge us over and above all creeds and frontiers.

— *A feminist Jesus*. To women, Jesus' attitude was revolutionary within the parameters of his culture and age. He was the "Son of man" who knew himself to be "son of woman," the "son of Mary." He let women follow him and become part of his itinerant inner circle. He was the close friend of Martha and Mary. He took the Samaritan woman into his confidence, in public. He was overcome by the widow of Naim's tears, let himself be rebuked by the Canaanite woman, felt at one with both of them. He made a woman, Mary Magdalen, the first witness to the resurrection—when his culture declared her witness, as a woman, inadmissible.

— *A conflictive Jesus*. His good news to the poor was at the same time bad news to the rich. He was not neutral or impartial. He defined his position in regard to social conflict and religious domination. He unequivocally took the side of the poor and the excluded. He did not waver in his stance *pro bono pacis.* All his life, from his childhood on, he was a "sign of contradiction."

— *A persecuted and martyr Jesus.* The political, economic and religious powers persecuted him. For most of his public life he was habitually defamed and persecuted. On several occasions he had to flee, to avoid the premature death he eventually could not escape. He lived "marked out for death." A price was officially put on his head and social, political and religious interests all had a hand in his death. He died murdered by the "absentee landlord" Sadducees, the Central Bank Temple and the imperial army. And he came to be known as the Crucified and the Faithful Witness.

— *Jesus, the way, the truth and the life of the Reign.* The Gospels show Jesus as a man on the way to "his hour," Easter. The "Galilean crisis" he went through in the process of discerning what the Reign was like and the subsequent disappointments he underwent at the hands of the people and his own disciples—who hoped and asked for a different Reign—as well as the agony in the garden and the abandonment on the cross: none of these prevented Jesus from continuing to be the witness to the Reign on its inexorable approach. He was, to an unparalleled degree, in life, one who "hoped against all hope," while at the same time the most failed of teachers and the prophet cursed by the very trees. And this is why he became, for us all, not only the way and truth, but also the resurrection and the life.

Where the list above has "Jesus," every one of us ought, humbly but with due responsibility, to put his or her own name. If we do not, following Jesus will be for us an empty formula or a clearly disorientated process. Just as we have to stand up for our eschatological hope, so we have to stand up for our historical following.

These are, we repeat, the features of the historical Jesus, and Latin American spirituality of liberation is specifically a spirituality of historical commitment, worked out in action, in taking up the crucial concerns of the poor majorities, in putting solidarity into action. We must make a continual effort to flesh out these features wherever our spirituality reaches, so that it is integral and harmonious: personal temperament, family life, the workplace, the church community, militant organizations. In this sense, the New Man and New Woman of the continent need New Christians. Oscar Romero the archbishop, Margarida Alves the peasant, Nestor Paz the student, Fanny Abanto the teacher and so many others have followed the historical Jesus in a way different—just because it is "ours"—from that followed by Ignatius of Antioch, Teresa of Avila, Domenico Savio or Maria Goretti.

The *basic option in Jesus' life*—the Father's will, the Reign,—is still *the* option for us too. And, under the power of the Spirit and in the face of the demands of the poor, we feel we have to work out this basic option by putting emphasis on the following *attitudes*:

— prophetic indignation;

— com-passion in solidarity;

— ongoing activity to cut free from every type of mooring: physical or spiritual, social or religious;

— promulgation of putting the poor first, in this history, on the way to the Reign;

— constant communion in filial communion with the father, with the *Abba*, "Daddy";

— family sharing with all, but above all with the poor, the outcasts, the non-citizens, the non-persons, the outlawed, those who "subvert" the various establshed (dis)orders;

— the poverty and renunciation of the Suffering Servant and his radical kenosis or self-abasement, leaving aside ties and interests, security and status, comfort and consumerism, good name and prestige;

— courage to take up our cross every day, without fearing conflict and without saving up even our own lives;

— confidence in the maternal tenderness of the Father, who looks after the lilies and the birds and even each hair of our head; and "hope against hope";

— keeping a constant spirit of community, always socializing our spiritual experience:

— in "popular reading of the Bible" and in confronting life

and politics with it; in our celebrations of faith, personal, in the family circle, in the liturgy;

— in the Eucharist, which, in Latin America above all, cannot fail to be both "fruit of the earth and work of human hands" and of struggle and blood: the pasch of Christ and the pasch of the people;

— in an integrated conjugation of personal and group experience, of cultural and political spheres, geopolitical ones too, within the macro-ecumenism that makes us journey and struggle with all those men and women who, knowingly or not, are basically working out the same option for the Reign;

— in that freedom of the Spirit that "blows where it will" and "makes all things new," as the Spirit of radical transformation (in personal conversion and social revolution) and as the Spirit of inculturation without frontiers and of utopic creativity;

— always, despite all contradictions, disappointments and failures, with that childlike trust that knows the Father is greater than all; that the Brother "is with us to the end," that the Reign is already here, and that beyond this first history and inevitable death, it will come to its eschatological fullness.

Contemplatives in Liberation

All that makes up the Christian liberation movement: liberation theology, church of the poor, base communities, Christian participation in popular movements, all the social and religious imagery of liberation—in poetry, music and literature—all the pastoral experience of working with the people built up over the years, the endless list of blood-witnesses who have validated this "journey" with their martyrdom . . . all this is inexplicable without the spiritual experience that forms the source-legacy inspiring and motivating this cloud of witnesses:

> Behind any innovative action by the church, at the root of all true and new theology, lies a typical religious experience that constitutes the word-source: all the rest springs from this all-embracing experience; all the rest is simply the attempt to translate it within the framework of a historically-determined situation. It is only by starting from this presupposition that we can understand the great syntheses of the theologians of the past, such as St Augustine, St Anselm, St Thomas, St Bonaventure or Suárez, and of the present, such as Rahner and other masters of the spirit. All spiritual experience signifies a meeting with the new and challenging face of God, which emerges in the great challenges posed by historical conditions.[1]

Earlier movements of spirituality experienced God primarily in the desert (anchorites, the desert Fathers . . .), in prayer and monastic work (*ora et labora*, pray and work), in study and prayer for preaching (*contemplata aliis tradere*, passing on what is contemplated to others), in apostolic activity (*contemplativus in actione*, contemplative in action).[2]

We believe that today, in creative fidelity to this living tradition, we are called to live contemplation in liberative activity (*contemplativus in liberatione*), decoding surroundings made up of grace and sin, light and shade, justice and injustice, peace and violence, discovering in this historical process of liberation the presence of the Wind that blows where it will, uncovering and trying to build salvation history in the one history, finding salvation in liberation. In the wail of a child, or in the full-throated cry of a people (see Puebla 87-9), we try to "listen" to God, to turn ourselves into the very ear of the God who hears the cry of his people (Exod. 3). (Contemplation, which has classically been defined as "seeing" without images, intuitively, can also be described as "hearing or listening" without images, intuitively, as an open radar in direct contact, as a solar panel face up to the sun, as standing before. . . .)

The earlier Christian tradition instructed us in a model of prayer that only went up, without coming down. This is graphically suggested in John of the Cross' title, *The Ascent of Mount Carmel*. The elevator of prayer could deposit us up there, in the clouds, doing nothing. This is not right, because neither does God need our prayers, nor is God up there in the clouds. The ones who need prayer are ourselves and our brothers and sisters, and we are not in the clouds either, but on the laborious and conflictive road to the building of the Reign. We believe we have to go up and come down, and that the farther up the mountain-side we get, the farther down we go and submerge ourselves in the *kenosis* of incarnation, of passionate concern for our history and surroundings.

So in speaking of being "contemplatives in liberation," we are speaking of the experience of God that is typical of Latin American Christians. This is the secret, the heart of, the key to our spirituality. Without realizing this, it is impossible to understand it; it would be misinterpreted as any old reductionism.

The Content and Context of Our Experience of God

We have already said that the spirituality of liberation is characterized typically by its "realism," by its "passion for reality," by its hammering insistence on "starting from actual conditions and going back to them." So is it strange that its experience of God starts in and goes back to actual conditions? This is the first new aspect: the content, the field, the place from which we experience God is not the "purely spiritual" or the "set apart from the world," nor the intellectual world of theological abstractions, but our actual situation as it presents itself to us in all its dimensions:

— the historical dimension: history itself, seen as the sphere of freedom, of human responsibility, of personal creativity in carrying out the task assigned to us by God;

— the political dimension: building up society, the tensions of living together, the balance of forces, the conflicts of interest between different sectors of society, with special emphasis on the "popular movement": the organized poor with their strategies, triumphs and defeats, their disappointments and hopes;

— the geopolitical dimension: national struggles for sovereignty and freedom, imperialism old and new, transnationalization and the global village, the wave of triumphalist neo-liberalism and the resistance of the poor, the readjustment of the old world order into a one-sided world with persistent efforts to introduce a "new world order";

— the daily problems of our lives: deteriorating living standards, shortages, the struggle to survive, the threat of social unrest, repression, unemployment, social fragmentation, street children, the drugs trade, the daily social consequences of the foreign debt burden, the shock of the "economic adjustments" imposed by international financial organs, the most real and "material" problems of our lives. . . .[3]

It is in this "material reality" that we find our experience of

God as contemplatives in liberation: "The liberating commitment has come to mean a genuine spiritual experience for many Christians, in the original and biblical sense of the term: a living in the Spirit that makes us see ourselves freely and creatively as children of the Father and brothers and sisters of one another."[4] We do not deny the value that "withdrawal," solitude, the "experience of the desert," has for us too. But if we stand aside, it is only for methodological, instrumental reasons, not for its own sake; we retreat "with the situation on our backs," with our hearts heavy with the world. We do not retreat from the world; we simply enter into its depth dimension, which for us is religious (see the section on "Political Holiness" below).

Agencies of This Experience of God

The first agency for bringing about this experience is, logically, *actual conditions*. We cannot experience God in our situation if we remove ourselves from it. So it is a matter of being present in our situation: openness to what is around us, incarnation, "insertion" in it. . . . This is the agency that provides us with the the matter or context in which we make this experience.

Another great agency is *faith*.[5] Faith gives us a contemplative view of our situation. It provides us with an "epistemological break": we see reality from another viewpoint, in a different perspective:

> When we see with the eyes of faith, we no longer speak of simple structural injustices, but of a real collective situation of sin; we do not only say that the social outlook is dismaying, but denounce the situation as contrary to God's plan for history. Liberation is not seen just as a global social process, but as a way of bringing about and bringing forward the absolute liberation of Jesus Christ.[6]

The contemplation we speak of is done in the light of faith. We experience God in our conditions and in history, but in faith, through faith. It is the light that reveals presences and dimensions that would otherwise remain hidden.

Another agency is *the word of God in the Bible*. God wrote two books: the first is the book of life (creation, what exists, history) and then, so that we could understand this one, God wrote the Bible.[7] To take the Bible as self-contained, reified, as the complete and self-sufficient reserve of all human and divine mysteries, is a new idolatry, and one now carried out with fanaticism. The Bible is a tool—certainly a special, most valuable and venerable one—given to us by the Lord to help us discern his living word, which crouches in any corner of history, ready to spring out and surprise us, because God is still carrying on the process of "revelation," still pronouncing that living word. If we shut ourselves up in the Bible, it is not possible to be contemplatives in liberation. "The Bible and the newspaper" are the two main pillars on which to set a liberatively contemplative Christian life.

The Bible—which is story, history, the experience of a people, of Jesus, of the first Christian communities—is, because it is all these things, a contemplative rendering of the presence of God at work in the world. In Latin America this active nature of the God of the Bible is emphasized as the essential note of the theology and spirituality of liberation. This is the new way we read the Bible among ourselves. It is a totally justifiable "re-reading," we maintain, since it is a return to the "reading" the Bible itself seeks to give us.

This reading has moved away from the hands and eyes of the specialists to become, prophetically, a "people's reading." Just as in politics the people have won the voice forbidden to them in society, so in the church the base communities have taken hold of the Bible. "The Bible in the hands of the people" is one of the potentially most fruitful spiritual manifestations for the church in Latin America. One can justifiably describe the "culture of the base church communities as a new biblical culture": the Bible spread through the day-to-day life of the people, in their prayers and struggles. Their experience and interpretation are not systematically written down, but are expressed in a multiplicity of ways, in liturgies and songs, in poems and dramatizations, visits and celebrations, meetings and assemblies, shawls and T-shirts: "Exactly like the word of

God itself before receiving its written form in the Bible."[8]

Other tools we use are the *various resources* we can lay our hands on to help us understand our situation: sociological and economic analyses, anthropology, cultural studies, psychology, the accumulated experience of popular education, mass media, the see-judge-act methodology, techniques of participation, the way the people analyze their situation, and so on. With all of this, we try to make our Christian discernment of conditions: "Recourse to the help of the social sciences does not stem from mere intellectual curiosity, but from a deeply evangelical concern."[9]

Together with all these agencies (some more illuminating, such as the Bible; others more analytical, such as social studies, theology and the various pastoral methodologies), the one that completes the picture is the assiduous practice of *prayer itself* (see Luke 18:1). The experience of God is, in effect, a contemplative experience: "The presence of God in us cannot be known other than by experienc; it cannot be expressed in words alone," in the words of the Dominican Office for the feast of St Thomas Aquinas. Or, as St John of the Cross put it: "Neither does human knowledge suffice to know how to understand it, nor experience to know how to tell it; because only those who go through it will know how to feel it, though not to tell it."[10] So personal prayer, communal prayer, the spirit of faith that makes us approach things virtually spontaneously from a depth perspective, a habitual "state of prayer" (see 1 Thess. 5:16-18), and reaching a certain level of contemplation, are also agencies of our experience of God in the here and now of our situation.

Our experience tends to run these agencies together. None of them is sufficient in itself. We have to read the two books: the Bible and the book of life. We have to be illuminated by the word of God, but equally we have to make use of the analytical and hermeneutical tools, in an inter-disciplinary approach (as sanctioned already by Vatican II: see GS 62; PO 16; OT 15, 20). We have to sink ourselves in the Bible, but also in conditions around us. We have to lend "one ear to the gospel and the other to the people," in the words of the Argentinian martyr-bishop Enrique Angelelli.

Contemplating . . . from Where?

What we contemplate as "contemplatives in liberation" is not equally accessible from anywhere, from any point of view. Analogously to what happens with normal spatial vision, there is also "perspective" in matters of the spirit: the place we choose to look from influences what will be in the foreground, the middle ground and background, what will be emphasized and what hidden. Each viewing point brings its own perspective: "You don't think the same from a cottage as you do from a palace."

Some viewing points are better and some worse. Some show nothing and some give a specially good view. The best place for viewing history and the history of salvation is from the social situation of the poor:

> The basic theological setting is the point of view of oppressed peoples in their struggle for liberation. Both because, this being the place where the meaning of human history is shown in greatest depth, it is natural for the divine presence to be shown there in its greatest depth, and because the choice of this place seems to be the geo-political transference most coherent with the evangelical option for the outcasts.[11]

The outlook of the powerful obscures liberation: "The metropolises are prevented from having hope: they are threatened by their 'establishments,' which fear any future that denies them a place. In order to think, in the metropolises, one has, first, to 'become' an inhabitant of the Third World."[12] Being contemplative in liberation supposes an option for the poor.

The Lord Jesus himself laid this down clearly: "I thank you, Father, . . . because you have hidden these things from the wise and intelligent and have revealed them to infants" (Luke 10:21). Jesus does not contrast "wise and intelligent" with "stupid" but with "infants." The "wise and intelligent" he is referring to are therefore those who "share the wisdom of the great." Instead of this wisdom, Jesus opts for the alternative, that of infants, the only wisdom capable of understanding "these things," at which Jesus rejoices and gives exultant thanks. So there are things infants see, understand, contemplate, and to which the great remain blind. What are these things?

For Jesus, "these things" are none other than those he continually dwelt on: the Father's preferences, the things of the Reign, what is involved in proclaiming the good news to the poor, the lowly ones' longing for liberation, the struggle for a just and sharing society, the building of the Reign of God. In reality, it is simply common sense that the powerful, the well-placed, the exploiters, the grandees of the system, should not be able to understand "these things." They don't even want to hear of good news for the poor. They don't look at things from the viewing point of liberation. They don't want to take part in the dynamics of the Reign: "How hard it is for those who have wealth to enter the Kingdom of God!" (Luke 18:24).

If we are to be able to contemplate "these things," we need to place ourselves in a setting from which they let themselves be contemplated, in the right social setting and with the correct perspective: that of "infants," that of the poor.

Contemplatives "in Liberation"

This means various things. The first is that we contemplate life from the standpoint of the greater liberation discovered by faith, the standpoint of the Reign (the "formal object" or "pertinence" of contemplation). The situation that forms the object of our spiritual experience, looked at in the light of faith and from the option for the poor (from "infants"), is seen in the light of the overall march of liberation, the very course of the Reign that envelops the particular historical movements of our peoples and of each of us as individuals.

The next thing it means is that our contemplation takes place in the midst of a process of liberation (the "place in which" we contemplate, an environmental or passive *locus ubi*), with its attendant convulsions, conditionings, risks, limitations and possibilities. Where it does not take place is outside the world, in the clouds, on a heavenly Olympus, or purely inside oneself, in the abstract, in political neutrality, in purely intellectual contemplation.

Then, it means that within the overall situation we focus especially on the actual progress of liberation (the specific material object of our contemplation): the liberative actions of our peoples, their struggles to create a new, free "world order."

It means, too, that we view the process of liberation not from outside, but from inside, "in liberation," in what it actually involves, involved in it, taking part in its struggles, taking up its causes. We contemplate in liberation bringing it about at the same time, "liberating" (an active *locus ubi*) and liberating ourselves.

We contemplate liberating. And by contemplating, we also contribute to liberation.

"Contemplatives": What we see, What we contemplate

Formerly, it used to be said that the "object" of contemplation was "divine things." So, according to St Thomas Aquinas, contemplation is "a simple and intuitive vision of divine things, which proceeds from love and leads to love." St Francis of Sales gave a similar definition: "a loving, simple and permanent fixing of the mind on divine things."[13] It was the very "eternal future glory" already present in anticipation in the soul through grace.[14] These "divine things," as described by the various classical schools of asceticism and mysticism, are in effect far removed from the things of this world. So St Teresa of Avila could write: "For myself, I hold that when his Majesty bestows this favour, it is to those who push the things of this world to one side." And Pseudo-Dionysius, so influential in Christian mysticism, puts it another way: "Separated from the world of sense and the world of understanding, the soul enters into the mysterious darkness of a holy ignorance, and, abandoning all scientific knowledge, loses itself in the one whom no one can see or grasp; united with the unknown by the noblest part of itself, and because it renounces knowledge. . . ."[15]

Even more, these schools often seem to propose a sort of competition or rivalry between attention devoted to "divine things" and that given to the "things of this world." So Blessed Henry Suso, pupil of Eckhart, influential spiritual director, inspirer of Thomas à Kempis, wrote: "Do not believe that it is enough for you to think of me for just an hour each day. Those who desire to hear inwardly my sweet words, and to understand the mysteries and secrets of my wisdom, should be with me all the time, always thinking of me. . . . Is it not shameful to have the Kingdom of God inside you, and to go out from it to think of creatures?" And even St Teresa could state: "I hold it to be impossible, if we were to take care to remind ourselves that we have such a guest within us, that we should give ourselves so much to the things of the world; since we should see how low they are compared to those we possess within us. . . ."[16]

Without denying the element of correct intuition in what these great mystics and theologians meant by these expressions, we, here and now, in the particular historical situation of this continent (and, truth to tell, in any time and place, if we are to move beyond dualism and dis-incarnation), with all the experience we have built up, base our experience of God on different approaches and categories.

For us, the "divine things" that form the object of mystical contemplation can be none other than "these things" revealed by the Father to "infants" (see Luke 10:21-4). These are "the things of the Reign" (see the section on "Reign-Focus" above for the Reign's capacity for transforming all activities and situations generally held to be Christian into their genuine Christian selves). They determine its progress, the obstacles in its way, its preaching, its building-up, the way the good news is proclaimed to the poor, the action of the Spirit arousing longing for liberation and raising the poor to their dignity as children and brothers and sisters in the longed-for coming of the Reign.[17]

These are certainly "divine things," but not in relation to any God—a God, for example, not essentially concerned in history and our situation, or one who can be appealed to without commitment. They are divine in reference to the God-of-the-Reign, to the God who has a plan for the whole of history and has called us to contemplation in bringing it about. That is, they are the "divine things" of the God of Jesus.

With the martyrs, the witnesses, the militants of the whole continent, radically committed to "these things," to the point of dying for them if necessary, for the sake of the Reign, we bear witness to our experience of God when we feel ourselves to be working with the Lord:

— in the unfinished creation, trying to continue and perfect it—as expressed in the theologies and spiritualites of work, of progress, of development;

— in cosmogenesis, biogenesis, noogenesis, cristogenesis: Teilhard de Chardin was not only a spiritual genius, but the spokesman for a spirituality latent in many Christians, much of which can be taken up by the spirituality of liberation, even if in different terms and opening its approaches out to new dimensions;

— in carrying out God's historical plan for the world, building the utopia of God's Reign: the "Reign-focused" re-reading of Christianity proposed above has undoubtedly made the greatest contribution to many committed Christians having a very deep experience of God in the midst of their struggles and political activities;

— in works that liberate from oppression, bring full humanity, redeem humankind, build a new world, "completing what is lacking in Christ's afflictions" (Col. 1:24);

— in pressing Jesus' cause: saying that being a Christian in Latin America today implies "following Jesus, carrying on his work, pressing his cause in order to achieve his objective . . ." is not just a happy phrase,[18] but an accurate account of the spiritual experience of so many Latin Americans who are passionately committed to liberative struggles, to living the gospel where they are, to renewing pastoral and church work in general, based on following Jesus;

— in social change—a spiritual experience authoritatively expressed by Medellín: "Just as Israel of old, the first people (of God) felt the saving presence of God when God delivered them from the oppression of Egypt by the passage through the sea and led them to the promised land, so we also, the new people of God, cannot cease to feel God's saving passage in view of 'true development, which is the passage for each and all, from conditions of life that are less human, to those that are more human'";[19]

— in discerning the signs of the times so as to find traces of the Reign growing among us.

Putting all this into more theological language, we could say that the fact of being "contemplatives in liberation" makes us:

— experience God in the actual situation;

— contemplate the advances made by God's Reign in our history;

— "feel" transcendence in immanence;

— discover the history of salvation in the one and only history;

— discern eschatological salvation being built up in history;[20]

— grasp the "geopolitics" of God behind changing historical circumstances.[21]

This contemplation loads our lives with a deep sense of responsibility by making us realize that they are shot through with divine responsibilities: at the same time as we "make our own soul," we also "collaborate in another work . . . the completing of the world."[21] We know that in our historical struggles, by making the Reign progress, we are already bringing the new world into being, giving present shape to the absolute future we hope for, heaven.[22]

So we can love this world, this earth, this history, because for us it is not a sort of stage set to be burned once the performance of the "great theatre of the world" is over, nor is it a blank canvas on which we paint a picture as an exam, and are rewarded for having passed this with a salvation that has nothing to do with our present circumstances (heterosalvation).[23] We can love this earth and this toilsome human history because it is the Body of the One who is and who was, who came and who comes, whom we follow in hope under the veil of flesh. And because, in this earth and its immanence, the transcendent Reign we bear in our hands is growing.

The course of history is not a matter of indifference to us. Although faith tells us that the final triumph is certain, we know it is subjected, in the course of history, to the attacks of its enemies, and we give our lives to the task of hastening its coming.

We love this earth with its history because for us it is the only possible agency through which we can meet the Lord and the Reign. Longing for God and the Reign does not make us detach ourselves from this world and what it brings; we have nowhere to build eternity except history: "The earth is our only road to heaven," in the words of a famous missiologist. No one can accuse us of being deserters, of escaping, of not committing ourselves, of not loving madly the cause of the human person, the cause of the poor, which is Jesus' cause, and indeed God's cause.

This is how we know that what we are going through, our struggles for love and peace, for freedom and justice, to build a better and oppression-free world, "the values of human dignity, brotherhood and freedom, and indeed all the good fruits of our nature and enterprise," will be found again, "but freed of stain, burnished and transfigured. This will be so when Christ hands over to the Father a Kingdom eternal and universal: 'a Kingdom of truth and life, of holiness and grace, of justice, love, and peace.' On this earth that Kingdom is already present in mystery. When the Lord returns, it will be brought into full flower" (GS 39). We know that what we contemplate in liberation under the signs of fleetingness and weakness, we shall find again in eternity.

> The promised restoration which we are awaiting has already begun in Christ, is carried forward in the mission of the Holy Spirit and through him continues. . . . The final age of the world has already come upon us (cf 1 Cor. 10:11). The renovation of the world has been irrevocably decreed and in this age is already anticipated. . . . However, until there is a new heaven and a new earth where justice dwells (cf 2 Pet. 3:13). . . [we dwell among] creatures who groan and travail in pain until now and await the revelation of the sons of God (cf Rom. 8:19-22),

[and although we have] the first fruits of the Spirit we groan within ourselves (cf Rom. 8:23) and desire to be with Christ (cf Phil. 1:23). (LG 48)

We feel ourselves to be present—and how present!—in immanence and transcendence, simultaneously, without conflict, though with a great tension in our hearts, deep down within ourselves: while on one hand we love this earth and its history so passionately, on the other we feel like "strangers and foreigners" (Heb. 11:13), citizens of heaven (Phil. 3:20) and at the same time exiled far from the Lord (2 Cor. 5:6); we bear within ourselves the image of this "world that is passing away" (1 Cor. 7:31) and at the same time view things *sub specie aeternitatis*; "raised with Christ" (Col. 3:1), we know too that "what we will be has not yet been revealed" (1 John 3:2; cf 2 Cor. 5:6).

The more physically rooted in history we are, the more longingly eschatological we feel: for the spirituality of liberation, the 1930s debate between eschatologism and incarnationalism has been decisively resolved by the full conjugation of the two tendencies. The more we look for transcendence, the more we find it in immanence: the Kingdom of God is not another world, but this one, though "totally other."[25] This is why we go on uttering the most valid cry that has been shouted out in this world: "Your kingdom come!" (Luke 11:2); may this world pass and your Reign come: "Come, Lord Jesus!" (Rev. 22:20).

We do not contemplate heavenly resting-places, but try to listen to God's cry in the shout of reality: "It is a very strong temptation for Christians to feel moved by beautiful passages of theology while the human caravan passes then by, walking on hot coals," wrote Emmanuel Mounier.[26] We try to contemplate God in the burning bush of the liberation process, in which we hear the word God sends us, as to Moses, to set our people free. We try to listen to it obediently, with *ob-audentia*. Contemplation of liberation is always a call to renewed commitment to our actual surroundings.

Prayer Life

Prayer, a Fact of Human Life

The human person is a mystery of unfathomable depths, and in the furthest depths of this mystery dwells the spirit. This is the source of our most intimate motivations, our fundamental choice, our ultimate attitude, our religious sense. . . . This personal core demands, by its very nature, reference to an absolute point. (Whether this is called "god" or not, whether it is considered an explicitly religious phenomenon or not, we regard it as such in the anthropological and existential sense of the word: on all this, see Part One.) On the basis of this absolute, we organize our consciousness and construct our own representation of the world, within which we distinguish and order different choices and values. In one way or another, according to our own psychology, education and religious and cultural potential, we all sense a call to turn inward to become aware of our own personal foundations, to feel now and again the rock on which our lives are grounded, to appreciate the deep certainties that are the sustenance for our journey.

On the other hand, this absolute is not a mere inward phenomenon or a subjective construction, but something that springs up out of real life, and is its foundation and principle of existence. Consequently we feel ourselves called, not only to rediscover ourselves in the presence of the absolute within us, but also to discover the absolute and trace its footprints in historical events, in everyday life.

As human persons, we all need to come into contact with the

absolute inside and outside ourselves. These are two calls of the Absolute which every person feels, in one way or another, in his or her own way. The contact that takes place, the explicit, conscious reference to it at the deep levels of the person, is always a form of "prayer," or "contemplation," in the broad sense of the term. To pray, in this sense, is something human, very human, deeply human, which corresponds to a fundamental human need.

In this broad sense, beyond the explicit religious definition of conventional religions, prayer is—and here we want to give a first definition—our turning toward our personal core, toward our personal roots, toward the rock of our personal certainties, toward our fundamental choice, toward our own absolute, even if we do not recognize it as a personal God like the God of conventional religions.

This "prayer," which is in fact much more contemplative than discursive, occurs in all of us, more or less frequently, at the most important and profound moments of our lives. But it also takes place, consciously or unconsciously, in many everyday forms of reflection, solitude and personal recollection. Many people regularly pray to God without being aware of it, or without coming to believe in God, without reaching a final explicit surrender, because they have been prevented in many cases by the negative witness that other Christians—or religious people in general—have given them. Many of our sisters and brothers feel themselves confronted by the Mystery without knowing if they are confronted by something, by Someone, by themselves or simply by the void.

This turning toward the depths is a phenomenon that occurs in all religions, and is also a question posed to modern atheism or agnosticism. The current proliferation of different modern forms of prayer, of "transcendental meditation," "Zen," and so on, is a response to this same permanent human need: "The conceptual presentation of religious truths very often no longer satisfies more sincere Christians. As a result many of them no longer look for answers in the study of theology but in faith experience, and look for them in different ways. This is a typical phenomenon of our time, and it would be wrong to regard it as a step backward, since at root it is progress. . . .

When we reduce our world to the compass of what is perceivable by the mind, we are probably perceiving no more than a third of reality."[1]

Christian Prayer

When we live from our deepest core with explicit faith in a personal God, this prayer becomes a mutually personal and explicitly religious relationship, and this in itself is already an explicitly religious sense of prayer.

More specifically, Christian prayer has to do, not with a general abstract God, but with a very specific God, Jesus' God, the Christian God, who is the God of the Reign. This gives rise to a set of specific criteria for Christian prayer, without which prayer may be very fruitful, but still not definitely Christian. Jesus told us not to pray like the Gentiles (see Matt. 6:7). We cannot, for example, pray out of sheer fear or self-interest.

What is important for us is not just prayer in itself, but that our prayer should be Christian. And prayer is Christian only when it is related to the Christian God and to this God's purpose (the Reign) and when, therefore, it includes God's daughters and sons (our sisters and brothers). It is not enough to address oneself to just any god, perhaps an idol, nor a God-in-essence who isolates us from real life and makes us hostile to the world. Prayer is not Christian if it does not incorporate the horizontal with the vertical in a harmonious incarnational cross. Prayer is not Christian if it is not pregnant with history, if it does not bring us to our brothers and sisters. Our prayer, in a word, must be "prayer for the Reign." The prayer Jesus taught us, whose central petition is just this, "Your Kingdom come," is the model. In the last resort, as we said in "Reign-Focus", prayer is another of the features of Christian life that liberation spirituality reformulates, transforming them "through the Reign."

Being Christian makes our prayer inherently biblical. Prayer always has been biblical in the life of the church in the most different theologies and schools of spirituality. But it is more biblical in liberation spirituality because it is biblical in a more popular way, as the Bible permeates all the communities' prayer. This prayer is increasingly taking place with a biblical base. The communities pray with the psalms, sing the Bible, use it skilfully, reaching for its images, events, and most striking phrases; they make Bible courses a habit, both for pastoral formation and for their spiritual life.

Of particular importance for us, alongside the lessons of the universal Christian tradition, are the great religious heritage of the peoples and cultures of Abya Yala. We must tap—though always with the necessary critical sense—the experience and wisdom the different religions have accumulated about methods and forms of prayer (see UR 3b; LG 8, 16; GS 22; AG 9, 11; NAe 2), because Christian prayer is not a nirvana-prayer, or a pure impersonal transcendental meditation, or a series of psychosomatic exercises for inner relaxation.[2]

Drawing on these (and other) basic principles, we have to say that it is impossible to imagine a non-praying Christian. Living in fullness as a person (from one's personal core, full of spirit) means living in a live relationship with the Absolute. Living Christian faith is to a large extent also praying. Christian prayer is the Christian way of living an essential dimension of being human. For us, then, it is important to pray, and it is important to us that our prayer should be Christian. The first aspect is important to us because of the simple fact that we are human beings, and the second because we are Christians.

We must live prayer, be advertisements for prayer, and also teach prayer. The disciples asked Jesus, "Teach us to pray." Pastoral workers must teach prayer. The "ministry of prayer" must of necessity be a constant concern of all those involved in pastoral work.[3]

Spirituality and Prayer

Spirituality is more than prayer. Prayer is a dimension of spirituality. Many people pray a lot and possess not a spark of Christian spirituality; all they possess is prayer, an arid, cut-off prayer, separated from life, segregated, isolated from history, which becomes in the end a prayer mechanism—or prayer to a different god. Spirituality is more than prayer.[4]

Nonetheless, spirituality depends to a large extent on prayer, on whether we pray or not, on what God we pray to and why. A reliable test to identify our spirituality (or that of any person, community, team or movement) consists in examining their prayer. Our spirituality will depend fundamentally on whether we pray, on what type of prayer it is, on how much we pray, but above all on what God and what cause our prayer serves. This means there must be a generosity that overflows and nurtures our prayer life.

Contemplation

Many people are contemplatives, even though they have not explicitly or deliberately gone through the well-known "steps" of prayer described by the classical schools. Many women in our communities, peasants, workers, activists, revolutionaries, pastoral workers, and fighters in Latin America are great contemplatives. And of course, the great indigenous religions of antiquity and of the present are deeply contemplative.

We see contemplation as an attitude of tranquillity in God's presence, without images:[5]

— focusing on God's purpose, the Reign, which can also be contemplated as a moral-political utopia;

— focusing on God's works, or focusing on nature, life;

— from the core of the person, focusing on the depth of the mystery of existence, both of human beings and of the world....

Contemplation is also a sort of disturbance that harmonizes with God's own compassion, with God's holy wrath.[6] Liberating Christian contemplation comes from a spiritual sensibility, a compassion, a capacity to share the suffering of human beings and even of God, a capacity to take on oneself the situations through which our sisters and brothers are going, a capacity to tune in to and harmonize with the spiritual state of salvation history at every moment. Compassion is at the origin of the theology and spirituality of liberation.[7]

Treatises, Schools, Teachers

Prayer has given rise to treatises, schools, teachers, methods, ways, roads, stages, steps, and phenomena. All models and schools have been (and will always be) conditioned by their context: historical, cultural, psychological, and theological. Eckhart, John of the Cross, Theresa of Lisieux will all go on being authentic teachers, valid references, but not all their prescriptions or methods will be valid for every time and place, and that includes us here and now in Latin America. The discoveries about prayer made by the great teachers of Europe or Abya Yala in the sixteenth century or in the seventh or in the tenth century before Christ may be helpful to us, but only after a careful and critical effort of discernment. They did not know Freud—who has taught us something—did not go through the cultural process of awareness-changing involved in the first and second Enlightenments, they could not imagine the world of our modern cities; they could not suspect the possibility of a politically and ecclesiastically committed Christian laity, nor could they imagine the rise of the poor in this America of ours. It would be disorientating to take these teachers of the past literally, or treat them as our only guides. Now we need also to receive the lesson the Spirit is directly giving us, here and now in Latin America and in every hour of our individual lives.

With regard to forms and steps of prayer, we should not want to distinguish with the mathematical precision of the classical writers between prayer and contemplation (vocal prayer, discursive prayer, the prayer of quiet, the prayer of full union, of ecstatic union, spiritual bouquets, spiritual marriage and so on).[8] These teachers sometimes give the impression that the only people who achieve contemplation are those who advance in an explicit progress through these methods of prayer and go through the different prior stages, apparently taking it for granted that most people do not achieve contemplation.[9]

The life of prayer is a process, a history. At all events, continual growth in our Christian life[10] is an obligation deriving from the call to holiness that the Lord himself made to us: "Be perfect, therefore, as your heavenly Father is perfect" (Matt. 5:48). Vatican II officially universalized what in another age seemed to be reserved for a few: the call to holiness (LG 39-42).

We do not disdain the teachers, the teachings of tradition, the treatises, the manuals. We value the "official pedagogy" of the churches, that is, the liturgy and the sacraments (though we ask for it to be made more incarnate). It would be absurd for a liberating Christian to ignore the Church's liturgy.[11]

We shall not be giving specific rules for the amount of time to be spent on prayer, since every person and situation are different, though one of us has written, "A pastoral worker who does not give at least half an hour a day to individual prayer, in addition to what takes place in the team, does not measure up to the standard required of a pastoral worker."[12] All of us, however, have the same need to recognize God's gracious giving in time generously given to prayer, something that overrides the search for efficiency. "Prayer is an experience of gratuitousness. This 'leisure' action, this 'wasted' time, reminds us that the Lord is beyond the categories of useful and useless."[13] We cannot forget that this generosity will help to determine the religious quality of the different elements of our lives. It is certainly true that prayer is an attitude that requires practice and development, a dimension that cannot be improvised, but one that demands an effort to cultivate: "For prayer a certain ascesis, a certain discipline, is necessary, because prayer is not something instinctive that comes from inside us automatically. Prayer demands its own time and place, even its own instruments. If we don't impose a certain discipline on ourselves, in the end prayer suffers."[14]

All this is not to say that we should slip into the easy simplification of saying, "Everything is prayer." Logically, we are not going to try to draw rigid boundaries, but nor must we lose clarity: action is action; it is not prayer. Liberation is liberation, and prayer is prayer. In the same way we do not allow it to be said that "the poor" include the rich whose wealth has not brought them happiness.[15] It is true that all Christian action genuinely carried out in faith, "in a state of prayer," is in some sense a living of prayer, but it is not comparable with prayer itself. Charity is charity, service is service, and prayer is prayer.

One of the goals of liberation spirituality, as of so many other spiritualities, is to achieve the ability to live in a constant "state of prayer." The distinctiveness of our Latin American spirituality lies in the fact that this habitual diffuse state of contemplation does not take the form of ecstatic flights, escapist desertions or solipsistic inner states, but takes place in the midst of everyday life, within a grand passion for the world and activity, immersed totally in history and its processes.

The great teacher of prayer for us is none other than Jesus, who withdrew into the desert (Matt. 4:1-2), who used to look for suitable places to pray (Luke 6:12), who prayed prostrate on the ground (Matt. 26:39), and on his knees sweating what looked like drops of blood (Luke 22:41-4), and who insisted that we should "pray always and not . . . lose heart" (Luke 18:1), prepared for death in prayer (Mark 14:32-42), and died in prayer (Luke 23:34; 23:46; Matt. 27:46).

True Christian prayer should always follow Jesus' own prayer. His exemplary prayer, the Our Father, should not only guide, but also judge, our prayer. The Gospels have made it totally clear to us that this prayer, in its content and its preferences, should be the prayer of every true follower of the Master. This prayer, with its content, was his reply, or attempt to reply, to the apostles, when they asked him how they should pray.

Subsequently, the community of Jesus' followers organized their prayer publicly in the liturgy, especially in the greatest Christian celebration, the Lord's Supper, the Eucharist. The divine office, the various devotions, praying the psalms, the rosary, the stations of the cross, novenas or days of prayer, praises or litanies, pilgrimages ancient and modern, celebrations of patron saints and other popular devotions, have gradually filled out over time the style and repertoire of the People of God's Christian prayer. But in every case, for this prayer to be truly Christian, according to the Spirit of Jesus, it must always express thanksgiving to the Father and a commitment to history, since this is worship "in spirit and truth" (John 4:23), the worship that is pleasing to God (Rom. 12:1).

Prophecy

All of us, through our calling as Christians, are prophets. We are quite used to categorizing as prophets some exceptional figures from the Old Testament or in the church. Nevertheless, all of us, by baptism, grafted as living shoots on to him who is Priest, Prophet and King, are priests, prophets and kings: a priestly, prophetic and royal priesthood.

In the Bible—as revelation, as history and as the history of a people—and in the Christian tradition—as doctrine, ministry and spirituality—the following features of the prophetic vocation have been singled out as most important. The prophet is:

— the person who speaks "in a name";

— the person who consoles;

— the person who challenges and proclaims;

— the person who anticipates the people's march towards salvation, sustains it and speeds it up.

Because of the way suffering, struggle and hope have become the experience of the majority of Latin Americans, among us these constitutive marks of the prophet have to be lived collectively. The spirituality of liberation has been defined as the spirituality of a whole people.[1] Prophecy belongs to a whole "spiritual" people.

What is important, if this prophecy is to have value as evidence and have a liberating effect, is that it should be specific, historical and, as it were, normal.

It is not a matter of guessing the future, but continually

creating it, within the coordinates of Christian utopia, in the conditions of life and death of our America, and in terms of the normal life which each one of us leads. The "abnormality" of the prophetic element in our lives must be the clearsightedness in the Spirit and the rapidity of response—to the same Spirit and to the people—with which we keep reacting to the signs of the times.

Moreover, what is required is not primarily prophecy in words, but in actions, with gestures involving our whole lives. The well-known gestures typical of the prophets of Israel, in the new Israel and more specifically here in Latin America, have to be reflected in social and political attitudes and actions, of pressure for alternatives and a utopian charge. There will be no need for us to tear our clothes, but we will be called upon to tear apart the dominant ideology and religious hypocrisy. Today, standing in the gate of the Temple (Jer. 7:1-15), will be prophecy within our own church community, and in the face of the ethnocentric or alienated structures of our own church. We will know how to find a modern equivalent for Amos' gesture against the royal sanctuaries (Amos 7:10-17) of the alliance between throne and altar, of economic power and ecclesiastical privilege, denounced as idolatry by God's prophets. This sinful alliance does not belong only to the past; in a more sophisticated form it continues today, and modern consciences are much more sensitive to this scandal. Referring to the alliance between the Church and the Spanish Empire in the conquest and colonization of America, the bishop and prophet Leónidas Proaño went so far as to utter, in his death agony, on 27 August 1988 at 2.30 a.m., these final chilling words: "An idea comes to me. I have an idea, that the Church bears the sole responsibility for this burden that the Indians have suffered for centuries. . . . What pain! What pain! I am bearing this burden of centuries."

First and foremost, the prophet listens to the living God and then speaks in God's name. Prayer, meditation on the word of God, openness to the demands of the Spirit, will give us the ability to prophesy legitimately, without giving ourselves greater credentials. When we are full of the Spirit of God, we spill it spontaneously around us. It must become normal for us to recall the aims and approach of the Reign before any sort of agenda or activity, and to appeal to what Jesus did and the demands his gospel makes.

The prophet next—though this "next" should not mean a split—listens to the real people, their cry, their needs, and their aspirations. In order to speak to God on behalf of the people, in order to speak to the new kings and to speak to the people themselves in language that really speaks to their condition, the first thing Latin American women or men must do if they wish to be aware and consistent, is to get to know their own people genuinely and by daily contact. In Latin America a situation analysis, local, national and continental, has become a necessary element in pastoral meetings and in the planning of pastoral work.

We must never claim an all-purpose mandate from the people if we want to avoid the well-known defects of some would-be radical leaders or pastoral workers infected with the messianism that is all too common among Latin American politicians. There is not a hair's breadth of difference between the omniscient national leader and a dictator. Christian prophets must have the modesty of such as Moses, who recognized that he was not a good speaker (cf Exod. 4:10ff; see also Isa. 6:4ff; Jer. 1:6ff.), and must never forget that they speak "in a name": "The word of the LORD," must be their word, and "the cry of the people" their cry.

The Argentinian martyr-bishop, Enrique Angelelli, had set himself as a constant rule of ministry to journey always with "one ear cocked for the people and the other for the gospel." The true Latin American prophet must proceed with one ear for God and the other for the people and with a mouth at the service of the people.

"No prophet is accepted in the prophet's hometown." That is what Jesus said (Luke 4:24). And it does not seem normal that a prophet should be killed anywhere except in Jerusalem. Jesus said that too (Luke 13:33). The many martyred prophets of America have given evidence with their blood of these warnings of the Master. The prophet's job is to challenge, and not only the great and the powerful, but also very often the people of the prophet's own house, fellow workers or political activists, perhaps the bishop or the parish priest. Or the prophet may have to embark, for civil or gospel-inspired conscientious objections, on attitudes of material disobedience, in society or the church: strikes and fasts, marches and manifestos, and on novel experiments, usually not understood. These challenges provoke the reaction of dollars and weapons, or of the civil or ecclesiastical power, or of baser interests.

"Shout out; do not hold back," was the instruction to the prophet Isaiah (58:1). In moments of discouragement or routine, this command given to the true prophet is even more necessary. All institutions tend to sclerosis, the institutional church among them. And all revolutions tend to become bureaucratic, including Latin American revolutions. The church is always exposed to the temptation to "interpret" the gospel, and there need to be many Francis of Assisis along its journey to proclaim to it, and in its name to the world, "The gospel without interpretation." The film made about the church base communities in Brazil, "Setting Out," was an attempt to depict and stimulate the attitude and action of the collective Francis who is emerging in the Latin American Church.[2]

The prophet offers a challenge, and is therefore irritating and destabilizing. The prophet dislodges us from our false securities and relocates us in utopia, which is always less comfortable. This should not lead us to intemperate attitudes, especially toward the "little ones," those who are isolated or excommunicated by life. Jesus did not dare even to quench the smouldering wick (Isa. 42:3), and Che Guevara wanted to "become hard but without ever losing tenderness."

It goes without saying that there are false prophets. Any of us can become one. We must never claim infallibility or forget to listen to the team, the community, the people, the church, the gospel, the Spirit. We must also listen to our enemies, in order not to forget the ancient wisdom of the refrain: "From your enemy take advice."

Liberation theology has taught us to use the interpretative tools of social, political and economic science, educational theory, and increasingly, the great communication medium of culture.[3] A Latin American prophet who wants to speak here and now in the name of God, and speak in the name of the people, to the people, must also always use these instruments. No amount of inspiration can replace them.

God is love (1 John 4:8). To love and make others love is God's will (John 15:12; Rom. 13:10). God loved the world so much that he sent his own Son (John 3:16; 1 John 4:9), not to condemn the world, but to save it (John 3:17; 12:47). And God's Son, become our brother, taught us once and for all that there is only one commandment, the commandment to love (John 15:12). Love is the agenda of the Reign of God. No spirituality will be in accordance with the Spirit of God and no prophecy will be faithful to God's Word if they do not put into practice and proclaim, first and foremost, the merciful and liberating love of God.

To be a prophet in the name of the God who has a mother's compassion (Isa. 49:15) means to be constantly a consoler. The Old Testament offers us whole pages of great beauty on this consoling mission of the prophets in Israel: "Comfort, O comfort my people, says your God" (Isa. 40:1). In the midst of a people oppressed for centuries, and condemned to ever greater hunger, poverty and exclusion, as the Latin American people are today, prophecy in Latin America must mean exercising tirelessly and with fraternal tenderness the "ministry of consolation." Nothing, not law or truth or justice or orthodoxy, gives us the right to forget, in the exercise of prophecy, this element of consolation, which is also essential to it. Men and women who are "perfect" in terms of church discipline or political activism have sometimes forgotten the human condition and the suffering of the people. In pastoral work we cannot give priority to an immediate goal or an impeccable timetable over a chronic situation of desolation and impotence. Sometimes prophecy means to be near, to be silent or weep with people. "You do not know what spirit you are of," Jesus tells us (Luke 9:55) whenever we offend a poor or unimportant person, and whenever we shout the inflexibility of our ideology more loudly than the Good News of the gospel.

All these characteristics of the Christian prophet, very specifically in this land "of death and hope," and in this "winter of the church,"[4] and "dark night of the poor," should combine to produce the attitude of com-passion that soothes the wounded and lifts up the fallen, and the ministry of consolation that restores faith in life and in the God of life, and the work of community support that sustains and carries forward the utopia of the Reign.

Putting Love into Practice

The primacy of organized activity, so much stressed by modern thinking and also so characteristic of the Latin American attitude (see Purposive Action), of our revolutions and our socially committed intellectuals, insisted on so much by the organizations and the popular movement here in America, does not come as much of a surprise to Christians. Indeed, one of the deepest and most strikingly original aspects of the Judaeo-Christian tradition lies in organized activity and history—in organized action in history: "Other peoples have chosen to approach God through nature, with its characteristics of majesty, unfathomableness, uncontrollability by human beings, or, at the other extreme, through subjective or inter-subjective inner experience. It can be said that history includes and surpasses both the realm of nature and that of the subjective and personal and, in this sense, far from excluding them, gives them a context and heightens them."[1] Christian spirituality of liberation must be able to combine, to their mutual enrichment, a theophanic experience of nature, so characteristic of our indigenous root-peoples, with the theophanic experience of history and action, the particular contribution of the Judaeo-Christian faith.

Israel—led by the hand of God's revelation—is the people that discovered historical thinking. In Christian revelation there is a whole pattern of thought in terms of history and action. The Old and New Testaments are the sacred books that tell of God's historicality. Our God is the God who reveals himself in history, "acting" in it. His word, *dabar*, is not just a sound, nor a mere rational concept, but a fact, something that happens, enters history, disturbs it and transforms it. God's word places before the people the utopia of a promise, offers them an encounter in the form of a covenant and so opens for them a space and horizon to enable them to journey, from promise to promise, from fall to pardon, from covenant to covenant, transforming history, conquering the Promised Land.

Yahweh's prophets never cease to reprimand the people of God when they stray into a cult that may be fervent but which, not supported by life, turns into idolatry. The gods are nothing; the God of Israel is life, love, history. "To know Yahweh is to work justice," the prophets repeat with an obsessive insistence (Mal. 6:6-8). The practice of love and justice is the supreme criterion of moral goodness, above any worship or sacrifice (Isa. 1:10-18; 58:1-12; 66:1-3; Amos 4:4-5; 5:21-5; Jer. 7 21-6) or any other moral security (Jer. 7:1-15; 9:24), just as the touchstone of Israel's religious faith and its very establishment as a people is God's liberating action in the exodus (Exod. 20:1; Deut. 5:6; Deut. 26:5b-9).

Jesus, "a prophet mighty in deed and word" (Luke 24:19) who first acted and then taught (cf Acts 1:1), who went about doing good (Acts 10:38), provoked the astonishment of the crowds who heard "all that he was doing" (Mark 3:8) as much by his actions as by his words, if not more, took up this prophetic theme and insisted—with increasing vehemence and total coherence until his death—that "Not everyone who says to me, 'Lord, Lord,' will enter the kingdom of heaven, but only the one who does the will of my Father" (Matt. 7:21-3), and "You will know [true worshippers] by their fruits" (Matt. 7:16; cf John 4:23), and "They who have my commandments and keep them are those who love me" (John 14:21).

Jesus' message attains its maximum clarity at this point, when he identifies the practice of love, especially "to one of the least of these who are members of my family", as the "eschatological criterion of salvation," by which "the nations" will be judged (Matt. 25:31-46). The parable of the Good Samaritan (Luke 10:25-37) stresses that putting love into practice takes precedence over distinctions of creed, cult or religion. John's Gospel never tires of insisting that practical actions, "works," are what give credible witness (John 5:36; 6:30; 7:3; 9:3; 10:25; 10:37-8; 14:11; 15:24).

The first communities collected the words and works of Jesus in unanswerable texts that run right through the four Gospels, the Acts of the Apostles, the Epistles and the book of Revelation. It would take too long to trace in detail this insistence on "putting love into practice" throughout the New Testament. For our purposes it is enough to mention the path-breaking texts in the Epistle of James (1:27; 1:14-26) and the Epistles of John (1 John 3:9-18; 4:7-16; 4:21-7).

Paul never preached faith without works, but denied that the "works of the Law" alone are sufficient (Romans, *passim*). And in his own life he gave abundant witness of apostolic activity and service to the community, from his sea voyages to his manual work as a tanner (Acts 18:3; 1 Cor. 4:12; 2 Thess. 3:8). The Protestant tradition in Latin America, with a Pauline influence that has not always been sufficiently recognized, has also developed a pastoral ministry with a deep social commitment and with outstanding exegetical and theological writing by figures such as Milton Schwantes, Jorge Pixley, Julio de Santa Ana, José Míguez Bonino, and Elsa Támez.

In Christian terms, this is the meaning of the great and valuable attack on "faith without works." Confronted with a church or a theology that "proclaimed" the Good News with little coherent action or sense of history, there has been a desire, an attempt, and real progress in Latin America, especially in the last twenty-five years, to construct a theology and a church that put the Good News into practice in history. The rise of the theology of liberation is itself the result of this accumulated wealth of liberating activity, experiences and martyrdoms. The Latin American church has not specialized in producing dogmatic formulas, but it has become a specialist in trying to put love into practice. As a result, both the revolutionaries and the prophets of Latin America can be regarded as, and are, coherent witnesses, who have set an example and carved out a path that is much more important than its immediate results and is transforming the continent.

There have been attempts to criticize the activities that have been collected under the Christian label of "orthopraxy," by presenting them as in contradiction to orthodoxy, whereas we think of them as proof of orthodoxy. Orthodoxy is only truly "ortho" when it also becomes "praxis." It is important never to forget the double etymology of "orthodoxy": *orthos* means "correct" or "good," and *doxa* can mean both "opinion," "idea," and "glory" or "manifestation." The "true glory of God" is not shown primarily in correctly proclaimed dogmas, but in love effectively put into practice. Once again, let us quote the definition of the real "glory of God" given by two martyr bishops of the church, one from the fourth century and the other from our own time, St Irenaeus and Oscar Romero: the real glory of God here on earth, said Irenaeus, is "that human beings should be able to live," and Romero: "that poor people should be able to live," or, as Jesus said: "that they may have life, and have it abundantly" (John 10:10). Jesus' Father, through the prophets, said in angry words that he wanted mercy and not sacrifice (Hos. 6:6; Amos 5:21ff.), and his Son made the same point with angry actions in the precinct of the Temple itself (Matt. 9:13). In Latin America the option for the poor, for the spirituality and theology of liberation, translates into the local and historical context of all the countries of this continent the option of the God of the Bible for the orphan, the widow and the foreigner. And day by day it translates into this context the effective com-passion of Jesus of Nazareth.

There is almost no anticlericalism in Latin America, and several Latin American churches have topped popularity polls. (This may not be not true of the majority, but in Brazil in 1991 a survey gave the church an 80 percent rating for credibility and reliability, much higher than the ratings for radio [48 percent] and television [43 percent]. Political parties [17 percent] and professional politicians [13.5 percent] have suffered the sharpest loss of confidence in recent years, and bottom of the poll came bankers and business leaders.) This is probably the result of the changes and renewal of the previous twenty years, when the churches put love into practice and took a firm stand in support of the needs and aspirations of the mass of the people, often risking their own security and accepting the consequences in misunderstanding at home and abroad. Typical features of Latin American church activity have been vigorous action on land, labour conditions, housing, migration and social exclusion, prostitution and abandoned children, education and political alternatives, the "Vicariates of Solidarity" and the "Fraternity Campaigns," involvement in community associations and development programmes and, in terms of distinctive Latin American issues, in ministries to the indigenous and the black populations. On the battlefield of action Christians and non-Christians have come together, in the service of the same greater cause, which some call the new humanity or the liberated society and others, also and explicitly, the Reign.

The return to the historical Jesus in the spirituality and theology of liberation is simultaneously a motivation and justification for this active faith, which means making the choices that Jesus made, doing what Jesus did. What was sometimes reduced, in a more traditional church, to a strict code of specific, sporadic and marginal "works of mercy" is presented to us in the spirituality and the theology of liberation as the immediate, undeniable, overriding imperative of living faith, credible hope and effective charity.

This activity, moreover, is not just a piling up of works, services and isolated forms of assistance. It has to be a structured activity, designed to transform the social situation of our oppressed and subjugated masses. This is the connotation of the term "praxis," so frequently used in Latin America, action that has a political dimension and is not simply assistential: it seeks to replace the structures of death with structures of life and liberation. Even the term "the civilization of love," which is often advocated as the church's great social utopia, and which Puebla made a slogan for Latin America, has to be properly understood, because "love" can become very vague and devalued by inflation. The 1985 Extraordinary Synod, in its message of 7 December, was more precise and more demanding: "There is a path opening up for the human race—and we can already see the first signs—leading to a *civilization of participation, solidarity and love,* the only civilization worthy of human beings."

Jesus passed through this world "doing good" (Acts 10:37),

and did everything well (cf Mark 7:37). Nothing other than this is the aim and the task of coherent revolutionaries and consistent Christians in Latin America. Being disciples of Jesus means that we must engage in the same activity as Jesus. "The very fact of reproducing to the ultimate degree the practice of Jesus and his own historical existence, because it is Jesus', means accepting Jesus as an ultimate criterion and thus declaring that he is something really ultimate; it is already, implicitly, but efficaciously, a declaration that he is the Christ, though subsequently this confession must be made explicit. . . . The area of greatest metaphysical density is action."[2] We should also remember the statement of the 1971 World Synod: "Action on behalf of justice and participation in the transformation of the world seem to us clearly to be a constitutive dimension of the preaching of the gospel for liberation from every oppressive situation." Making the revolution also brings about the Reign, although the latter is first and foremost a gift and a hope.

To put it in very practical terms, not being an active member of a party, a trade union, and the popular movement (and sometimes we shall have to be members of all of these at once) in Latin America means not to be politically aware or coherent in one's social activism. And not to be an active member of a committed social ministry is, in the Latin American church, to lack an understanding of the structural and political dimension of charity and to lack social consistency in love. Logically, this applies to all of us according to our position and gifts.

The utopia lived in Latin America is still being lived, in spite of all the exhaustion and steps back, because it is a utopia in the process of being created. It is not just being written about; it is being constructed. The spirituality and theology of liberation have taught us, in a new way, to sense the three theologal virtues of faith, hope and charity as a single, profound experience that welcomes the mystery of God, God's family and creation (faith), devotes itself to exploring and bringing it about by purposive activity (charity), and continues to dream dreams that surpass all achievements and overcome all frustrations (hope).

To sum up, in the form of guidelines, we should remember:

—In Latin America it is impossible to live a Christian spirituality without living spiritually as a Latin American.

—It is impossible to be a good Latin American Christian without applying the option for the Reign in attitudes and actions that make it credible, celebrate it coherently, help to build it in the here and now of the continent and allow us to hope for it in the greater land to come.

—We Christians, who have an experience of the Reign given to us uniquely through faith, must also translate it into cultural, family, social, political and economic forms.

—For the sake of the Reign, Christian communities in Latin America that wish to be consistent must be active in the popular movement, in defending indigenous peoples and in support of Afro-Americans, in the cause of the liberation of our peoples, in the communion of solidarity and in the establishment of a new world order without grinding poverty and imperialism, without destruction of nature and without an arms race.

—A Latin American woman cannot be a good Christian without fighting for women's liberation. A Latin American peasant cannot be a good Christian without fighting for agrarian reform. A Latin American worker cannot be a good Christian without fighting for a workers' revolution. And none of us—layperson, priest, pastor or bishop—in Latin America will be good Christians if we do not fight for a church that is communitarian, participatory, socially committed and liberating.

The Option for the Poor

The Relationship between the Option for the Poor and the Option for the People

We are about to consider one of the pillars of Latin American spirituality, one of its "trade marks." The option for the poor can be regarded as one of its greatest and most famous contributions to the universal church, although, strictly speaking, it is not the introduction of something new, rather the rediscovery of an essential dimension of the Christian message that belongs to the core of the church's tradition.[1] As we noted in connection with the option for the people, at the origin of the option for the poor is the phenomenon of the breakthrough of the poor, which has caused so much upheaval in society as well as the church.[2] "The breakthrough of the poor in Latin American society and the Latin American church is, in the last resort, a breakthrough of God into our lives. This breakthrough is the starting point and at the same time the motor of the new spirituality."[3]

Latin American Christians, for the most part poor, who were the leaders of this breakthrough, active participants in the liberation struggles that have been breaking out on the continent for several decades, asked themselves in the light of faith what the gospel brought to their option for the people and their participation in the process of liberation, and how they should live their Christian identity inside this process; and at the same time they asked what difference this option for the people made when they came to read the word of God and live their Christian lives. This interactive process of action and reflection is what produced the theology of liberation, and what also gradually produced a precise formulation of the option for the poor, which, before it had a theory, was essentially a spiritual experience.

In the precise sense we are here giving to the terms, the "option for the poor" is the Christian version of the "option for the people". They are a single spirit, a single attitude, considered from two different points of view. The option for the people includes moral, political, geopolitical, hermeneutical, cultural, and pedagogical aspects, and is shared by believers and non-believers. The option for the poor includes this option for the people, with all the aspects just mentioned, but adds the perspective of faith, explicitly religious motivation. The option for the poor includes the option for the people, although the latter does not include the explicit faith perspective of the former. Some people come to the option for the poor from the human experience of the option for the people, and others come to the option for the people from the religious experience of the option for the poor.

The explicit faith perspective that is a feature of the option for the poor does not turn it into something completely different from the option for the people. On the contrary, there is an underlying continuity between the two. The motivation of the option for the poor is neither distinct from nor reducible to that of the option for the people. It is not in a simple sense a new set of reasons. A better way of describing it is to say that the reasons that inspire the option for the people, seen in the light of faith, without losing their own autonomy and coherence, gain a new look and acquire a theological and theologal status in the option for the poor: the intolerable situation of injustice becomes a situation opposed to God's plan; it becomes sin. The struggle for justice becomes a mission in the service of the Reign of God. The historical potential of the poor acquires a link with God's plan of salvation. Faith gives a distinctive fullness and a fundamental radical quality to these existing reasons.[4]

The Spiritual Experience of the Option for the Poor

What inspires Latin American Christians to live the option for the poor as one of the deepest dimensions of their human and Christian lives is an explicitly religious spiritual experience. How can we describe this spiritual experience? What sort of experience is it?

We have the experience of making God's own option for the poor. We are imitating God, the Father-Mother of compassion. God made the first option. All through the history of salvation God always appeared on the side of the oppressed, as the liberator of the people, a role summed up in the Old Testament term *goel*, the one who secures justice for the poor and the excluded. Our option for the poor is rooted ultimately in God: to use a technical term, it is theologal.[5]

We experience an encounter with Christ in the poor. We recognize the "suffering features of Christ the Lord" in "very concrete faces," which are all too frequent on our continent: the faces of children blighted by poverty, the faces of young people disorientated and frustrated, of indigenous people and Afro-Americans in sub-human situations, underpaid workers, people under-employed or unemployed, people in the cities, excluded and overcrowded, old people . . . (Puebla, 31-9). "The poor are the living mediation of the Lord, his real expression and not just an intermediary between him and us."[6] Jesus identified with the poor to the point of making them the one absolutely necessary and absolutely universal sacrament of salvation.[7] The poor become our evangelizers (Puebla 1147).

We experience the Spirit of Jesus, strengthening the resistance and struggles of the poor, rousing them, inciting them to take history into their hands and organize to transform the world. We discover the action of the Spirit in the liberating struggles of the poor.[8]

We experience the option for the poor as practical discipleship of Jesus: it is doing what he did. It is taking up his cause, continuing his struggle, prolonging his own solidarity with the poor and excluded. It is carrying out his mission in the mission of the church, proclaiming the Good News to the poor, in an attempt to hasten the coming of the Reign for the poor and, through them, for everyone.

We experience a principle of Christian discernment, that apart from the Good News for the poor there is no "gospel" or true church of Jesus, and this enables us to see possible limitations in many trends in spirituality in previous periods of history. The option for the poor becomes a "mark" of the true church, of discipleship of Jesus, of Christian spirituality.

We experience an encounter with the poor that is deeper than the naive or pragmatic view that sees each poor person as a particular case, not structural, which simply calls for alms or kindness. The option for the poor reveals the poor as a collective phenomenon, a source of conflicts and alternatives.[9]

The option for the poor leads us to adopt the social position of the poor.

Simultaneously the option for the poor leads us to a rediscovery of charity: we go beyond individual, immediate almsgiving that is simply kindness. The new experience of charity starts from justice and from the desire to create the structures of the Reign of God in society, and realizes that people live in society, in a nation, in collectivities structured by culture, politics, economics, and religion.

The Experience of the Option for the Poor

We live the option for the poor first as a break with the attitudes of the dominant classes, which we have usually absorbed. We don't break with any person; we break—and radically—with the mind-set of those who dominate society. By now everyone should realize that the universality of salvation and of the Christian mission cannot be achieved without the radical exclusion of the sin of domination and injustice.[10] This is a departure from our own class, a difficult sacrifice, a kenosis. The option for the poor demands this break of all of us, including those who were born in the world of the poor, because this does not make them free of the attitudes of the powerful. As the bishops put it at Puebla, the option for the poor is an invitation the church extends to "all, regardless of class" (Message to the Peoples of Latin America, 3).

After this break, the option for the poor leads us to an exodus, makes us go out to meet the other person, go to the poor quarters of town, enter the world of the poor and accept it as our own. It is an incarnation, an identification with the world of the poor.[11] It is adopting the social position of the poor, as a chosen setting from which to look at events and transform them to bring them closer to the poor.[12]

The option for the poor also requires us to take up the cause of the poor consciously and actively: "We invite all, regardless of class, to accept and take up the cause of the poor, as though they were accepting and taking up their own cause, the cause of Christ himself" (Puebla, Message to the Peoples of Latin America, 3). This means active solidarity with the struggles and activities of their movements, actively defending their rights, a clear commitment to their total liberation, an unconditional affirmation of life and an equally unconditional rejection of injustice.[13] It also means rejecting wealth in the sense of a civilization based on privilege. "In the economic order, Christian utopia, seen from Latin America, arising from real historicized prophecy, . . . proposes a civilization of poverty to take the place of the present civilization of wealth. . . . The civilization of poverty, . . . founded on a materialist humanism transformed by Christian light and inspiration, rejects the accumulation of capital as the energizer of history, and the possession-enjoyment of wealth as a principle of humanization, and it makes the universal satisfying of basic needs the principle of development, and the growth of shared solidarity the foundation of humanization."[14] Its aim is not universal pauperization, but universal participation. In this way, the option for the poor introduces us into activity in history for liberation, for universal transformations: "The church has always made the option for the poor. Nevertheless there is now something new in this option for the poor: we are now making an option for their processes, for the people's processes. We are making an option for the poor as individuals, as classes, as majorities, as a people, as an organized people, as peoples in process. That is the new element."[15]

Taking up the cause of the poor brings with it accepting their destiny, that is persecution and martyrdom, something that is not a random event, but the culmination of the option for the poor. Jesus' cross gains its full historical realism when it spontaneously overtakes followers of Jesus and fleshes out their following of Jesus in terms of the option for the poor. We meet the cross when we fight against the cross, against the unjust poverty imposed on most of the world's population.[16]

The option for the poor includes a large measure of discipline and purification at all these levels: it requires us to put aside our old mentality, constantly analyze the social situation, increasingly identify ourselves with the cause of the poor, be strong in the daily struggle to endure persecution and to be ready for martyrdom: the Second Vatican Council called on all Christians to be always prepared for martyrdom (LG 42), and this call acquires permanent force through the option for the poor. That is why Puebla solemnly declares: "We affirm the need for the whole church to be converted to a preferential option for the poor, with a view to their integral liberation" (1134).

The option for the poor challenges us not to accept limits to our spiritual growth. At the beginning we shall still retain paternalistic, uncritical and perhaps romantic attitudes. Our spiritual growth will go through various stages: direct contact with life in the raw, constant analysis, learning from action, the disappointments of events, incarnation in the cultural world of the poor for those who have not been born into it, incorporation into their spiritual experience, the discovery of the strength of the poor and of the fact that our contribution is not essential, overcoming the "them and us" attitude. "[We] are being asked to make [our] own the experience that the poor have of God..., [to make] our own the world of the poor and their manner of living out their relationship with the Lord and taking over the historical practice of Jesus . . ., to rise to life with the people in its spirituality."[17]

In the option for the poor our spirituality acquires various dimensions at the same time. It gains a moral dimension because it includes a shout of anger at the situation of unjust poverty. It gains an additional political dimension, because it situates us in a particular position within society alongside the poor and against their poverty (see Political Holiness, below). It also gains a geopolitical dimension inasmuch as it shows us that the poor are also peoples occupying a subordinate position in relation to imperial transnational powers. It is also a hermeneutical option in that it is one we make in order to reach the best position to live out and understand our faith: "Latin American Christology believes that the best place for the theologian to be is in the world of the poor and the church of the poor, and that from this committed position theological understanding functions better, and acquires a better grasp of the totality and its meaning."[18] There are other dimensions, too, educational, cultural and others.

The option for the poor is, in short, a key element of our spirituality. It is a fundamental option. It is a fundamental human option because for many men and women it is the most basic way in which they understand themselves and formulate the meaning of history and human life. It is a fundamental religious option in itself, since such a deep fundamental option is always religious in nature, even if those who make it are not conscious of this religious character and even think of themselves as atheists. But it is a fundamental religious option in the sense that we live it simultaneously as an expression of our explicitly Christian option: for us "to make the option for the poor" becomes a symbolic expression that encapsulates our religious identity. And it is a fundamental Christian option because it gives meaning to discipleship of Jesus for us, "living and fighting for the cause of Jesus." For Latin American religious the option for the poor is equally crucial: "The option for the poor is creating a new understanding of religious identity itself. It is a sort of reinterpretation of the meaning of our mission from the point of view of the poor that challenges our way of life, the motivation of our activity, our apostolic works, the structure of our spirituality and, finally, the meaning of being disciples of Christ today. The option for the poor permeates the whole meaning of religious life, because it corresponds to the attitude of Jesus' own option."[19] Puebla also noted that the option for the poor is the strongest tendency among Latin American religious (733).

Cross/Conflict/Martyrdom

Being a Christian means following Jesus, and following Jesus means going with him day by day, carrying one's cross. "If any want to become my followers, let them deny themselves and take up their cross and follow me."

The crucifix—the cross with the figure of the crucified Jesus—has become the most universal symbol of Christianity, and unfortunately the most trivialized also, as jewelry, displayed in banks and unjust courts, on showy buildings and in the deadly company of the swords of so many conquerors.

In the next section, "Penance and Liberation," we explain what the cross is and is not, particularly in relation to making reparation for sin and to self-control. In this section we want to focus on five major aspects of the Christian cross:

— poverty;
— suffering and death;
— self-denial and sacrifice;
— conflict;
— martyrdom.

Poverty

The majority of human beings, some 80 percent, survive in poverty. In Latin America 44 percent of the population struggle to live in extreme poverty, according to a statement by the secretary of the UN Economic Commission for Latin America in March 1992.

Meanwhile poverty and destitution are here, in Latin America, in its streets and fields, in the flesh of our people. This poverty too has to be lived with spirituality. How?

Of course, we must condemn it and fight it ferociously as contrary to the will of God our Father and Mother, as the cause of many premature and unjust deaths and of an accumulated weight of suffering and despair. The spirituality of liberation, because it is Christian and liberating, must take up the war on poverty as a fundamental virtue of its prophetic attitude, of its fraternal solidarity and service to others.

When poverty lives in our own house, we must also, first and foremost, discover its causes and possible solutions. The first form of love for one's family is to fight against this poverty, so that our home may be a place of life and happiness. We cannot be poor without spirit: it was to the "poor in spirit"—in Matthew's version—that Jesus promised his beatitude.

Second, we must fight against this poverty by joining with other poor people in an organized way. We are not poor by accident, or individually. We are a vast impoverished collectivity, a product of domination and exploitation. It is not the God of Life who makes us poor or wants us poor; it is the gods of death, capital, public corruption, dependence and, sometimes, hereditary factors or our own passivity and exhaustion. Whatever our situation, in an attitude of faith, and in communion with Jesus, who was poor, we can always make our poverty, in any circumstances, our cross within the great Cross. Conformity with the will of God—which does not mean conformism—is a fundamental feature of the poor of Yahweh in the Old Testament and of those who are "crucified with Christ" in the New.

At the same time, and within this clear and constant process of denunciation and war on poverty and its causes, structures and consequences, those of us who are not poor in Latin America—and in any place where there are poor people— must be constantly on the watch for poverty and seek it out, in order to suffer with the poor and share their deprivations, their demands and their struggles. We cannot insult them by any type of luxury or superfluity in our lives, in our families or our institutions, civil or ecclesiastical. The poor must not be able to blaspheme the name of God on account of the scandal of a faith that is extravagant and shows no solidarity. It is inconceivable for a church, a religious house, a priest, a pastoral worker, but also a family or any Christian lay man or woman, to squander things most people lack, or to refuse to share with this majority, not just alms or an occasional visit, but one's whole family, religious or church life.

Being a Christian in Latin America means being close to the poor, taking up the cause of the poor and, to some degree, living like the poor. Otherwise what we do belies the new commandment, and solidarity and the gospel become a bitter joke.

Being a Christian in Latin America means living the option for the poor constantly and in an organized way: being poor in a different way, through the Spirit, or, through the same Spirit, becoming poor with the poor, in the beatitude of gospel poverty and in the fight against inhuman poverty. Poor and non-poor, but all living the option for the poor, we must make it a regular practice amongst us to observe the distinction and exhortation of Medellín in its document, "The Poverty of the Church": to fight real poverty as an evil, to live spiritual poverty as renunciation and availability to the will of God, and to turn solidarity into everyday fraternal contact and struggle.

Suffering and death

Suffering, in the form of pain, physical or mental illness, inherited or acquired disabilities, loneliness, accidents, natural decline and in the end, death, is simultaneously a mystery and something inherent in our condition as finite and mortal beings. Every day brings its own problem (Matt. 6:34), and each age its own sufferings.

Humankind never has been and never will be able to remove suffering from its path entirely, though we do have the basic right and duty to fight it and reduce it constantly (GS 34). Job's suffering runs through all human history, in every civilization. Gustavo Gutiérrez has given us a dramatically vivid and powerfully evangelizing sense of the Latin American people as a collective Job.[1]

Human beings always have wrestled and always will wrestle with the question of the meaning of suffering, innocent or apparently pointless or blatantly unjust.[2] The challenge for us as Christians is to discover the meaning of suffering and live it in accordance with God's will, perhaps stripped to bare faith, in order to experience God too through suffering and to talk about God out of suffering, in order to bring all suffering into the movement of the Reign, as the cross of liberation and not the cross of damnation. We know for certain that we can pass from death to life (1 John 3:14), from suffering to joy, through the word, life, death and resurrection of Jesus. Through Jesus, the suffering servant par excellence and "the firstborn from the dead," we have the understanding and ability to suffer well, and we must help others to suffer well. This means being open, without anxiety, to the vicissitudes of life, in health, finance, social position, or in painful accidents of any sort. The first Christian response to suffering is to see God's liberating action even there.

Second, when confronted with suffering, we must be able to combine trustful prayer—which will sometimes be the prayer of Gethsemane, "Remove this cup from me; yet, not what I want, but what you want" (Mark 14:36)— with all the human solutions in our power. Jesus did not look for suffering. The cross is not passivity.

Third, with generosity of spirit, we must avoid making others suffer by offloading our own suffering on to them. It is one thing to be a Simon of Cyrene, another to force others to be one. This ability to bear our own suffering, without dramatizing it and creating an atmosphere of suffering around us, is particularly necessary within a family, because of the closeness and permanence of the relationship.

Fourth, we have to be able to organize even suffering. This may be a matter of the rhythm of our own lives or may mean taking part in activities or organizations promoted by the various ministries that deal with suffering: the ministry to the sick and those with disabilities, to refugees, the displaced, the excluded.

Toward death, the only truly Christian attitude is a paschal one. Death has been conquered (1 Cor. 15:54-7) in him who died with all our deaths and for all of us (1 Thess. 5:10; 1 Cor. 15:3). Christian spirituality, even more especially in Latin America, where death is such a massive, daily and absurd occurrence, must learn to live with death and teach others to face it and transform it. First we must fight it, because it goes without saying that our spirituality, the spirituality of the Spirit of Life, can never be one of suicide. Second, we must help to bear it in the cases of our relatives or friends afflicted by death, above all when it is an unjust death, a case of persecution, social exclusion or any sort of violence. Third, when faced with death we must always learn, and help others to learn, lessons of life, about health care, social measures, health and safety at work, and the like. Finally, the approach of death and the hour of death are above all a *kairos*, regular or sudden, to live hope. For us who have died through baptism and entered the death and resurrection of Jesus, death, someone else's or our own, must be a sacramental experience, a witness to Easter.

Self-denial and Sacrifice

In the history of Christian spirituality, "carrying one's cross," in response to the invitation of Jesus in the gospel, has also meant, especially in the various types of religious life, giving up some rights or comforts normal in "non-consecrated" life. It has also meant, in a more general way, self-denial, denying oneself, mortifying oneself. Practices known to everyone, such as fasting, physical mortification, vigils, and so on, have given this self-denial a content.

"Denying oneself" and giving up possessions or rights, interests or comforts, "for the sake of the Reign," continues to be valid, relevant and urgent in Christian spirituality, today especially to confront consumerism, hedonism, extravagance, when the extreme poverty of the majority of people is steadily increasing, and the opportunities for pleasure and enjoyment by a small minority are steadily expanding. And naturally it remains, and will continue to remain necessary for us to accept the sacrifice and self-denial required of us to be faithful to God and other people, to control our passions, and fulfil our private or public duties.

We have already said that there are certain constants, which include this area of voluntary sacrifice, that all religions and cultures advocate and even ritualize. Holiness, in whatever place and in all periods, is a process of purification and self-giving, a sacrifice of self and a disciplined race toward the fullness of love (Phil. 3:12). The spirituality of liberation, in the twofold emphasis it gives to the following of Jesus and the option for the poor, must be a spirituality of generous sacrifices "for the Reign."

These constants nevertheless change, and must change their forms according to period and place. One of the serious mistakes of so-called "traditional" spiritualities was to over-formalize a discipline and a mysticism that belonged to a particular context in the belief that they were building the house of the Spirit for all times and places.

All of us will have to carry the cross of sacrifice and self-denial in family life, at work, and in our commitment to the people. Indeed, we will have to be present in the three spheres simultaneously, accepting them coherently and even as an act of witness. Christians who are not capable of daily self-denial, even in small details, and with cheerful readiness, are not living their spirituality coherently, however heroic they may occasionally appear in social activism or ministry. Married life, relations between the generations, education, courtship, the discipline inherent in teamwork and service, the ability to understand and forgive, like the vagaries of the weather, journeys or unexpected tasks, or having to go without food or sleep, all these are the first cross we have to bear constantly, with spiritual flair, without fooling ourselves by looking for exotic crosses or saving ourselves exclusively for the cross of public responsibilities or extraordinary tasks (see "Penance and Liberation" and "Everyday Faithfulness," below). The guerrilla warfare of the Reign is waged, not only, or even principally, in the mountains of heroism, but above all in the lowlands of daily life.

As pastoral workers or facilitators of communities, all of us—lay people, religious, priests, pastors, bishops, men and women—must make ministry itself a liberating and redeeming cross, which we bear consciously and generously. We are not mercenaries or officials or dilettantes. We cannot treat ministry as a job for our spare time, nor can we select at our convenience the pastoral tasks that appeal to us, though we have the right and duty to use discernment on the basis of our attitudes and the priorities of the people and the church. Ministry is a cross. The Good Shepherd warned us in advance and with his supreme witness that all good shepherds are ready to give their lives for their sheep (John 10:11), and not just at one possible painful moment, but day by day.

This pastoral cross includes all the little irritations of working in a team, to do with planning, disciplined implementation and evaluation. We may have to give up leadership ambitions and accept with spiritual grace the incomprehension of colleagues or superiors, or even the ingratitude of the people. We will sometimes have to volunteer for areas or tasks that others don't want, or carry on with self-denying persistence in a ministry or task even when no immediate results are visible, or when the results seem to disprove our assumptions. We must not forget that failure can be a cross. We must not forget that the grain of wheat first dies, in the ground, and only later bears fruit (John 12:24). And we must not forget that we are trying to follow a failure in Jesus of Nazareth.

The people themselves, in their cultural diversity and complex family situations, struggling to survive and bombarded with contradictory suggestions and social and religious fashions, are a cross for any committed pastoral worker. To run away from the cross of the people would be to run away from the cross of Christ. In the last resort, the "supreme penance" and the greatest reward for us as pastoral workers, is the people, whose parents we have become (1 Cor. 4:15). Nor can we fall into the temptation of respecting the people only when they belong to the already organized popular groups. Our pastoral com-passion and any self-denying service it claims should be spontaneously directed to the mass that has become anonymous and wanders "like sheep without a shepherd" (Matt. 9:36).

Today more than ever, if we want the phrase "the new evangelization" to come alive and be more than a slogan, ministry, and very typically in Latin America, requires us to give up any ethnocentrism and to make constant efforts of creativity, which are easily misunderstood, at real inculturation. For some the greatest sacrifice may be having to abandon contact with one's own culture, native or adopted, in order to incarnate oneself, like the Word, in the culture of the pastoral area to which we are sent. For others, the daily self-denial will be the struggle against all the odds, in their own marginalized or banned culture, to enable the gospel and the church to be freely inculturated. This cross of inculturation, as old as it is new, is only just beginning to be publicly recognized by the church as a cross that bears the fruitfulness of the gospel (see "Incarnation," above).

Moreover, ministry, worthily exercised, in addition to all the urgent tasks, demands of us the self-denial involved in study, being informed, continuing education. And first and foremost, ministry that is liberating in a Christian way demands of us the self-denial—silence, listening, darkness of faith, risks of availability—of an intense and sustained prayer life.[3]

In Latin America in the last few decades, religious life, under the wise stimulus of CLAR, the Latin American Confederation of Religious, has found a way of situating in the Latin American context the sacrifices and surrender that are the basis of religious life. (Inexplicably, CLAR, which has existed since 1959, is now experiencing suspicion and sanctions that in our view it does not deserve, but we hope that in any case these will not fail to be another cross that purifies Latin American religious life.) Through communities "inserted" in poor communities, religious have shifted old houses and energies to the frontier and the margins of society. With the poor of the earth and the activists in popular causes, they are putting at risk their peace of mind, their reputations, their health and even their lives. Innumerable religious, men and women, have already shed their blood for the Reign on this continent. The time for the religious life is not over, least of all in Latin America. New experiments and a greater interweaving of religious life and lay life hold out the promise of a providential flowering.

And in the religious life, both in the past in the Egyptian

desert and today in Latin America, the three vows of poverty, chastity, and obedience were, are, and will be the embodiment of the cross accepted in community of life, witness and evangelization. All three, however, will have to be increasingly understood with reference to the way of life of the poor and the task of effective service to these masses, and to the need to challenge the idols of pleasure, possessions and power. The fact that this religious life is essentially developed in community necessarily demands the constant self-denial that is the essence of properly lived life in common. A "really common life," not only within our own religious community, but also with the great community of the poor, is a prophetic actualization in our time of the ancient "supreme" penance, whatever the particular charism and ministry of our congregation.[4]

Conflict

As individuals, as a society, as a church, if we faithfully live our spirituality and its radical consequences, we will inevitably have to shoulder the cross of conflict. Conflict, which was an essential feature of Jesus' life in history, continues to be an essential feature of the lives of his followers in history. This conflict can be divided into three categories:

— conflict with his own relatives and companions (Luke 2:41ff; 4:28; 4:19-20; 8:46; Mark 8:31ff; John 12:4);

— conflict with the powers and interests of this world (Matt. 17:24-7;27:59ff; Mark 8:33ff; 10:35ff; 12:1-12; 14:53-4; 15:1; 15:6ff; Luke 20:1-19;22:66; John 10:24,31; 11:45; 18:12ff);

— conflict with the synagogue and the Temple controlled by a closed curia or burdensome regulations or an exaggerated hierarchical system or clericalism.[5]

Since our peoples awakened with a new awareness of their situation of captivity and began to look for liberation, Latin America has become the continent of conflict. Popular organizations and church base communities, activists and pastoral workers at their different levels, intellectuals, artists, and liberation theologians, whole villages and anonymous masses of the Christian people of Latin America have carried this cross of conflict daily, during military dictatorships or during the current reign of neo-imperialism, at home or in exile, in city or country. Escaping from ignorance and conformism forces people to join the conflict that is inseparable from history.[6]

We all share Archbishop Romero's conviction: "Believe me, my friends, those who commit themselves to the poor have to face the same fate as the poor. And in El Salvador we know very well what the fate of the poor is: to be 'disappeared,' to be tortured, to be seized, to turn up as corpses."[7]

Like him, for the same reason, we "are glad" that the Latin American church is taking part fully in this conflict that brings martyrdom: "I am glad, my friends, that our church is being persecuted specifically for its option for the poor and for trying to become incarnate in the interests of the poor."[8] And what he said of his country we can say of the whole continent: "It would be sad if, in a country where such horrible murders are taking place, we could not find priests among the victims. They are the proof of a church incarnate in the problems of the people."[9]

For Christians, of course, this cross of conflict is more painful and less understandable when we meet it in the institutional church.[10] Archbishop Romero, as in so much, is a model in his experience of conflict in the church at various levels, as his personal diary records. But, wherever it comes from, the cross of conflict—with our family, with the system, with the church—will be a Christian cross only if we are able to carry it with spirit, in the Spirit, as Jesus carried it.

Martyrdom

Jesus of Nazareth accepted conflict to the point of death, death on the cross. Often conflict for the sake of the gospel and liberation will bring us to the point of martyrdom.[12] Latin America stands out as a collective witness to this. In the early years of the church this situation seemed natural. Origen said that the catechumens prepared simultaneously for baptism and martyrdom. Vatican II acknowledged this challenge for our own day when it declared that all Christians have to be prepared to witness to Christ with their blood if necessary (LG

42). Today in Latin America, whole churches have won the cross and palm of martyr churches: to be a Delegate of the Word in Central America or work in the ministry to abandoned children in any city on the continent, or in the ministry to indigenous peoples or in the land ministry in almost all Latin American countries, to take a few examples, is often to be a Christian candidate for martyrdom. "Blood for the people" is one title in our continental martyrology,[13] and is a constant reality in various parts of the continent, when people accept the responsibilities of a Christian spirituality that is both contemplative and political, both free and a force for freedom.

The subversive memory of so many martyrs is nourishing food for the spirituality of our communities and for our peoples' resistance, which is the path to liberation. The celebration of that memory, so efficacious as a sacrament, is the best expression of the gratitude that fosters courage and commitment. Peoples or churches who forget their martyrs do not deserve to survive. This memory, this celebration, is made visible constantly in names, faces, words, relics, and even the motif of bloodstains that is so frequently seen in houses, meeting rooms and churches, on posters, ponchos, murals and T-shirts.

To be a Christian, we said, is to be a witness to Easter. "Martyr" comes from the Greek word for "witness," and the two meanings coincide again today. Martyrdom, beginning with the death of Jesus, is the supreme model of the Christian cross. "No one has greater love than this, than to lay down one's life for one's friends" (John 15:13).

Penance and Liberation

It is well known that a distinctive feature of our spirituality is realism: we try to live in truth, to start from the reality of life and remain immersed in it. And the reality is that the world is in a state of sin and that we ourselves are sinners and in need of conversion. Because of this, penance and conversion are fundamental ways of recognizing this reality.

Over thirty years ago Pope Pius XII said, "The greatest tragedy of our age is the loss of the sense of sin." The spirituality of liberation has not lost the sense of sin. Quite the opposite, it is keenly aware of it, declares war on it, fights fiercely against it on both the social and the personal and individual levels. Penance is a way of fighting against sin, and does not consist only (negatively) of combating personal and social sin, but also (positively) of a determined effort to construct personal virtues and "social virtues."

We have already said that current developments in theology make it possible for us to relocate the concept of sin with reference to that focal point to which everything has to be referred, the Reign. All sin is sin against the Reign. And it is sin to the extent that it goes against the Reign. Nothing is a sin by the mere fact of being forbidden, but because it goes against the Reign. The classical formula is, "Things are not evil because they are forbidden, but they are forbidden if they are evil" (St Thomas, ST I-II, 71, 6 ad 4). And the spirituality of liberation is clear that things are not good or bad by virtue of a legalistic external moral principle (being forbidden or not), but as judged by an inherent moral criterion: being in conflict with God, with God's liberative plan, with the Reign.

Just as we confess God's glory (God's love for us, for humankind), we also confess our sin (ingratitude toward God, malice toward our sisters and brothers).

Personal Sin

In first place, sin is in each one of us. We are light and dark, grace and sin. There is an ambiguity in the substance of human beings. The drama of human history passes through each one of us. It takes place in every individual human being, the whole battle, in every heart. The Christian doctrine of original sin stresses this radical fact that sin is in each of us, in our hearts and in the "atmosphere of sin."

There is no saint who is truly human and has Christian insight who does not have to say every day, "My sin is ever before me" (Ps. 51:3). "Unless you repent, you will all perish" (Luke 13:5).

Social Sin

Sin, however, is also present in society as well, very present, excessively present. Here it shows itself as hunger, exclusion, poverty, destitution, lack of housing, health care and education, unemployment, abandoned children, exploitation, aggression against the poor, concentration of land ownership, oligarchies, the First World, imperialism and the like.

The doctrine of "original sin" can be reinterpreted simultaneously both in individual personal terms and in social personal terms. The point is the radical presence of sin in us, and at the same time a sort of "atmosphere of sin," in which the existence of sin is greater than the mere sum of individual sins.

Sin or evil is in society as a structure of iniquity (the sin of the world, social sin). Grace too becomes present on both personal and social levels. Both sin and grace can be experienced on an individual personal scale and on a communal and social scale. We know that there are social sins and social virtues. Medellín, especially in its chapters "Justice" and

"Peace," and Puebla (specifically sections 28, 73, 487) have clearly recognized the reality of social, structural sin.

The Interaction between Social and Personal Sin

There is an inevitable interaction between social sin and personal sin. We are beings both structured and structuring. We live in society, and are the product, the victims, of its structures. We are "structured": for good or ill we carry within ourselves these structures. At the same time, however, we are "structurers," creators of structure. We make society: each of us contributes—if only minimally—to shaping and structuring society. We share responsibility for the structures because, inevitably, we make them, we tolerate them, we reinforce them, legitimate them or combat them; it is impossible for us to be detached from them.

There has been a futile polemic between some Christians and one school of Marxism about the starting point of conversion and the new world. Social sin derives from personal sins, but personal sins in turn are conditioned by social structures. They mutually strengthen and feed off each other. It is a vicious circle that has to be broken wherever this can be most effectively done, without time-wasting discussion about where to start.

In this classic polemic conservative Christians, connected with the national and international bourgeoisies, have insisted that the primary need is for a "conversion of hearts," before and (in practice) to the exclusion of any "change of structures." From the opposite standpoint, some Marxist traditions insisted that the first (and in practice the only) need was for structural change in society.

The supporters of "conversion of heart," generally the powerful, the moneyed classes, well placed in the status quo, bitter enemies of all change, have made political use of religious language to avoid, discredit or at least postpone structural change. Personal conversion then becomes an alibi for religious opposition to social change. Far too often, the Christian churches have played into the hands of these social groups, in the mistaken belief that they were defending an article of faith or a demand of human nature.

On the other hand, the extreme advocates of structural change in society claim that conversion of heart is not possible without prior social change, and that conversion comes spontaneously when change occurs. On this view, everything would be reduced to achieving social change, after which conversion of heart, the New Man and the New Woman, would come automatically.

Neither side in this argument is right. The truth lies in a synthesis. A conversion of heart that is not reflected simultaneously in a struggle for a change of structures is not complete or authentic, but an alienating deception. On the other hand, any structural reform will be useless and doomed to failure if at the same time a conversion of heart is not taking place, if the New Man and New Woman are not emerging. "It is true that structures (and persons) must be converted, but the transformation of structures does not automatically engender the liberation of persons. That is, the liberation of the individual does not depend on the collective liberation of humanity."[1]

For centuries now, institutional Christianity, allied with the powerful, has been preaching "conversion of heart" to contain the rebelliousness of the poor against oppressive structures, so soothing the consciences of the oppressors and damping down the revolutionary energies of the Christian masses. On the other hand, we have by now ample evidence in Latin America that a simple change of structures does not change hearts. There is an original residue of sinfulness in human hearts that is resistant to the influence of social structures. The New Man and Woman do not come into being by revolutionary decree. Without a profound mysticism, without New People, the best social reforms and the best revolutions will not get anywhere.

Penance, as a struggle against evil and sin, must be personal and in the heart, on the one hand, but at the same time social and structural as well. Any approach from one end alone will be either fraudulent or ineffective.

Conversion

Life in the Spirit is a process. One of its dimensions is penance, a dimension consisting of permanent conversion, a process of eradication of the evil that exists in us and in the world, a process that tries gradually to win new spaces of light and authenticity. It is a historical process of war against the evil that inhabits our hearts, which are both structured and structuring, and society, itself too both structured and structuring.

Conversion has to be permanent for various reasons:

— Because sin is not only the evil we do, but all the good we fail to do. We always sin at least by omission. We shall never be able to say that we have given the Reign all we have to give. All that we fail to do is omission, from which we have to be constantly turning away.

— Because sin is failure to love, or failure to love sufficiently. We can always love more. (St Thomas said that love is a commandment that in a sense cannot be obeyed, since it can never be regarded as satisfied.) The Christian commandment consists not simply in loving, but in loving "as I have loved you" (John 15:12).

— Because Christ invited us to follow our adventure through to the end: "Be perfect, therefore, as your heavenly Father is perfect" (Matt. 5:48). And the Vatican Council reminded us of the universal call to holiness (LG 39-42).

— Because the same Council reminds us that the church is called to a "continual reformation" (UR 6; cf LG 8; GS 43; 21).

Conversion means:

— "Turning," being turned upside down or inside out, making a complete revolution with our whole being, stirring things up from the bottom, shaking the whole plant, from root to fruit.

— Turning every day to the One who made us, who calls us, inhabits us, inspires us, calls us together.

- Turning every day with an attitude of welcome toward our sisters and brothers, especially the poorest, the persecuted, the little ones.

— Turning every day toward ourselves, to our personal "core," to our depths, to our fundamental choice, to the decisions and convictions that are the rock on which our lives are based, to strengthen the roots that feed them.

— Turning every day with fresh resolve toward Jesus' cause.

Penitential Elements in Christian Life

There is a fundamental penitential dimension, essential to the Christian life, that is part of what it means to be Christian. Within this we can distinguish different elements:

(1) A first step in this penitential process is recognition of sin. It is not easy to recognize that we are personally sinners and share responsibility for the sin of the world. It is easier to see "the speck in your neighbor's eye but not the log in your own" (Matt. 7:3). It is easier to discover social sin than personal sin. Very often we fail to realize our personal contribution to social sin.

This recognition brings with it repentance, sorrow for sin, a sense of guilt. As well as an acceptable sense of guilt there is another that is mistaken, unhealthy and liable to appear in a wide variety of pathological forms: obsessions, scruples, psychological traumas, neuroses and so on. We have to distinguish clearly between the psychological sense of guilt and the one that is genuinely religious and inspired by God. The advances of psychology will help us to overcome unnecessary or clearly unhealthy guilt complexes more easily. True remorse or repentance is liberating. It is important in this connection to remember that Jesus is the "liberator of oppressed conscience."[3]

(2) Another penitential element is the uncovering of the roots of sin. The structural mechanisms of social sin, like the deep roots of personal sin, are very often obscure. Neither society nor our conscious mind (still less our subconscious) are transparent. The spontaneous explanations we give or are given do not reveal the real causes of the problem. The constant effort to be vigilant, to analyze the context (both personal and social) are penitential attitudes. If truth is suppressed by injustice (cf. Rom. 1:18), the spirituality of liberation tries to live in truth and set the truth free, exposing the open and hidden mechanisms of injustice.

(3) The very fact of being a Christian, a follower of Jesus, brings with it other penitential elements. These include:

— The painful, but valuable effort to control our own personal passions (self-esteem, self-assertion, anger, sex . . .)

so that they do not degenerate into pride, egoism, violence and lust. A first, basic form of discipline consists in an effort to channel these energies toward good, toward the Reign.

— Taking up the cause of Jesus, the cause of the Reign, with the whole penitential dimension involved in living and fighting for it; affirmation of life and love, absolute rejection of injustice and death, keeping up hope against all hope.

— The following of Jesus in its dimension of kenosis and incarnation. This often includes an element of breaking with the past that has to be expressed in a change of position, physically or socially, a deliberate move to make contact with different ways of life, in poor areas, identifying with the world of the poor.

— The option for the poor as active solidarity with their grass-roots struggles and activities, actively defending their rights, commitment to their total liberation, action in history for liberation, and so on.

— Communion in Jesus' fate, by sharing the same risks that he shared in his historical struggle: persecution by the powerful, discrimination and even excommunication by the powers of institutional religion that are not inspired by the gospel, death threats and sometimes even the premature and unjust death of martyrdom. "If they persecuted me, they will persecute you" (John 15:20; cf Mark 13:13).

Following Jesus is the first penance. Discipline is not only for professionals or religious. "Whoever wishes to come after me, . . . must take up a cross" (Matt. 16:24ff).

This penitential process of personal transformation is the context within which we must place the explicit celebration of reconciliation, in its various forms: personal or communal gestures of reconciliation, communal celebrations of penance and the sacramental celebration, individual or communal.[4]

In addition to the fundamental penitential dimension, we are all familiar with positive penitential or ascetical "practices" that exist in all spiritualities and cultures. Their very universality shows that they are genuinely human. In every age, in every personal or group psychology, in every spirituality, the dimension of penance and self-control finds different forms.

In this connection, nowadays in Latin America new forms

of penance are popular, both personal and communal: marches, collective fasts, various forms of prophetic condemnation, public celebrations of penance in the streets, risks accepted in solidarity (accompanying refugees, human rights monitoring, having a presence in conflict areas or war zones), an "inserted" life in poor districts, presence in neglected areas or areas on the front line of ministry.

The "political holiness" we seek as part of our spirituality brings with it its own forms of penance and discipline:

> But the liberation process has created the matrix of another type of holiness. Christians must continue to battle against their own passions. This is clear. But now they battle against the mechanisms of exploitation and destruction of the community as well. New virtues emerge, different but genuine: solidarity with one's sisters and brothers, the members of the impoverished class, participation in community decisions and fidelity to these decisions once they are made; victory over one's hatred of the agents of the mechanisms of impoverishment; an ability to see beyond the obvious, and work for a future society not yet in sight and perhaps never to be enjoyed at all. This new type of asceticism makes its own demands and calls for particular sacrifices if one is to remain pure of heart and celebrate the spirit of the Beatitudes.[5]

Our spirituality has its own questions or criteria with regard to these penitential or ascetical practices:

—In the first place we cannot forget that Christian penance is not something deliberately sought, something we choose to add to our lives, but something that comes spontaneously when we seek the essence of Christianity.

—The message of the Bible continues to be a decisive guide when we have to discern true penance. The fasting God wants is that people should come to know him and act justly (Isa. 58:1-9; Jer. 22:16). "He has told you, O mortal, what is good" (Mic. 6:8). "I have had enough of burnt offerings" (Isa. 1:11). "I desire steadfast love and not sacrifice" (Hos. 6:6; Matt. 9:11-13).

— In the light of this, it is a matter for particular regret that we fall into so many contradictions and so much incoherence by looking for "additional" forms of penance instead of living the supreme penance inherent in love of other people.

— There is quite enough suffering in the world already, and God doesn't want us to increase it. Quite the opposite, he wants us to fight it. "'God wants me to help him to take this cup from me.' To struggle against evil and to reduce to a minimum even the ordinary physical evil that threatens us, is unquestionably the first act of our Father who is in heaven; it would be impossible to conceive him in any other way, and still more impossible to love him."[6] Living and fighting for the cause of Jesus includes fighting suffering and creating happiness, overcoming evil with good (Rom. 12:21). The cross that the Lord Jesus invites us to take up if we wish to follow him is not a cross that needs looking for; it is the cross that comes from fighting against the cross,[7] "that cross which the world and the flesh inflict upon those who seek after peace and justice" (GS 38). "Seek truth; the cross will find you soon enough." "A curse on the cross . . . that cannot be the cross of Christ."[8]

— We have to overcome the latent Manicheism, the unconscious hostility to pleasure present in penitential practices that has come down to us from one tradition. Sex is good, as the gift of God that it is, and pleasures are not bad in themselves; what is bad is misuse, abuse, of them. Pleasures are gifts of God that we can and should love: ". . . We are able to love the things created by God, and ought to do so. We can receive them from God and respect and reverence them as flowing constantly from the hand of God. Grateful to our benefactor for these creatures, using and enjoying them in detachment and liberty of spirit, we are led forward into a true possession of them as having nothing, yet possessing all things" (GS 37). God made us for happiness, not for pain or frustration.

— We have to overcome the sadism or masochism concealed in very traditional expressions that lend themselves to misunderstanding, such as that of Thomas à Kempis, "The more violence you do to yourself, the holier you will become." The Reign of heaven requires violence (Matt. 11:12), but not masochism. Christian penance cannot consist in deliberately seeking pain for its own sake, nor in sacrifices to gods thirsty for blood, nor in neurotic victimization. God loves life, not death. Our God is not sadness, but lasting happiness.

— The Christian attitude par excellence is not a cold "indifference" or a Stoic calm in the face of the realities of the world and history. For the sake of our faith we have the right and duty to be passionate about the things of the earth, once we see them as the *oikos* or dwelling of the human family, the tent and the body of him who came and is to come, the dough and the oven in which the beautiful but battered Reign is coming to perfection. Because of this, ecology (which has its root in the word *oikos*) is for us the practice of a virtue, a matter of faith and a challenge to spirituality.

— The mere cultivation of willpower through ascetic practices has its own Christian value, not for the renunciation in itself, but in function of the love for the Reign that it expresses and makes possible. Renunciation in itself does nothing for salvation.

— The example of Jesus, whom we follow, will always be the ultimate criterion. Jesus retired into the desert (Matt. 4:1-2), used to look for suitable places to pray (Luke 5:16), got up early (Mark 1:15) and spent the night (Luke 6:12) in prayer, learned obedience through suffering (Heb. 5:8), sweated blood in the garden (Luke 22:44). Yet at the same time Jesus does not seem to be an Essene, withdrawing from life, but lives among his people (Luke 2:50-2), takes part in their festivities (John 2), goes away to rest with his disciples (Matt. 14:13ff), and exults with joy at the Father's works (Luke 10:21, and elsewhere.)

Macro-Ecumenism

Throughout the world the spirituality and theology of liberation are famous for their openness to and sympathy for a range of liberation movements. It is also a well-known fact that this spirituality and theology have been enthusiastically welcomed and supported by many sectors of the population, groups and institutions traditionally regarded as unsympathetic or even hostile to the churches and religion in general. This openness and acceptance is part of an attitude, a spirit, which we will call total ecumenism or "macro-ecumenism," because it goes beyond the dialogue between Christians referred to by the term "ecumenism."

This is not just an attitude of mind, but a spirit that inspires attitudes and derives from a spiritual experience, and experience of God in the world and history, and from a particular way of understanding the world and its processes.

God's Ecumenism

We could say that in our religious experience we have encountered God's "ecumenism." God is ecumenical. God is not racist, or linked to one racial group or culture. God does not belong exclusively to anyone. The New Testament revelation breaks down the walls of the "Jewish" God and shows us the universal God, the God who wants all human beings "to be saved and to come to the knowledge of the truth" (1 Tim. 2:4).

After a period in which many versions of the image of God

in the ambit of Western civilization had been too closely tied
to one culture—or to a set of hegemonic cultures, Greek, Latin,
Saxon—Christian thought and discernment in recent times
have given us back a clearer view of the ecumenical face of
God. For Catholics the Second Vatican Council was a crucial
moment in this process, especially in its decrees on the church,
the modern world, ecumenism, mission and the lay apostolate.
Today we see more clearly the presence of God's Spirit down
through history, in all peoples and all cultures.

Today we realize much more easily that the Spirit is present
in all peoples, long before the explicit arrival of the gospel
(Puebla 201), because the Triune God is the first missionary,
who sows the Word and makes it germinate in all peoples.[1] The
Spirit is present and active in the heart of every culture, which
is always a glimmer of the Spirit's light. The Spirit is alive and
present in the heart of every human being, including those
who—so often without fault or even in good faith—ignore or
even deny this (Puebla 208). The Spirit takes salvation along
paths known to no one else—"My ways are not your ways"
(Isa. 55:8; cf GS 22)—far beyond the narrow limits of institutional Christianity; we should recall again Karl Rahner's
remark that non-Christian religions, being the most universal,
are the ordinary way of salvation. In the face of this we rejoice
and do not begrudge the generosity of the Father and Lord with
the workers of all vineyards at the most varied times: "Am I
not allowed to do what I choose with what belongs to me? Or
are you envious because I am generous?" (Matt. 20:15). This
experience of God, of a God who does not tie himself to any
ghetto and who acts and saves throughout the universe and in
all of history, broadens our vision and our sense of belonging.
We too cannot feel tied exclusively to one race, culture, people
or church. God's ecumenism makes it impossible for us to treat
channels such as our own church or institutional Christianity
as absolutes. We realize that in God's eyes a church has existed
"since the just man Abel,"[2] and that, as St Augustine put it,
"The substance of what we today call Christianity was already
present in ancient times and has been present since the origins
of humanity. Finally, when Christ revealed himself in the
flesh, what had always existed began to be called the Christian

religion" (Retr. 1.12, 3). Whoever is not against us is for us (cf Luke 9:49-50).

The Ecumenism of Mission

The new experience of God that we have had through discovering Jesus also makes us realize the ecumenical nature of our Christian mission. We mean the fundamental mission of every Christian, beyond any particular vocation or charism. This mission consists of "living and fighting for the cause of Jesus, for the Reign," and this, clearly, is the most ecumenical mission possible because the Reign is peace, justice, fraternity, life and love among all men and women, and human communion with nature and with God.

This fundamental Christian mission is nothing other than the mission of every human being. It is the "great mission," the meaning of human life on this earth. Christians do not have a different mission; they have the same mission. The only difference is that Christians have a new light that enables them to understand it better and a new power to carry it out, the light and the power of Jesus Christ. The essence of the Christian mission, however, coincides with the essence of the human mission. The human mission is ecumenical, and is ecumenically accessible to every man and woman who comes into this world, through their consciences, by the light of their reason, and through the generous impulses of their hearts. Non-Christians are not fundamentally disadvantaged for carrying out the great human mission. And we know very well that there have been countless people in this world and its busy history who have been generously faithful to this mission. Would God be just if he placed the majority of his sons and daughters in conditions that were so unfavourable or dangerous to salvation? Does God not want the salvation of all?

Whenever men or women, in whatever circumstance or situation, under whatever banner, work for the causes of the Reign (love, justice, fraternity, freedom, life), they are fighting for the cause of Jesus, they are fulfilling the purpose of their lives, they are doing God's will. In contrast, those who call themselves Christians and live and fight for their churches are not always doing God's will. The final criterion by which God will judge human beings (Matt. 25:31-45) is just this: totally ecumenical, non-ecclesiastical, non-confessional, not even religious, wider than any race, culture or church.

Discovering this, experiencing the God of the Reign, seeing in this way what God's will is, is a vital foundation stone of total ecumenism, macro-ecumenism. We have no reason to feel superior because we are Christians, nor can we look down on others because they are not. What is really important is not being a signed-up member of a church, but joining the movement of the Reign, our relationship with it, being fighters for its cause. This is the decisive criterion by which the Lord will judge all of us, and this is also the criterion by which we too must assess each other, in preference to any religious or denominational label.

The objective, the cause, is the Reign, before any other objective or distinction. That is why we have to unite our struggle with that of all men and women who seek identical ends of justice and liberation, and be "united with all who love and practise justice" (GS 92; cf GS 43; 93; 16; 92; 57; 90; 77; 78; UR 12; AG 12; AA 14). There is no sense in the attitude of people who want to stress church divisions or divisions between believers and unbelievers when they could be joining forces to achieve the values of the Reign, especially when the world is calling urgently for life and peace, freedom and justice, and is moving inevitably toward unity (cf LG 28; GS 5; 33; 43; 56; 57; DH 15; NΛe 1; PO 7).

If our real passion is the aspiration for the coming of the Reign ("Your Kingdom come," "Come, Lord Jesus"), and we measure everything ecumenically by this measure, probably we shall feel more united to people who work for the cause of Jesus even without knowing it than to those who—perhaps even in his name—oppose it. This is tremendous because it is real. And it comes from the gospel. Jesus himself felt this greater closeness. He identified more with the Samaritan than with the priest and the levite, more with the liberation of the poor than with the Temple worship (Luke 10:25ff), more with the lowly sinners than with the self-satisfied Pharisees (Luke 15:11-32; Matt. 21:31-2), more with the person who does the will of God than with the one who says, "Lord, Lord" (Matt. 7:21), more with those who feed the hungry, even without knowing Jesus (Matt. 25:37ff), than with those who have done miracles in his name (Matt. 7:22), more with the son who said No, but did what his father wanted than with the one who said Yes but did not (Matt. 21:28-32).

The Lord wants us to let ourselves be guided by this real order of salvation, by the priority interests of the Reign, before and in preference to any other criterion. This is the light in which we must assess everything. This new light produces results very different from those that first appear: as to being inside and outside the church, we can say that not all those who are really one or the other appear to be, and that not all those who appear to be are. This perspective produces an earthquake and a new landscape of solidarities, with a structure defined much more by total ecumenism. This sort of ecumenism is very annoying to those who are imprisoned in a church-focused outlook, a view that turns the church's mediating role into an absolute, that makes them in fact put the church, its world and its interests before the interests of the Reign, even though they do not realize this and even theoretically maintain the opposite. We do not deny or minimize the value of the gift of belonging to the community of Jesus. Belonging to the true church, for us, is both a grace and a challenge. Feeling the great human family as our own does not rule out feeling grateful, from within, for being in the Christian family.

"Not everyone who says to me, 'Lord, Lord,' will enter the kingdom of heaven, but only the one who does the will of my Father in heaven," says Jesus (Matt. 7:21). Those who "do" the will of my Father means those who live and fight for the Reign of God. Acting in the spirit of the Reign is the criterion of salvation. In other words, the Lord is telling us clearly in the gospel that the real order of salvation is at issue in the carrying out of God's will, that is, in the building of the Reign, in the establishment of justice, love and freedom. Just saying, "Lord, Lord," does not of itself bring salvation. This is the distinction already mentioned on a number of occasions between the "order of salvation," into which we have all been incorporated, and the "order of the knowledge of salvation," to which only some gain access. The first is decisive for salvation, the second not. This does not mean that the second is pointless, but that its point is precisely that of helping to ensure the "doing" of God's will. A totally ecumenical approach must be attentive to the crucial order of salvation, the order involving the "doing" of God's will, the order of Reign activity.

Jesus did not say that those who do the will of God are already Christians, not even anonymous Christians; what he said, simply, is that they will enter the Reign, which is what is important. We cannot measure all this in terms of institutional Christianity or the church, but in terms of the Reign. What is important is not being a paid-up Christian, but entering the Reign. "What is important, in the last resort, will not be being or not being a Christian. The important thing, in the last resort, will be living like Jesus Christ, making the choices that Jesus Christ made, 'working for the Reign,' as we Christians would say."[3] We all have a calling to enter the Reign; not everyone in fact has one to be in the church or to be an explicit Christian.

Ecumenical Attitudes and Criteria

There is a series of attitudes that derive from this ecumenical outlook and both give it substance and prove it.

— *Contemplation.* This is essential to this sort of ecumenism, an enhancd capacity to contemplate God in history, in life, in people who do not yet know Christ, in the processes through which peoples go, in the struggles of the poor, in the efforts of so many generous activists, including those who declare themselves remote from any professed God or from a recognized church or religion. "Missionaries are either contemplatives and mystics or they will never be genuine missionaries. True evangelizers are imbued with faith in the active presence of the Trinity in every fold of the cloth of history, despite the blurring which results from human perversion. In the highly socialized patterns of the lives of the Aztecs, in the communal work of the Brazilian Indians, in the profoundly egalitarian sense to be found in most Brazilian indigenous tribes, missionaries will see sacraments of the Trinitarian communion and marks of the presence of the Father, Son and Spirit in the world."[4]

— *Optimism about salvation.* This means believing in practice that God wants all human beings to be saved and to come to know the truth (1 Tim. 2:4), and that this desire is effective. It means believing that all our human caprices and even our religious conflicts are like childish games in the sight of God, our understanding and loving Father and Mother, always ready to forgive and accept. It means believing that God will give every human being, even those apparently most closed to God's grace, albeit "in ways known to God alone" (cf GS 22; LG 16; AG 7), a generous chance of salvation. For many, death itself will be the sacrament of their salvation.[5]

— *Involvement with the world, permanent contact with it.* Nothing human is alien to us. The joys and hopes, the sufferings and distress of human beings, especially those of the poor, are also ours. And these lead us constantly to examine the signs of the times (GS 4; 44; 62; AG 11; ChD 16; 30).

— *Positive openness.* This means that we feel predisposed in principle to accept and value the work and effort of our fellows, activists, peoples, rather than to look at it with caution or reject it. Interchange with the world and positive openness to it was exemplified by the spirituality of Vatican II, which tried to apply "the medicine of compassion." "The ancient story of the Samaritan was the Council's model of spirituality," said Paul VI.[6] We know that our message corresponds to the deepest desires of the human heart (GS 21), and that there is only one ultimate calling for human beings, a divine one (GS 22).

— *Cooperation with all who in any way fight for this universal cause which is the Reign.* Everyone who is not against the Reign is with us. All who fight for a good cause are taking part in the fight for the Kingdom and deserve our support in their struggle (GS 43; 93; 16; 92; 57; 90; 77; 78; UR 12; AG 12; AA 14). We shall not try to obstruct the good that any groups do simply because they are not from our group (Mark 9:38-40).

—*Institutional disinterestedness.* Our absolute is the Reign, not its means. Our absolute passion is to ensure that God should be all in all, and that all creatures, means, mediations and institutions should surrender completely to God's reign, place themselves completely at its service. That is why we are not "church-focused," and do not place any other institution or intermediary at the core.

—*New evangelization.* Yes, our spirituality generates a new model and a new method of evangelization, a new apostolic attitude. We can no longer accept in our day models of evangelization that have nothing to do with ecumenism, like the attitude of those who used to think that without the missionary there could be no salvation for those who died outside the church,[7] or of those who in fact imposed faith. The new evangelization will not impose Christianity, nor will it treat non-Christian religions as evil, nor talk only to the so-called "higher religions," but also to the so-called "minor religions" of indigenous minorities, and will engage in religious dialogue with any people, and culture and any religion, for mutual enrichment and in order to offer them freely and in a spirit of freedom and respect the fullness we have known in Christ Jesus.

— *A move toward humanity.* The new spiritual experience of the church has made us realize that the most important thing is not theories or dogmas, or canon law or rites, but love, love of God and of God's sons and daughters. We have also realized that not everything has the same importance, that there is a "hierarchy of truths" (UR 11) and that we cannot sacrifice charity for a theory. That is why we understand that there is no point in sectarianisms, because they never lead us to a greater love for our brothers and sisters.

In all these attitudes we are doing no more than imitating God. God is for us the model of truly total ecumenism.
    The Reign unites.
    The church divides

when it does not agree
with the Reign.

All these ecumenical ideas upset traditional ideas about evangelization and the apostolate.

— No missionary arrives before the first missionary, the Triune God. "The Spirit, who filled the whole earth, was also present in all that was good in pre-Colombian cultures. That very Spirit helped them to accept the gospel. And today the Spirit continues to arouse yearnings for liberative salvation in our peoples. Hence we must discover the Spirit's authentic presence in the history of Latin America" (Puebla 201).

— God has other words besides the Bible, and can write other sacred books.

— No people and no individual is lost or condemned for lack of missionaries or through the absence of institutional Christianity.

— Mission has a purpose, but not the purpose of bringing salvation to the nations, but that of perfecting it, of offering the fullness of that salvation as we have known it in Jesus.

— It is not as important to spread the church as to build the Reign.

— The goal of evangelization is not the church but the Reign.

— Everything to do with the church that is not directed towards the Reign or that in practice comes into conflict with the Reign is wrong.

— To make Christians who are opposed to the cause of the Reign or the Good News for the poor (their liberation) is an absolute contradiction.

— What is important is not denominational "proselytism", but to win fighters for the Reign.

— All sectarianism and all fundamentalism is anti-ecumenical, a breach of solidarity, inhuman and contrary to God's will.

— Without macro-ecumenism the inculturation of the gospel, and even harmony between human beings, is impossible.

In other words, the criterion of the Reign is the supreme ecumenical criterion and that which measures the ecumenism of all the others.

Political Holiness

"Political holiness" is an expression that has been very successful in recent years in Latin America. There is no doubt that it accurately expresses a very strong intuition in Latin American spirituality. "The Christian tradition," Leonardo Boff tells us, "is familiar with ascetic saints, in control of their passions and faithfully keeping the laws of God and the church. But it has very little acquaintance with political saints and activist saints."[1] In other words, this is certainly something new, responding to a felt need, although at the same time this is a development that is already mature, consecrated in the lives of many witnesses and sealed by the blood of many martyrs.

Latin American political holiness is the holiness of all times, the traditional holiness of baptism and grace, of prayer and penance, of love and ascesis, of the eucharist and examination of conscience. It is, though, a holiness that expresses and channels the ethical-political "virtues" that the Spirit is calling forth in Latin America inside and outside the churches, absorbs them and allows itself to be transformed by the action of the Spirit fermenting underneath all the changes and reformulations in theology and biblical studies that have taken place in the churches of Latin America.

First of all, it is an outgoing holiness. It is a holiness that comes out of itself and looks for its brothers and sisters. The goal it sets itself is not to attain its own perfection, but to achieve life in abundance (cf John 10:10) for others. It is a holiness completely directed outside itself toward God's plan for our history. It is a holiness that does not run away from the struggle, from modernity, from the big city, but faces them in the power of the Spirit. If the Spirit could do things in Egypt, or in Nineveh or in Babylon, it must be able to do things in São Paulo, in Bogotá, in Lima or Los Angeles; in steelworks, in the revolution. If God is among the cooking pots, as St Teresa said, he is also among the trade unions, the political parties, and demands of the poor.

It is a holiness beyond the pale, in the world, in the midst of the world that God loved so much (John 3:16), the world to which God sent his Son to save it (John 3:17), the world to which God sends us (Matt. 28:19). It is a holiness of "being in the world," being world, not being part of the evil world (which is what Jesus meant). It is being in the world with our feet firmly planted on the ground, longing for the world to be different, for the world to become Reign. It is not a holiness that tries to save itself from the world, nor even to be saved in the world, but to save the world, and to save it with the world's help, in the sense that this holiness doesn't think that it is Christians alone who will save the world.

It is a holiness of the major virtues such as truthfulness, the struggle for justice and peace, for human rights—all human rights, not just individual human rights, civil, political and cultural, but the so-called third generation of human rights, economic and national—the struggle for international law, for the transformation of the community of the children of God, for the creation of new structures of fraternity (a socialized world, the New International Economic Order, a new United Nations, a world without a First and Third World). Political holiness turns all these into major virtues to correct or complement the classical virtues, which are more domestic, more individualistic, conventual or spiritualistic in their emphasis: modesty, custody of the senses, purification of intention, custody of the presence of God, visits to the Blessed Sacrament, ascetic sacrifices and mortifications, repetition of pious exclamations. These major virtues restore to a gospel context some canonized virtues of bourgeois education that are usually limited to one-to-one relationships, to the private sphere, (bourgeois) family life, the obsession with sexuality.[2] The political holiness of the spirituality of liberation is also the spirituality of the "structural" or "social" virtues, of the major virtues. We use these terms to make a parallel with the terms "structural sin" and "social sin" to refer to the practice of the Christian virtues which transcends the sphere of the individual or group and seeks a social application of them within the structural mechanisms of society. It should be noted, however, that the major virtues are not in conflict with the minor or domestic virtues; it is inconsistent to fight for the major virtues and fail in the essence of the domestic virtues. There is also no contradiction with the individual virtues; it is not enough to fight for a just society without being just oneself.

It is not a holiness that locks us into a narrow world of trifles.[3] It is the holiness of great causes: justice, peace, equality, fraternity, love fully realized and socially structured, the "civilization of love" in the full sense of the term, liberation, the new man and the new woman, the new world. . . . In other words it is the holiness of those who try to live and fight for the cause of Jesus.

It is a contemplative holiness. Faith gives it a contemplative vision of the world, enabling it to discover the presence of God in the events of the world. In the complex detail of the historical formation of the world it is able to contemplate the presence of the One who is and is to come, who guides history as its Lord. It is able to see the history of salvation in the history of every day. "Christian activists, used to the complexity of social phenomena, which are today extremely sophisticated and accessible only with the use of scientific methods, have to reinforce enormously their faith-vision in order to be able to detect in socio-historical mechanisms the presence or absence of God and his grace. As never before in history, there is a need for prayer combined with political shrewdness, a mystical sense allied with critical analysis of events."[4]

In essence, it is a holiness-for-the Reign, formed by active hope for it, the struggle to make it come, waiting for it as an eschatological event, but one made credible by historical achievements; by the search for instruments to hasten its coming. Here as in other things, the Reign is the reference, the Christian absolute, which gives a new shape to all Christian categories (see the section "Reign-Focus, above). Where until quite recently spirituality talked about "the life of grace," "supernatural life," "the quest of perfection," "the cultivation of the (inner and private) virtues," Latin American spirituality of liberation talks about the Reign as the ultimate reference point, of history as the site for the building of its utopia, of the real world as its starting point and destination, of historical action for transformation as the commitment it demands, of "incarnate contemplative prayer" as the way to perceive and detect the Reign in the obscurity of history, of liberation as a synonym for redemption and of the poor as its principal beneficiaries (cf Luke 7:18ff; Matt. 25:31ff).[5] It is a holiness "lying in wait for the Kingdom."

It is a holiness that confronts the sin of the world, looks it in the face, condemns it prophetically and commits itself to correcting it. It does not flee from the world. Nor does it view the world with the optimistic eyes of the First World, as though the only evil in it consisted of minor accidental upsets. It goes into the world, gets its hands dirty, gets splashed with mud (and tears and blood). With this holiness believers bear the sin of the world, like the Servant of Yahweh (Isa. 52:13 - 53:12). They try to "take away the sin of the world" like the Lamb of God (John 1:29).

It is a holiness that does not run away from ambiguity. That is, it does not avoid commitment on the pretext that the causes at issue are not absolutely pure. It does not insist on angelic purity in the particular immediate choices among which it has to move before committing itself. It knows that in politics there is nothing perfect and nothing final. Politics is not for angels, and there are no germ-free choices in it. Political holiness does not shirk from supporting causes that in themselves are neither perfect nor totally holy. It does not put the purity of its own image above all else. "Clean hands" are the prerogative of those who don't get involved. This is a holiness that does not flee from conflict. It enters the world, and, since this world is marked by sin, divided and at odds, believers are challenged by the conflict, badmouthed by all sides. And in the conflict it declares itself always, without hesitation, on the side of the poor.

It is a holiness starting from a new position in society, from the social setting of the poor. (On the idea of "social setting," see "Option for the People" and "Contemplatives in Liberation," above.) For centuries holiness was thought of (in theology, in the churches, in the monasteries, in treatises on asceticism) as something detached from any social or political context. The model of holiness cultivated was the monastic model, a model allegedly a-political and a-historical, though many of those monks—following one political interest or another—led crusades, agrarian reforms and economic and educational transformations.[6] And it is a fact that those Christians who have been publicly recognized by the church as saints were mainly from a particular social class.[7] Political holiness places itself, consciously and critically, in the social setting of the poor (see the section "Option for the Poor," above).

It is a holiness characterized by a sensitivity to the majorities in our society, thinking according to the "logic of the majorities," and able to look at them whole, without letting the tree of the individual stop it from seeing the wood of the masses, without being an obstacle, through the assistentialism of aid, to effective justice and charity. This critical sensitivity is able to see the collective poor, not as a mere sum of individuals, but as an organic unit, as a class, as the people, as a marginalized race, as an oppressed culture, a subjugated gender.

It is an intelligent holiness, one that wants to act out an intelligent and effective love, analyzing situations, making use of analytical tools and ideological interpretations, used always with the necessary critical sense. It is an intelligent holiness, which tries to go to the causes and the structures, and not stop at the symptoms or momentary situations (cf Puebla 28-30; 41), which does not want to give as charity what is due in justice (AA 8). It is an intelligently "interdisciplinary" holiness, not narrowly clerical or modest and churchy, or timidly pious.

It is an ascetic and disciplined holiness, one that accepts the demands of politics, the need for organization, austerity, the exercise of the political virtues, the constant practice of discernment, analysis, teamwork.

Political holiness is also explicitly political. It does not claim to be a-political. It does not fall into the trap of believing that you can be non-political or neutral. It has broken with the taboo on politics imposed in recent centuries by those who wanted the churches to engage in politics without realizing it or without admitting it. It has rediscovered the connection between faith and politics, as has the universal church: "The Spirit is leading us to see more clearly that today holiness is not possible without a commitment to justice, without solidarity with the poor and oppressed. The model of holiness for the lay faithful has to include the social dimension in the transformation of the world according to God's plan" (1987 Synod, Message, 4). It has rediscovered an understanding of politics as "one of the highest forms of charity" (Pius XI), as "long-distance love" (Ricoeur) or "macro-charity" (Comblin).

Let us remember the sayings of three great witnesses. Emmanuel Mounier insisted, "Everything is politics, but politics is not everything." Mahatma Gandhi said, "Those who say religion has nothing to do with politics don't know anything about religion." And Desmond Tutu observed, "There is nothing more political than saying that religion has nothing to do with politics."

Political holiness is also the leaven of a holy politics. Many politicians have received their training in the journey of the churches with the poor, and have been educated in close contact with the base communities or with the various church bodies devoted to defending human rights, workers, peasants or indigenous peoples. This social ministry of the churches has encouraged the development of a typically Latin American method of popular education for transformation, internationally associated with the name of Paulo Freire.[8] It has made more obvious the need for a new type of politics (in contrast to the type of politics usual in Latin America: careerist, corrupt, unscrupulous, unprincipled, and lacking any genuine interest in serving the people). In some parts of Latin America this political holiness of the spirituality of liberation has made the church the institution that has accumulated most experience of working with the people, in the political holiness, the political *diakonia* of Christians.

It is a holiness that takes very seriously the priesthood of all believers (LG 2, 10ff). Political holiness also includes the realistic nature of holiness stressed by Vatican II (esp. LG 41): a holiness that must be worked out in everyday life, in our own situation and with our own responsibilities, without looking for esoteric paths. Traditionally holiness was understood in a very churchy way, spiritualistic and spiritualized (the "sanctification of the world" through the right intention, highmindedness, through the quasi-sacramental presence of Christians in the world). But there is no genuine sanctification if there is no real transformation. A sanctification that left the world as it is, giving it religious legitimacy, would be a blasphemy. The true sanctification of the world implies its real, tangible transformation to make it more like the Reign of God.

Political holiness is a holiness of active hope, which is able to overcome the defeatism of the poor in the face of the status quo, the established powers, the regrouping of capitalism and imperialism, in the face of the wave of neo-liberalism, the thrust of capitalism against labour, North against South. It is a holiness capable of enduring the hours of darkness for the poor, upholding the asceticism of hope against all hope. It is a holiness that knows we shall never on this earth reach the total fulfilment of the utopia of which we dream (the Reign), and that no particular achievement, no instrument, must be confused with the goal. The Reign is always more, greater and always further on.

It is an ecumenical holiness, able to join forces with all those who fight for these greater causes, believers and non-believers, Christians and non-Christians, Christians of one denomination and another. It can do this because it never loses sight of its goal and its great central cause, the Reign: that they may have life and have it abundantly (John 10:10).

A New Way of Being Church

The subject of the church in the spirituality of liberation is crucial, and it often involves conflict, because it challenges not merely individuals, but the institution itself. The vision, the conception, the perspective, the attitude, the love, the spirit, with which the spirituality of liberation envisages the mystery and the fact of the church enable us to talk of a "new sense of the church," or of a new spirituality in living the mystery of the church in Latin America. Typical phrases often used—quite legitimately—in Latin America to describe this development are "the conversion of the church,"[1] "a new way of being church," and even "a new life-style for the whole church, communal from top to bottom," which is particularly associated with the base communities of Brazil.[2]

Church and Reign

The most important point to understand in order to appreciate the essence of this spirituality is the relationship between the church and the Reign. There was a time when the church was identified with the Reign of God on earth, and was described as a "perfect society." The first draft of the Dogmatic Constitution on the Church prepared for the First Vatican Council said: "We teach and declare that the church has all the marks of a perfect society. It is so perfect in itself that this is what distinguishes it from all other human societies and places it above them." In our time, however, we are much more conscious of the centrality of the Reign of God and see the church as an instrument in the service of the Reign (see "Reign-Focus," above).

The church is not the Reign, but the "seed and beginning" of the Reign. It is an instrument. It is at the service of the Reign. Its only purpose is to serve the Reign and prepare for its coming, hasten its coming, be a channel for it, encourage it. This is a constant theme of the documents of the Second Vatican Council: "The church receives the mission to proclaim and establish among all peoples the Kingdom of Christ and of God" (LG 5); "Its goal is the Kingdom of God, which has been begun by God himself on earth and is to be further extended" (LG 9); "For this the church was founded, [to spread] the Kingdom of Christ everywhere" (AA 2); "The church has a single intention, that God's Kingdom may come" (GS 45). It is entirely dependent on the Reign. Everything in the church, including its very existence, has to be at the service of the Reign, at the service of God's cause, which is also the cause of human beings: "Christians cannot yearn for anything more ardently than to serve the people of the modern world ever more generously and effectively" (GS 93); "The church claims no other authority than that of ministering to people" (AG 12); "The church has declared itself, as it were, the servant of humanity. The idea of service occupied a central place. All this wealth of teaching leads in one direction: serving human beings."[3] To spend itself, and wear itself out, for the Reign of God, even if this takes its life, this is the purpose and deepest meaning of the church. This takes us far away from any "church-focus" such as existed in the past: "Unfortunately it has happened that (the church) became more interested in its own problems, in its own advantage, and did not concern itself with the problems of justice and freedom unless they affected the church, its structures or its internal ecclesiastical structure. As late as the time of Pius IX, the church of the clergy was more interested in itself than in the world's problems, which it often did not react to or discuss."[4] The Reign is the absolute, and everything else is relative (*Evangelii Nuntiandi* 8). Everything in the church (its organization, its resources, its assets, its law) must be always at the service of the Reign.

The Reign is Jesus' cause, which is justice, love, freedom, mercy, reconciliation, direct contact with God. Whenever human beings work for the victory of these causes, they are making the Reign, and carrying forward Jesus' cause. On the other hand, when people say that they believe in the name of Jesus or belong to his church, it does not always mean that they are carrying forward his cause. The most important thing is the Reign, not the church. The church is important too, but its importance is rooted in its continually building the Reign until it comes to fruition.

In this new sense of what the church is, as in the other elements of our spirituality, we do not rely on a "new theological theory," but on our eagerness to be guided by Jesus. Jesus' aim was not "to found a church," but to serve the Reign.[5] No church would be really the church of Jesus if it did not, like him, place its life at the service of the Reign as an absolute. We believe in a church that is a "sacrament" (LG 1), the flesh of Jesus in every time and place, the visible, incarnate and inculturated sign of the presence of Jesus: "It is the function of the church, led by the Holy Spirit who renews and purifies her ceaselessly, to make God the Father and his incarnate Son present and in a sense visible" (GS 21).

This becomes as tangible as Jesus' own flesh. To be the church, to be "the church of Jesus," for us can be nothing other than to live and fight for Jesus' cause, for the Reign of God, that is, to transform this world by bringing it closer to the utopia that God has shown to us so that we may build it in history: the Reign of God, which is "life, truth, justice, peace, grace, love, reconciliation, forgiveness, knowledge of God."

The Church and Salvation

The church is not the Reign, but a servant of the Reign. The Reign is greater than the church. The idea accepted in the dark ages of the past, that outside the church there could be no salvation, is not true. In 1442 the Ecumenical Council of Florence declared, "We firmly believe, profess and teach that none of those who are outside the Catholic Church, not only pagans, but also Jews, heretics, schismatics, will share in eternal life. They will go to the eternal fire prepared for the devil and his angels (cf Matt. 25:4), unless, before the end of their lives, they are incorporated into the church. . . . None, however great their alms, or even if they shed their blood for Christ, can be saved unless they remain in the bosom and the unity of the Catholic Church."[6] This view led the church to positions of intransigence and intolerance, to vilify other religions—as the church did with indigenous religions when it came to Latin America in the sixteenth century[7]—and to condemn the modern world.

Today we recognize that the Triune God is present in all peoples, in all religions and in all cultures. Vatican II consecrated this openness of spirit when it recognized this presence of God and salvation beyond the limits of the church (LG 16; UR 3; GS 22). From that moment the mission "to the pagans," and the relationship of the church and of all Christians to the boundaries of the church changed. The goal now is not to "bring salvation" for the first time to a place where there was never any presence of salvation (LG 17; 16; 8; UR 3; GS 22; AG 7; 9; 11; NAe 2), but to recognize its presence in a respectful dialogue that helps it to grow.

"The true evangelizer is imbued with faith in the concrete presence of the Trinity in every crease of the fabric of history, despite the splotches and blotches of human perversion. In the highly socialized forms of life of the Aztecs, in the communal work of the Brazilian Indians, in the profoundly egalitarian sense prevailing among most of the native tribes of Brazil, the authentic missionary will see sacraments of the trinitarian communion, and signs of the presence of Father, Son and Holy Spirit in the world. The missionary always comes late; the Holy Trinity has already arrived, revealing itself in the awareness, the history, the societies, the deeds and the destiny of peoples."[8] This is true not only of the mission to the "pagans," but also of the rest of our evangelizing service to the modern world.

The boundaries of the church do not coincide with the boundaries of salvation. Not everything that is in the church is only salvation (there is also sin), nor is what is outside the church necessarily beyond salvation. To personalize, we can say "Not all its members are in it and not all those in it are its members." St Augustine put it like this: "Some people seem to be inside (the church) when in reality they are outside, while others seem to be outside when in fact they are inside" (*De Bapt.*, V:37-8 [PL XLIII, 196]). The important thing, in any case, is not so much to be in the church as to be in salvation.

The church is not a necessary, indispensable, instrument of salvation. Outside the church too there is salvation; Karl Rahner said that the ordinary way of salvation—because it is that of most people—is the non-Christian religions. We recognize the presence of salvation in many men and women throughout history, as individuals and as peoples, who in their lives have groped for God and have given their all in the struggle for the values of the Reign, outside the church, against the church, and even as declared atheists (GS 22; 19; LG 16; 8; 17; AG 7; 9; 11; UR 3).

Outside salvation, however, there is no church. That means, outside the service of the Reign, outside the Good News for the poor, the church of Jesus Christ does not exist. There may be an ecclesiastical institution, the name of Jesus may be used (or misused), but his Spirit will be far from there. What is of the church and what is valid in the church is not of the church or valid simply because it formally belongs to the church, but because it shares in the church's mystery and its life, because it really embodies holiness, which is love, which is liberation, which is salvation. In the church what is not the presence of salvation is not the presence of Jesus, is not "the church of Jesus," is not the church as Jesus wanted it to be.

The church is necessary for the full knowledge of salvation in this world. In Jesus God has revealed in all its fullness the plan of salvation. This enables us to know in faith what so many men and women, as individuals and peoples, strive for but do not come to know.

All this gives us a new attitude, a new spirit, in our relationship with the world. Paul VI said of Vatican II: "A wave of sympathy took it over . . . , a current of affection and admiration went out from the Council to the modern world."[9] It was a spirit of humility, of openness, of dialogue (GS 4; 44; 62; AG 11; ChD 16; 30), of optimism,[10] of recognition of the presence of the Lord in everything good that exists in the world (LG 8; 16; GS 22; AG 7; 9; 11; UR 3; NAe 2), of cooperation with all who fight for the same cause (GS 43; 16; 93; 92; 90; 57; 77; 78; UR 12; AA14; AG 12), of a sort of total ecumenism (see "Macro-Ecumenism", above).

We regard the church as a mystery of communion: communion with the Father, with the Son, through the Spirit (1 John 1:1ff). It is communion with the mother of Jesus, first companion of the journeying of the people of God. It is communion with the saints, with the martyrs, with our sisters and brothers in the faith, with all men and women who have encountered God down through this busy history of the human family.

The Church, the People of God

The new idea of the church that is part of our Latin American spirituality is deeply marked by the new view of the church that emerged from Vatican II, a view that amounts to a "Copernican revolution" in relation to the earlier view of the church. This view starts from the people of God, from being a Christian, this basic equality, and not from hierarchy, having an office, the differences. The deepest significance and essence of the church are not its organization, its apparatus, its legal aspects, its authority, but the community of believers, formed into "a single people" (LG 9).

With Vatican II, we think of the church fundamentally as a community of equals, of believers, of followers of Jesus, in which, compared with this shared, overwhelming dignity, holding this or that office pales into insignificance. With Vatican II, we believe that the local church is the principal embodiment of the church, that the local communities give the universal church its existence, and not the other way round.[11]

Perhaps Karl Rahner was the first to see section 26 of *Lumen Gentium* as "the greatest innovation in conciliar ecclesiology, and a really promising approach for the church of the future." According to this section, "The church of Christ is truly present in all legitimate local congregations of the faithful which, united with their pastors, are themselves called churches in the New Testament." These local churches are the church in its fullness, because the fullness of the church exists where "the faithful are gathered together by the preaching of the gospel of Christ, and the Lord's Supper is celebrated. In these communities, though frequently small or poor, or living far from one another, Christ is present. By virtue of Him the one, holy, catholic and apostolic church gathers together."

The spirit of our church community has expanded into a vast flowering of Christian communities, base communities, from the base of society and from the base of the church, that are participatory, creative and full of new ministries.[12] There is a whole process of renewal, a "journey," to use the expression which the Brazilian church has made famous, of a new way of being the church or, better, a way of being the church to which the whole church is invited.

This new attitude in the church is characterized by a new equality: it is a church of adults, without junior or second-class members, united in communion and participation, structured more horizontally in a circle of sharing than in a vertical pyramid. In this church we all share responsibility, all of us with our individual gifts and tasks, including laypeople and women. We form the church and it forms us; it is simultaneously our mother and our daughter.

We think of the church primarily as local and as such incarnate in time and space, in every people, in every culture, not uniform and not monolithic, in a real sense "this church."[13]

The Saints and Mary

In this new vision of the church, the people of God, on both sides of the total history of salvation—on earth and in heaven—becomes a communion of saints which is closer and more united in the adventure of the Reign. The saints—whether canonized or not—continue the journey with us, as a pilgrimage, at the same time as they wait for us at its end. We do not make distinctions between them either in time or status. St Sebastian and St Romero, for example, are both very much of today. What is important about them and about us is what makes us a "communion," is the Spirit of Jesus and our living as members of the Reign, whether militant or triumphant. The realism of our spirituality can both invoke the saints and "use" and imitate them.

Mary, the mother of Jesus, whom Brazilians commonly call "the saint," and whom all Christians recognize as the first of believers after the Faithful Witness, is popularly invoked in Latin America as a kinswoman from Nazareth and the best "companion" on our journey, who shares the hopes of the poor.[14] Her countless traditional titles, with their wealth of creativity and tenderness—very often a legacy of Iberian, or general Latin, piety[15]—have been increased in Latin America by a plethora of titles deeply rooted in popular affection.

The first, and most Latin American of all of these, is Our Lady of Guadalupe. It is not just a title, but a genuine Marian revelation and revolution. As Puebla put it, "The gospel, fleshed out in our peoples, . . . has brought them together to form the cultural and historical entity known as Latin America. And this identity is glowingly reflected on the mestizo countenance of Mary of Guadalupe, who appeared at the start of the evangelization process" (446). The title belongs not just to Mexico, but to the whole continent—Mary has acquired continental status. She anticipated and challenged the use the conquerors later made of her name and image when they linked massacres with supposed victories of Mary—that so frequent title "Our Lady of Victories"![16] In Tepeyac, by her apparition so imbued with alternative indigenous symbols, Mary disowned the evangelization of the colonizers and heralded the dawn of a new, liberating, Latin American evangelization, and championed the centrality and leadership role of the poor, the laity and women in the church of her Jesus and her America. The Mary of Guadalupe is a pregnant indigenous woman, free from hierarchical prejudices, and a consolation for rejected natives. Ever since then, true Marian devotion in Latin America has had an unchallengeable model to appeal to. From Tepeyac, from that first "image" of a Latin American Mary, via many other images—many of them still imports and attempts at colonization—our theology, our spirituality, our communities have succeeded in finding Our Lady of Liberation, the authentic Mary of the *Magnificat* and Pentecost. We have come "from Mary the Conquistador to Mary the Liberator," for the good of Marian devotion and for the good of an ecumenism based on solidarity.[17]

A Church of the Poor

The church of Jesus must always be a church of the poor because the cause of Jesus is the Reign, which is good news for the poor.[18] The poor occupy a central place in the church: this centrality is the total given by adding together the centrality of love, justice, and human and divine reality.

When we talk of a "church of the poor" we mean that in this church the poor are autonomous, leaders, the central point of reference, with rights and authority,[19] that they are no longer objects in the church. Traditionally the church has joined with the dominant classes to help the poor through its alliance with the rich. What is new about the church of the poor is that the alliance is now directly with the poor: the church welcomes them, lets them take their place in the church, recognizes them as shapers of history in the church. The church undergoes a conversion to the poor.[20]

If the poor are the church, they are no longer a mass, but communities, aware and organized, a people. The "popular church" is obviously not in opposition to the hierarchical church, but to the bourgeois church, the church taken over by the élites who dominate the people. It is a church undergoing a conversion to the people, to their interests, their culture, their cause, giving them a welcome and a leadership role in making history.

The Ecumenical Church

Perhaps nowhere outside Latin America, nowhere even in the Third World, is this new style of church life lived, at least so publicly and very often officially, in its ecumenical dimension. The Christian churches, some churches, are true sisters in the practice of solidarity, in joint institutions, jointly signed statements, important pastoral activities, in committed, popular interpretation of the Bible, in training, in publications, in public demonstrations and everyday work, in the face of persecution and to the point of martyrdom. This new practical ecumenism of the Latin American church has beneficial consequences that we cannot yet foretell for the church throughout the world.

And this ecumenism, without denying its Christian distinctiveness, develops into a macro-ecumenism that crosses the boundaries not only between churches but also between faiths (see "Macro-Ecumenism," above). This attitude, lived with authenticity, and above all in struggles for liberation and human rights,[21] tested in the fire of persecution, exile and martyrdom, has restored to the Latin American church, on the continent and beyond, its title to credibility.

The Bible

This new church life, as we have seen, is rooted and fed theologically, pastorally and historically by the theology of liberation, by the social ministries and by the interpretation of history from the point of view of the poor.[22] In addition, it now has an increasingly strong and coherent—and always ecumenical—base in a liberationist and popular interpretation of the Bible. In Latin America today the Bible, which among Catholics remained for centuries the preserve of the authorities and scholars, and among both Protestants and Catholics very often became infected by "fundamentalism," is becoming popular and committed. The Bible is a people's book and a people's instrument. Fine biblical scholars, organizations and publications are building up a great biblical movement of spirituality and ministry that is leaving its stamp on the new Latin American church.[23]

In addition, in Latin America the Bible has acquired ministers of the church and the people, sealed by the Spirit of God, who spread the gospel as missionaries and even bear the witness of martyrdom. These are the "Delegates of the Word," a ministry first instituted in Choluteca, Honduras, in 1968 which has subsequently spread through Central America and now exists in various forms all over the continent. Today the Bible is really the book of the people of God.

The Church, Judged by the Reign

Our love for the church is a love "for the sake of the Reign," which therefore makes us want to see the church increasingly converted to the Reign. This is what was meant by the phrase *Ecclesia semper reformanda*, the constant reform of a church that is a "chaste prostitute." This is the position of Vatican II (UR 6; see also LG 7; 9; 35; GS 21; 43), but it has not always been held in the churches. Pope Gregory XVI declared, "It is totally absurd and deeply insulting to say that some restoration or regeneration [of the church] is necessary to restore it to its primitive integrity and give it new strength, as if it were thinkable that the church can suffer defect, ignorance, or any other human imperfection" (*Mirari Vos* 10). Mature love of the church must always be critical, especially when the church is dominated by interests other than those of the Reign. We must grow out of any naively triumphalist love of the church, which ignores its historical defects, ancient and modern (GS 19; 36; 43; DH 12). "We ought to be conscious of them, and struggle against them energetically, lest they inflict harm on the spread of the gospel" (GS 43).

A similar critical attitude springs from Christ's love and prophetic role, which all members of the church share through their baptism. Often this critique is also based on "the evangelizing potential of the poor. For the poor challenge the church constantly, summoning it to conversion; and many of the poor incarnate in their lives the evangelical values of solidarity, simplicity, and openness to accepting the gift of God" (Puebla 1147).

Everyday Faithfulness

God's Spirit, especially since God became time and history in Jesus of Nazareth, wants us to live God's present in our human present. Christian spirituality, which is immanently eschatological, and especially the spirituality of liberation, is constantly trying to anticipate, as it lives out its hope, that "full simultaneity of life" (Boethius' *tota simul et perfecta possessio*) which we shall enjoy eternally in God. By faith we know that "every road is a harbor and time is eternity."

The Bible and the liturgy constantly invite us to live a new life, to do things in a new way, in that bold everyday renewal which is conversion: "O that today you would listen to his voice! Do not harden your hearts" (Ps. 95:7-8). In other words, we are holy today, tomorrow and the next day, or we are never holy.

The Second Vatican Council, in chapter 5 of the Constitution on the Church, on the universal call to holiness, describes a type of sanctification bound up with the detail of daily life. When it examines the holiness appropriate to the various states of life (41), in each case it insists on the need to reach holiness, not so much through extraordinary actions and occasional heroic feats, but above all by daily fulfilling our particular responsibilities "in the conditions, occupations or circumstances of [our] lives."

The very fact that we live in time demands that we have this day-to-day realism in achieving our aspirations and meeting our responsibilities. Every day we decide the meaning and fate of our lives: "I am today."[1]

Jesus, whom we seek to follow, did "everything well" (Mark 7:37). The evangelists have recorded in hundreds of sayings and parables the supreme value of little, everyday things. The gospel invites us to live with personal consistency even the smallest details: "You have been trustworthy in a few things, I will put you in charge of many things" (Matt. 25:23). Whoever does one of the least of these commandments and teaches others to do the same will be called great in the Kingdom of heaven (cf Matt. 5:19). "Not one stroke of a letter will pass from the law until all is accomplished" (Matt. 5:18). Even in ordinary things we cannot be ordinary—*in ordinariis non ordinarius*, as the classical tag puts it—and even in ordinary things we must be revolutionary. And Paul tells Christians of all times to make their aim the sanctification of everything we do in the complexity and simplicity of life: "So, whether you eat or drink, or whatever you do, do everything for the glory of God" (1 Cor. 10:31). Our own bodies, our whole everyday lives, have to be worship which is acceptable to God (Rom. 12:1ff), our universal priesthood (1 Pet. 2:4-10).

The spirituality of liberation, in wanting to make its distinctive feature the gospel option for the poor, not only rejoices in God who "looked with favor on the lowliness" of the girl Mary (Luke 1:48), and revealed the secrets of this world to the lowly and uneducated of this world (Luke 10:21), but also tries to become "lowly" by constant fidelity to the little things of every day. This means the often painful, but also battling and hopeful sharing that characterizes the lives of the poor majorities who make up our people. The great causes of liberation are achieved in the little acts of everyday life. This is another of Jesus' lessons: we have to be concerned with great issues, but without ignoring the little ones (cf Matt. 23:23).

Utopia belongs to us, because we are hope and liberation. but utopia only becomes credible when it is built day by day, just as the day-by-day routine only becomes bearable through the power of utopia.

In "Everyday Faithfulness" in Part One, we went into detail about many practical aspects of individual, family and social life that must be part of this faithfulness if the spirituality of liberation is really going to liberate individuals and society. Here, as we develop the Christian aspects of this spirituality, we must recall, on the one hand, the basic demands and potentialities of an authentic human spirituality in Latin America and, on the other, the specific responsibilities and possibilities of a spirituality lived in faith, hope and love.

God's present in our human present requires us to pray every day, without ceasing (1 Thess. 5:16). It would be incomprehensible, and in the end fatal, if Christians, and especially pastoral workers dedicated to liberation, abandoned regular prayer because of the demands of work or the many calls on their commitment. Either we pray every day, to receive every day God's present—God's word, God's forgiveness, God's Spirit—or in the end we lose our own present: personal fulfilment and apostolic mission.

God's present in our human present calls on us to be open every day, with bowels of mercy and justice, to every need, to any cry for help, any demand or struggle, at home, in the street, at work, on the street corner, in the next street or anywhere in the world. We cannot restrict our mercy to the fixed times or the services planned in the pastoral plan or the popular movement. Very often plans and pressure, action and revolution, make us pass by the victim who has fallen by the roadside (Luke 9:29-37).

God's present gradually permeates our human present insofar as we become whole, as persons in our own right, as persons in interpersonal relationships and as persons in society. Christian faithfulness, in the spirituality of liberation—and let us not imagine that this is a task for religious or a First-World luxury—should commit us to fruitful study. Reading and personal study, participation in courses and meetings, not arriving late, paying attention, assimilating for our lives and activity, with a critical gospel spirit, what is offered by the media and political, social and cultural agendas.

God's present asks us, as the church of Jesus that we are, because it is the Father's will (Eph. 1:9-10) and his Son's paschal legacy (John 17:11), to make progress in practical ecumenism in our everyday contacts with other Christian sisters and brothers, in joint activities of different churches, in the liberating push to make ecumenism move faster, which must come down from the level of broad principles and interdenominational congresses to everyday activity. In all this we must not lose heart at the contradictions and even disappointments that go with ecumenical cooperation. We must also be able to distinguish—in ourselves and others—between evangelization and sectarianism, the fervency of witnesses and the frenzy of fanatics.

God's present, for the human society that we are, requires our political commitment to try to achieve social alternatives, the possibility of utopian socialism, the new world order we dream of, in the practical affairs of our locality or field of work or cooperative. The only people who bring about revolution are those who work at it all the time.

In this respect, we Christians, who over the centuries have been criticized, and with good reason, for locating the Reign entirely in eternity, must display a resolute commitment to the gradual establishment of the Reign. Here, as in no other sphere, only unfailing day-by-day faithfulness will give adequate witness to our hope. Eternity gradually becomes the present.[2]

From the word and historical activity of Jesus of Nazareth, we can be sure that we are called, and are, sons and daughters of God (1 John 3:1). This awareness that faith gives us enables us to live the pressures of everyday life with that attitude of spiritual childhood which is at the heart of the gospel: "unless you change and become like children, you will never enter the kingdom of heaven" (Matt. 18:3), with what that great prophet Bishop Sérgio Méndez Arceo called the "unconcerned concern" of the birds and the lilies of the field that Jesus recommended to his disciples: "Do not worry, saying, 'What will we eat?' or 'What will we drink?'" (cf Matt. 6:31-3); "today's trouble is enough for today" (Matt. 6:34). The classical self-surrender into the hands of the Father is fully justified in our world of despair and violence. And the advice of the old spiritual teachers, on the lips of Ignatius Loyola, may help us to combine dialectically the child's trust with the passionate dedication of the activist: "Act as if everything depended on you, but realize that everything depends on God." Or, in verse:

My advice is for me:
Don't try to suffer today
what is in store for you tomorrow.
What you can't get done today
leave for tomorrow
or even, maybe, for yesterday.[3]

The Easter Hope

We believe that we have passed from death to life because we love one another (cf 1 John 3:14). With even greater reason, we believe that Jesus has passed from death to life because he loved all men and women, and gave them the supreme proof by dying for them, dying for us.

Faith in the resurrection of Jesus is the historical and eschatological basis of our faith. He is the teacher and Lord, the truth and the life because he rose after being crucified. But, in addition, faith in the resurrection of the dead, in our own resurrection, is the ultimate ground and daily strength of our hope, the guarantee of our struggles and the final answer to lies, injustice and death.

Paul, the persecuting Pharisee who was converted, was a member of "the security forces of the theocratic state," before he had his self-sufficiency shot from under him by the teacher from Nazareth. He tells us that if Jesus had not risen, and we were not to rise in him and through him, we would be the most stupid of humanity.

The Christian faith is specifically faith in the resurrection of Christ and of everyone, and faith in that total transformation that will bring "the new heaven and the new earth." The testimony of Christians is witness to Easter. The risen Lord, still with his wounds, still open but now glorious, gave his first disciples this mission: "You are witnesses" (Luke 24: 44-9), witnesses to my struggles on earth, witnesses to my death on the cross, witnesses to my resurrection. In the dark nights of life and of history, each of us as a Christian has the mission of the deacon at the Easter vigil, to proclaim Jesus' victory over sin, slavery, and death.

It is hard to find a word that sums up with more force, more subtlety and more hope the Christian faith and the mission of Jesus than this word with its ringing echo of alleluias—Easter.

With the same furious conviction that as revolutionaries we believe in life and the future of history, we Christian revolutionaries believe in the resurrection of Christ, in our resurrection and in our eschatological fulfilment as the people of God. This belief has all the dynamic obscurity of faith, of course, but also all the demanding certainty of hope. The Easter hope is a personal and communal synthesis, for history and transcending history, of the supreme dialectic of life and death.

The churches have quite rightly been criticized throughout history when they have appealed to the resurrection and argued for hope without simultaneously appealing to history and justice. The use of hope, stripped of its incarnation in social and political commitments, would be ample justification for Marx's dismissal of religion in general, and Christianity in particular, as "the opium of the people."

Fortunately, in these last few decades many Christians, individuals and whole communities, and some local churches, have succeeded in combining the purest faith in the resurrection with the most realistic and passionate involvement in liberation struggles. The same has been true of whole ecclesiastical regions and bishops' conferences, in their pastoral letters and statements on social issues. Recent papal social encyclicals have made eloquent appeals, especially John XXIII's *Pacem in Terris*, and in Latin America the decisive documents have been Medellín and Puebla. Perhaps not all Christian activists everywhere—especially when brothers or sisters, groups or communities, have been dramatically isolated or harassed by crises of the struggle—have done it with the necessary openness and balance. This has been particularly hard when the local churches have been hostile to changes in society and the church, and clung to established privilege or a lifeless traditionalism, or when the countless premature deaths, structural injustice, ruthless state violence, the failure of utopias and the apparent victory of the market and arrogance, have tempted them to doubt their hope. Jesus' cry on the cross, "Why have you forsaken me?," has been heard more than once in Latin America, all too sadly justified. A young Colombian's confession, in a confidential letter, "What an effort it is to believe in the Reign!," reflects the depression and exhaustion of so many Latin American activists. And it is true, our hope is "against all hope." Christian hope is not cheerful optimism. It is, all at once, promise, work and waiting. Even the Bible, in its Old Testament, with the promises such as those of the psalms, of success, prosperity and happiness for the just and doom and failure for the godless (see Pss. 1; 3; 7; 9; 10; 11), if not read in the light of the New Testament's cross and resurrection, can produce empty illusions and, in the end, frustration. The rich, the powerful and the oppressors are not always punished or ultimately unsuccessful, nor are the poor or the just happy in life, even the just Jesus of Nazareth.

Nevertheless this is the challenge to our faith and the task for our charity, which can only be sustained and made effective by true Christian hope.

"This is our alternative, death or resurrection." And before that, every day, life and struggle for life, as we cling to time and history, and plant and build, amid risks, looking to the future, facing death. Latin American martyrs by the thousand have already given this witness, first with their faith and action and finally with their blood. And, in the shade and the light (cf Exod. 40:36-8) of this "cloud of witnesses" (Heb. 12:1), our communities continue on their way and multiply, and our peoples organize as they march toward the promised land, and Latin America, the continent of death, is at the same time, the continent of hope.

The only proviso is that all and each one of us remember that "giving an account of our hope" must be translated into everyday attitudes and actions, personal and community, in our families and our work, in prayer and politics, struggle and celebration.

The Seven Marks of the New People

The New People is born of New Women and New Men

1. Critical Clarity

* Deciphers events and structures, by the light of faith and with the use of social, political and economic theories.

* Studies, evaluates, and is dialectical.

* Is not deceived by appearances, promises or charity.

* Can interpret the local, continental and world situation and gets to the foundations of the structures of domination and alienation.

* Walks with its feed on the ground of the real world, with ears keyed to the cry of the poor and the sophisms of the rich, with eyes open to the processes of history and the horizon of utopia.

* Is clearsighted and spreads clarity.

2. Contemplation on the March

* Is constantly open to the mystery of God that is life and love

—in God's Trinity, the perfect community,

—in history, which is also God's Reign,

—and in the universe, which is also God's dwelling place.

* "Bumps into God in the poor," professes God in the practice of justice and charity and celebrates God in individual, family and community prayer.

* Goes on its way entranced by nature, its bride, accompa-

nies all who journey in intercultural exchange and with the tenderness of grace, and loves its people, its land and its time with a heart ecumenically young.

* Dreams, laughs, sings, dances, lives.

* Dresses in symbols and rituals, old and new, preserves subversive memory and engages in alternative creativity.

* Cultivates ethnic-cultural identity, social sensitivity and a political sense of history.

* Instead of a television screen has the eyes of conscience, the wisdom of life and the revelation of the Bible.

3. The Freedom of the Poor

* Stripped of privileges and accumulated wealth, and throwing in its lot with the poor of the earth, it promotes the civilization of humanizing poverty against the civilization of inhuman wealth.

* Is poor in order to be free, and is free in order to spread freedom.

* Shares poverty accepted out of solidarity and fights poverty imposed by injustice.

* Makes freedom its spirit and song, and makes liberation its battle and its victory.

* Is biased like the God of the poor, radical like the Jesus of the beatitudes, and free like the Spirit of Pentecost.

4. Fraternal Solidarity

* Makes solidarity the new name of peace, the new way of putting love into practice, and the new force of politics.

* Welcomes, shares and serves.

* Suffers, becomes enraged, campaigns, celebrates in common.

* Does not discriminate by sex or race or creed or age.

* Because it knows itself to be a child of God, tries to be brother and sister to all.

* Fights to make the different worlds one human world.

* Promotes organization at all levels, but without fanaticism, dogmatism or proselytism.

5. The Cross of Conflict

* Knows that to exist is to be an activist, and that the Reign is taken by violence and that the cross contains life.

* Embraces the saving cross of Christ, but destroys all oppressive crosses.

* Never flees from self-denial for the Reign, or forgets self-control, or shirks companionship, work or liberation.

* Adopts great causes without fear of conflict, despite persecution and even to the point of accepting martyrdom.

6. The Gospel Insurrection

* Fired by the Good News of the gospel and tireless in the building of the Reign, rebels against the mechanisms of profit and weapons, consumerism and cultural domination, fatalism and complicity.

* Is decision, activism, prophecy.

* Fights against all social and religious idols in rebellious fidelity to God and humanity.

* Rises in revolt constantly, out of personal conversion, in a communal and ecumenical renewal of the church, and for the sake of a democratic revolution of society.

7. The Stubborn Easter Hope

* Hopes "against all hope," among disappointments, in the monotony of every day, despite failures and in the face of all the evidence of the triumph of evil.

* Maintains the consistency of the faithful witnesses, spreads the "perfect joy" of the utopians, and organizes the hope of the poor.

* In pleasure and pain, at work and play, in life and death, it keeps being Easter within Easter.

* Advances in the conquest of the promised land, along the roads of the Great Motherland, toward the Greater Motherland.

Constants of the Spirituality of Liberation

1. Spiritual Depth

The spirituality of liberation is a real "spirituality": it consists first and foremost in "living with spirit," and cannot be reduced to outward routines or theoretical interpretations. It operates at the deepest level of our humanity, where we make fundamental choices and draw our primary motivation; this is true for individuals, groups and communities. It is an ethos, an attitude, an energy, something we absorb into our lungs, inspiration, "spirit."

Liberation movements and activities, and the theology of liberation itself, have their root and creditability in something prior to themselves, the rich spiritual experience so obvious in Latin America.

2. Reign-Focus

The spirituality of liberation is a spirituality of the Reign of God. The Reign of God is the cornerstone of the whole structure, because this spirituality regards it as the only absolute. The spirituality of liberation is "Reign-focused."

The spirituality of liberation is marked by the rediscovery in theology of the historical and eschatological character of Jesus' message, the cause of Jesus, that for which he lived, died and rose again. The Reign of God was the real core of his preaching and activity. Because its essence is following Jesus, the spirituality of liberation makes the Reign of God its focus, its mission, and its hope. It understands all Christian life in terms of the Reign.

Because it is Reign-focused , the spirituality of liberation subjects any self-absorbed society to criticism. It also criticizes the church whenever, in its structures, it yields to the temptation of a church-focus that denies the centrality of the Reign. There have been, and still are, in the Christian churches, many spiritualities that are not exactly Reign-focused. The spirituality of liberation believes, however, that the church is the "initial budding forth" of the Kingdom, and is at its service (LG 5).

3. A Spirituality of Christianity's Essence and Universality

Because it is a "Christian" spirituality of liberation, the spirituality of liberation seeks to be a spirituality based on Jesus' own spirit (or Spirit—the *ipsissima intentio Iesu*). It tries to make its primary focus following Jesus and continuing the struggle he waged. It does not give importance to side issues in the Christian universe.

At the same time, as a spirituality "of liberation," it concentrates on what is most universal, urgent and decisive in the human universe: the situation of the poor and their plea for life, for justice, for peace, for freedom, against domination and oppression. No one who does not hear and absorb this central demand of the real world can understand the spirituality of liberation or make it coherent and credible.

The spirituality of liberation is a spirituality for all. It is not just for alleged professionals in spirituality. It is for all Christian women and men, without adjectives, before and during any specific state of life, calling or ministry, because it is focused on "the Christian calling."

4. Rooted

The spirituality of liberation seeks to live the mystery of the incarnation by rooting itself in various dimensions:

* In the real world

Its methodology always starts from the real world, which it tries to understand and interpret to the best of its ability. Its relationships are always marked by this ever-present "realism," and in its action it always also seeks to return to the real world, to act on it and change it. It makes this real world the stuff of the experience of God.

* In history

The spirituality of liberation always examines the "signs of the times," the "moment," the *kairos*, "God's present" and the human present. It pays attention to the current situation. It tries to understand and live out the movements of history.

* In a place: Latin America

It is "the most Latin American spirituality," not because there are no others in Latin America, but because it started there and is the spirituality that most faithfully accepts the identity, the challenges and the hopes of the continent. That is also why it is the spirituality that most forcefully champions the indigenous character and distinctiveness of our peoples and churches.

* In the poor

This spirituality is marked crucially by the poor; it takes up their cause, shares their struggles and raises them to the position of leaders and shapers of society and church. It takes its direction from the option for the poor, from the logic of the majorities. And in the face of every new situation, in order to remain faithful, it asks, "What does the gospel say?" "What will this mean for the poor?" The poor are its "social setting," because they are the most universal and most clear-sighted social setting, because this is the social setting of most Latin Americans and the social setting where the gospel locates salvation.

* In politics

As a consequence of its Reign-focus, the spirituality of liberation is part of an interpretation of the Bible and the church that is also historical and political. It understands human life as a call to build in history the utopia that God revealed to us in Jesus, the Reign.

Beyond all private issues, it opens itself to politics, to geopolitical parameters, to the shaping of human life into national, continental and world society.

It brings with it a concept of "political holiness."

5. Criticism

An heir, at a distance, of the first and second Enlightenments, armed with intellectual "suspicion," hardened in the fire of revolutionary experience and having learned also from the crisis of "real socialism," and, at a distance, from post-modernism, the spirituality of liberation, like the theology of liberation, is innately critical and rejects the pre-critical naivety of idealism and structuralism.

Like the theology of liberation, the spirituality of liberation tries to be always aware of the social setting it occupies, of the game it is being drawn into, wittingly or unwittingly, within the correlation of social forces. Accordingly it examines its premises, and questions the role the church, the institution, faith, religion, play in society and in history, and judges it in the light of the gospel and the movement of the Reign.

It is aware that between the gospel and our faith there are always, inevitably, "mediations," cultural, ideological, hermeneutical.

It knows that there is no such thing as neutrality. To understand is to interpret, and every interpretation is guided by interests. The spirituality of liberation does not claim an impossible "sterile" neutrality, nor is it taken in by those who claim to be neutral. The spirituality of liberation knows that it is an interested party, but for that very reason it examines its interests as part of a new spiritual discipline, trying to make sure that they coincide with the interests of the gospel: liberation for all. It does not claim any other objectivity than that of coinciding with Jesus' objective, or any other neutrality than that which Jesus showed himself to be a passionate supporter of, the neutrality of life, of which he made himself the Good News for the poor.

6. Action

The primacy of action over any merely speculative or abstract schema, so characteristic of modern thought, also characterizes the spirituality of liberation. Its ultimate objective is that the Reign may come, that is, the gradual transformation of all history, by means of integrated activity, so that it gradually becomes the utopia that God himself wants.

More important than the influence of modern thought, for the spirituality of liberation, action is a family inheritance, from the ancient liberating actions of God and the demands of the Old Testament prophets, to the actions of the martyrs and activists of Latin America today, all refracted through the whole life of Jesus of Nazareth.

Injustice conceals truth and produces untruth. Christian truth "is produced" in charity. Following Jesus means "producing Jesus."

7. Wholeness: without Dichotomies or Reductions.

The spirituality of liberation treats reality as dialectical and therefore one and whole. That means:

* It is not divided vertically: into natural and supernatural, material and spiritual, secular history and sacred history;

* It is not divided horizontally: into this world and the next, time and eternity, history and eschatology;

* It is not divided anthropologically: into individual and society, person and community, inner and outer, private and public, religious and political, personal conversion versus structural change.

* It is not transcendentalist, but is transcendent; it is not immanentist, but does accept and live commitment in immanence. The dimension of transcendence makes it "transparency" in immanence.

* Nor is it spiritualist, believing in a God without a Reign, nor materialist, believing in a Reign without God. It lives the integrated synthesis that Jesus lived and revealed to us: for the God of the Reign and the Reign of God.

Epilogue

Destination Known

Inspired by reading the preceding pages, I should like to go back to Pedro Casaldáliga's first word (pro-logue).

There he recalled the figure of a great mystic who also had the gift of poetry, and was able to describe to us in language of great beauty the toils, the anxieties and the joys of the ascent of Mount Carmel. Though free like all mystics, and also with the freedom of all true poets, he nonetheless submitted, for our benefit, to the steady course of explanation and instruction. "Declaration," he calls it, as we are reminded by his disciple and fellow poet, Pedro Casaldáliga. And yet he cannot avoid telling us in the end that; "For the just there is no law," and that all he could do was to share the experience of the God who gave comfort to his soul.

This is the experience and activity of many Christians in Latin America. While they may not reach the heights of eloquence of a John of the Cross, there is nonetheless great beauty in the way in which, with words and gestures, they communicate their experience of God. It is an experience of the God of life in the midst of a situation marked by despoliation and premature death, the dark night of injustice through which the people of Latin America are passing.

This night is especially dark for those Christians who believe that the poverty present among us is contrary to the will of God, and that solidarity with the poor and the struggle for justice are inescapable demands on Christians. This renders them liable to persecution and even suspicion as regards their fidelity to the church in which they were born, with which they enjoy communion and whose proclamation of the Reign they take as the basis for understanding the situation of our continent.

For all these reasons the testimony of John of the Cross may help us to understand better the spiritual journey undertaken by many in Latin America. But what can there be of interest to us in the saint of the Ascent of Mount Carmel, of the nights and purifications, of betrothals with God, that seem so remote from daily life? What interest can we find in the mystic for whom issues such as social justice seem strange, who never discussed or quoted Luke 4:16 or Matthew 25:31, texts so important in the lives of Christians in Latin America and in our reflection? What can there be of interest to us in this great and admirable Christian who nevertheless seems so remote from our concerns?

Better Indies

It is tempting and attractive to play at might-have-beens. We could, for example, imagine John of the Cross in Mexico (where he was due to go, sent into a sort of exile), living his faith in a continent that in previous decades had lost a large part of its population. Nonetheless, the saint, with his health ruined and aware of his meagre energy, finally turned down the appointment. He wrote to the friar in charge of the project, "that the idea of the Indies had already come apart, and he had come to Peñuela (where he died soon afterwards) to embark for other and better Indies . . . that the true Indies were these others and so rich in eternal treasures." How would the Carmelite mystic have lived his experience of God in Mexico?

It would also be tempting, and rather more serious, to recall his experience of family poverty, and the persecution he suffered for his reforming zeal. Perhaps this is where we might find a bridge, something to make a connection between him and us in Latin America. We could also poke around in his writings and turn up texts like the one in which he denounces the satisfied, those who are revolted by the poor, which, the saint says, is contrary to the will of God.

But, to be honest, I don't think that these things represent the greatest relevance of John of the Cross for the present situation of Latin America. I think we have to look for this in a different area, not because these things are not important, but because it is not exactly here that his witness and work are relevant to us.

There are people who are universal by the extent of their knowledge, through the immediate influence they had in their time, or through the diversity and number of their disciples. But there are also people who are universal by virtue of the intensity of their life and reflection; rather than travelling the earth with their ideas, they go to its core and thus reach a position equidistant from everything that happens on the surface. John of the Cross is one of these, universal by being singular, possessing concrete universality, as Hegel would say. If this is so, if John of the Cross is a universal man for these reasons, he ought not to be alien to what is happening in Latin America today. And he is not.

In Latin America today we ask ourselves an agonizing question: How do we tell the poor, the oppressed, the insignificant, "God loves you"? In practice, the everyday life of the poor seems to be the result of the negation of love. The absence of love is, seen through faith, in the last resort the cause of social injustice. The question how we are to say to the poor, "God loves you," is much broader than our capacity to answer it. Its breadth, to use one of John of the Cross's most-used words, makes our answers very small. But this question is there, inescapable, demanding, insistent. Is not John of the Cross's work a titanic effort to tell us that God loves us? Is it not here, at the very heart of the Christian revelation, that we find what there is of interest to us in Latin America in this witness and work? Was not John of the Cross someone who made a huge effort to tell us that when everything comes to an end, our "care" will be left "forgotten among the lilies"? Our care about how to tell the poor that God is love?

Gratuitousness

In the witness and work of John of the Cross something deeply biblical appears with great force: the gratuitousness of God's love. But note: there is nothing more demanding than gratuitousness. Duty has a ceiling: it goes to a limit and is satisfied by fulfilling an obligation. This does not happen with the gratuitousness of love, because it has no boundary. When Paul says to Philemon (in that letter that Christians forget so completely), "[I know] that you will do even more than I say," it is an open suggestion of permanent creativity. There is nothing that demands more than love without strings.

John of the Cross has reminded us that to be a believer is to think that God is sufficient. The night of the senses, the spiritual night, should in the end free us from idolatries. Idolatry in the Bible is a risk for every believer. Idolatry means trusting in something or in someone who is not God, giving our lives to what we have made with our own hands. Very often we offer victims to this idol, and for that reason the prophets make a close connection between idolatry and murder.

St John of the Cross helps us to discover a faith that is not based on idols, on mediations that obscure God. This is why the biblical figure of Job is so important to him. It is not strange that he should call him a prophet. He is right: he was. A study of the language of the book of Job shows it to be much closer to the prophetic books than to the Wisdom writings. In a situation of extreme marginalization and poverty, Job finds the appropriate language to talk about God: the language of gratuitousness. The great message of the book of Job is this: God's gratuitous love is at the beginning of all things and gives meaning to everything. It is God who makes it rain in the desert, where nobody lives, simply because he likes to see it rain. The book of Job does not give us a reason for suffering; it gives us a framework in which to live it and to begin to understand it. In this connection our saint's interest in another biblical figure, Jonah, is also important. The gratuitousness of God's love leads to a pardon which the nationalist Jew Jonah is unwilling to accept.

In Latin America we are convinced that our greatest problem with regard to belief is not rejection of God, but idolatry. The danger for the believer is treating power and money as idols; this idolatry of power and money is always, seen through faith, the reason for poverty, destitution and injustice. We must not forget that Latin America is the only continent which is at the same time Christian and poor. In this fact there is something that is not working properly: the same people who proclaim their faith in the God of Jesus forget or rob the immense majority of the population.

We are also convinced, and John of the Cross helps us to understand this, that in the process of liberation we can create, manufacture, our own idols. For example, the idol of justice. It seems strange to speak in this way, but justice can become an idol if it is not placed in the context of gratuitousness, if there is no friendship with poor people or daily commitment to them. Gratuitousness provides a context for justice, and gives meaning to history. Social justice (however important it may be, and it is) can also be an idol, and we have to purify ourselves from it in order to declare clearly that God alone suffices, and in this way give justice too the fullness of its meaning.

Equally, the poor to whom we wish to commit ourselves, with whom we wish to be in solidarity, can also become an idol. One example of this is the idealization of the poor some people engage in in Latin America, as if they had to demonstrate to themselves and to others that all poor people are good, generous and religious and for that reason we have to be committed to them. In fact, the poor are human beings touched by sin and grace like all other human beings: idealizing the poor does not lead to their liberation. The reason for our commitment to the poor is not that the poor are necessarily good, but that God is good. As is only to be expected, among the poor we find all sorts. The poor and poverty can turn into a subtle thread that binds us to a type of idolatry. Here John of the Cross's striving to overthrow everything that does not leave God and God alone distinct is important.

I am not talking just about the idols of money and power, but also about those who are in solidarity with the poor and can themselves also manufacture other idols. Not only this—and here I want to express myself carefully because this is something I feel very strongly—: our own theology, the theology we are trying to construct in Latin America out of the suffering and hope that makes up the life of our people, can be another idol. It can also become separated from the realities that gave it life and become, for example, a fashion in the universal church. The authors of the best-known works of this theological position appear as the representatives of the Latin American church that is trying to be committed to the poor. But this is not necessarily the case. The deepest experiences are expressed by the Christians of our poor and mistreated people. They are anonymous for the media and for many in the universal church, but not for God. They live day by day their commitment to the most insignificant and weakest people in our countries. Here too I think there is a danger of idolatry: even our own reflection on faith, honest though it be, can become a hindrance. And once more John of the Cross, with the scalpel of his experience and his poetry, cuts out what is infected, what clouds our vision of God. That is why he is important to us.

To end this point—for me the most important— I should like to recall a line from Luis Espinal, who was murdered in Bolivia: "Lord of night and emptiness, we want to be able to snuggle down confidently in your soft lap, with the trust of children." This is our final goal in what we call the liberation process. We have always thought of it like this.

The Journey

This is a theme particularly vivid and eloquent in St John of the Cross. It is also a rich biblical image. The journey implies time and history, and this time and history are present in John of the Cross in such a special way that they can go unnoticed. The title of a novel by Manuel Scorza, a Peruvian writer, is a good description of the feeling we have when we read him: "the motionless dance." There is something of this in John of the Cross. There is movement, a change of position, advance, and yet we are in the same place. There is a very great mobility and a sense of history and time that is very deep, and at the same time a rootedness in God. He naturally appeals very often to the Jewish people's great faith experience, the exodus, as he might also have referred to that very unusual term in the Acts of the Apostles, unique in the New Testament, "the way," used to refer to the church and the Christian faith. In the Bible, in that book of theological reflection on the exodus which we know as Deuteronomy, we are given the answer to an apparently trivial question which we Christians sometimes ignore, but which preoccupied the Jews. Why forty years? The event took place between Egypt and Palestine, a short distance.

I will ignore the symbolic explanations. Deuteronomy gives an explanation: it was for the sake of a twofold knowledge, so that the people should get to know their God, and so that—in anthropomorphic terms—God should get to know his people. This is the reason for the long crossing. Deuteronomy, chapter 8, explains to us that this double acquaintanceship took place on the journey. This is also, I think, what we find in John of the Cross. On this journey there is a double acquaintanceship: as he says, the point of the departure is the arrival. We do not leave to go on a journey, we go on a journey to get somewhere; we leave to go to another place. This acquaintanceship takes place in a dialogue with God.

We in Latin America try to understand the process of liberation as a journey not only to social and political liberation (which is crucial), but also, and above all, toward full friendship with God and among each other. This again is what we mean by the phrase "the preferential option for the poor": this is the way, and I think it implies time. The preference cannot be understood outside the context of the universality of God's love: no person is excluded from that love, but the poor and oppressed have a privileged place. To prefer means that something comes first, that it comes before other things. The preference for the poor presupposes the background of universality, and this preference has an ultimate justification: "the God of Jesus Christ." It is not our social analysis or our human compassion, or our direct experience of the poor; they are valid and important reasons, of course, but they are not the final reason. Ultimately the option for the poor is a theocentric one, a life focused on God. That was John of the Cross's goal.

In addition, in one of his writings John of the Cross reminds us of a fundamental biblical datum: love of neighbor grows in proportion to love of God, and vice versa. This is not something static; it is a process. At the root of the experience of commitment to the poor which many Christians in Latin America have is a very deep desire to meet God in that Pauline face-to-face encounter that John of the Cross rightly applies to Job, to whom God speaks personally to reveal to him the gratuitousness of his love.

Freedom

The famous phrase, "This way there is no path," does not denote the easiest section of the ascent of the mountain, but the most difficult. Hitherto we have been able to follow markings; from this point we have to continue creatively and with determination. John of the Cross lived out this freedom when he chose to be a Discalced Carmelite, when he refused to give way to the pressures to abandon that state, when he escaped from prison. We can call this freedom, but this attitude could be given a different name, stubbornness. John was famed for his stubbornness, like all the saints (which does not mean that all obstinate people are saints . . .). It is a spiritual attitude: "where the Spirit is, there is freedom," in St Paul's famous phrase.

In Latin America we think of freedom as the goal of liberation. Liberation is not our end; it is a process, it is a people's journey, not the destination. We have discovered in the same way during this time that this journey to freedom is not something marked out in advance. The biblical image of the desert that John of the Cross uses is there to tell us that there is no route traced out, either in the desert or in the sea. Among us, in the same way, this journey of liberation to freedom presupposes creativity, making our path, creating our route. "Free to love," is a phrase we use frequently to describe our way of understanding what it means to be Christians; it is inspired by Paul's letter to the Galatians (cf 5:1, 13). No one takes my life from me, "but I lay it down of my own accord," says Jesus (John 10:18) in an extraordinary expression of freedom. This is the freedom we are interested in and that is why John of the Cross, like every spiritual person, is a free person and therefore very often so dangerous. This is what many of his contemporaries felt about him. This is how many

Christians are seen in Latin America.

Joy

"Delight" would be St John of the Cross's word. Delight is very clearly present in the songs, in the Spiritual Canticle, in which the image of love in the human couple, the deep experience of happiness, enables him to speak of the delight of meeting the Lord. At the same time this is a joy experienced in the midst of difficulty, climbing a mountainside in the midst of suffering. I believe that Juan de Yepes' experience of poverty, having been poor, must have left him with a deep sense of pain. What the poor experience is being insignificant and excluded. Seeing his mother beg, begging himself, these were very deep experiences; our contact today with the poor shows us that their lives are left with a stamp, not of sadness, but certainly of deep pain, and that is why, more than others, they value any reason for happiness. John of the Cross's experience of prison, when he even feared he would lose his life, also forms part of this suffering; as a result, his delight is, to put it in Christian terms, paschal, at suffering overcome, at the transition to happiness. I would say that today in Latin America there is no way of being close to the poor without sharing their pain and their reasons for happiness. As Christians we feel that we are loved by God, and this is the well-spring of our joy.

But, as I said a moment ago, suffering does not necessarily mean sadness. I learned this from a person who said in a Christian community: "It is possible to suffer and be happy; what is not possible is to be sad and to be happy. That cannot be." She was quite right. Sadness is a turning-in on oneself situated on the edge of bitterness; suffering, on the other hand, can create a space of solitude and personal deepening in us. Solitude is another important theme in John of the Cross, solitude as a condition of authentic communion. After all, Jesus' cry, "My God, my God, why have you abandoned me?" was uttered on the eve of the greatest communion in history, that of the resurrection, of life conquering death. Solitude is, then, a condition of communion. John of the Cross and many people in Latin America know this very well.

Language

John of the Cross states that he is trying to get inside the subjects he deals with on the basis of experience and science, but above all, as he delightfully puts it, by "cuddling up to Scripture." The result is poetry in verse or prose. Poetry is beyond doubt the greatest human gift that a person can receive. How can we talk about love without poetry? Love is what has always inspired poetry. We, from a continent marked by unjust and premature death, also think that experience is a condition for being able to talk about God and say to the poor, "God loves you." The experience is the experience of the mystery of God.

I have always been amazed by those philosophers and theologians who talk about what God thinks and wants as though they had breakfast with God every day. . . . John of the Cross reminds us, on the contrary, that this is not possible. We can only talk about God and his love with great respect, mindful of what Thomas Aquinas said: "What we do not know about God is more than what we know about him." Without being able to understand things well, but convinced that he had a duty to love, a Peruvian poet and dear friend, Gonzalo Rose, said, "Why have I been forced to love the rose and justice?" Nonetheless, this is our calling in Latin America, to love justice and beauty. God is the source of both. Our language about God, that is, our theology, must take into account these two aspects: it must be prophetic and contemplative at the same time.

This is the language we find in Job when he speaks to God from the "dunghill," as John of the Cross says, using a vivid and exact translation of the Hebrew term (unfortunately, more recent translations soften the word). Here, from the dunghill, from what is outside the city, from what is excluded, there arises, as in Latin America, a new language about God. Latin America is a continent in which there is a people with a rich religious experience. Out of that experience, even if we do not call it mystical, the poor of our continent show a deep sense of God. This experience is not in contradiction with their poverty or their suffering. I think it is also a continent in which there is much holiness, generous and anonymous self-sacrifice. Many people live in extremely difficult areas at the risk of their lives.

A couple of years ago in my country a Good Shepherd sister, María Augusta Rivas, was killed. They called her "Aguchita"; she was a woman of seventy. Shortly before going to work in the place where she was murdered, which was playfully called La Florida, she wrote a letter in which she said: "I want to go and work with the poor of La Florida because I do not want to appear before the Lord with empty hands." If she appeared with full hands, it was because she believed in her humility that they were empty. There are many cases like this here.

To end this after-word, this epilogue, I should like to say that there is something that is felt with great intensity nowadays in Latin America, the value of life. Ignacio Ellacuría often used to say, "Here in El Salvador life is worth nothing." He was wrong. His own legacy refutes his statement. The lives of the Salvadoreans must have been worth a great deal for him and his companions to have stayed in El Salvador. They were people of high intellectual level and at the same time committed to that country at the risk of their lives: the lives of the Salvadoreans must have meant a great deal for them to have done that.

I am ever more convinced that death is not the last word of history, but life. That is why Christian celebrations are always a mocking of death: "Death, where is your victory?" Every feast is an Easter. Perhaps that is why in the Hispanic tradition we call all feasts Easter. We are the only people in the world who say "Happy Easter," at Christmas (and Epiphany), and in the past Pentecost was also an Easter. Every Christian feast is an Easter because we celebrate the conquering of death.

We Christians have to say with Bartolomé de Las Casas: "the tiniest and most forgotten creature is fresh and alive in God's memory." This fresh memory and life is what enables many poor people in Latin America to hold their hope high. Many among us can say with that other great Peruvian poet, César Vallejo, "All I have to express my life is my death." This is the situation of many Christians in Latin America, and that is why John of the Cross, the poet of the nights, of solitude, of the journey, of the encounter with God, is no stranger to us.

Gustavo Gutiérrez

Notes

Introduction: Spirit and Spirituality

1. J. Comblin, *Antropologia cristã* (Petrópolis, 1985). Eng. trans. *Retrieving the Human: A Christian Anthropology* (Maryknoll, N.Y., 1990; *Being Human: A Christian Anthropology*: Tunbridge Wells, 1990), pp. 58-60.
2. Cf. X. Zubiri, *El hombre y Dios* (Madrid, 3d ed. 1985), p. 40.
3. S. Galilea, *El camino de la espiritualidad* (Bogotá, 2d ed. 1985).
4. Cf. C. Boff, *Teología de lo político* (Salamanca, 1980), pp. 295ff.
5. There is a section devoted to "Macro-Ecumenism" in part Two.
6. There are many different spirits, as evidenced by book titles such as *The Spirit of Democratic Capitalism*, by Michael Novak, and *The Protestant Ethic and the Spirit of Capitalism*, by M. Weber.
7. See Paul Tillich, *La dimensión perdida* (Bilbao, 1970) on the anthropological dimension of "Depth" and its religious significance.
8. "There is no reason for the Christian to reduce [the concept of spirituality] to the context of Christianity": H. Urs von Balthasar, "The Gospel as Norm and test of all Spirituality in the Church," *Concilium* vol. 9, no. 1, Nov. 1965, p. 5. In the same issue, A. M. Besmard comments more fully: "Let us openly acknowledge that not only non-Christian but also non-believing systems of spirituality can and do exist." "Tendencies of Contemporary Spirituality," p. 16.
9. J. M. Vigil, "¿Qué es la religiosidad?," in *Plan de pastoral prematrimonial* (Santander, 1988), pp. 179-85.
10. Cf. J. L. Segundo, "Revelation, Faith, Signs of the Times," in *Mysterium Liberationis* (Maryknoll, N.Y., 1993), pp. 328-49. (Eng. trans. of *Mysterium Liberationis*, 2 vols (Madrid, 1991).
11. Vigil, "¿Qué es la religiosidad?," p. 187.
12. *Confessions of St Augustine*, Book III, 6, 4.
13. K. Rahner, *Hearers of the Word* (London and New York, 1967).
14. See, e.g., F. Garrigou-Lagrange, *Perfection chrétienne et*

contemplation (Paris, 1930); A. Tanquerey, *Précis de théologie ascétique et mystique* (Paris, 1932). Both refer to to the view of Thomas Aquinas that Christian moral virtues are "infused" and not to be confused with the highest moral virtues described by the philosphers.

15. See J. Comblin, *The Holy Spirit and Liberation* (Tunbridge Wells and Maryknoll, N.Y., 1989; cf also *idem*, *O tempo d'ação* (Petrópolis, 1982), pp. 35-9.

16. As it is called in P. Casaldáliga, "Missa dos Quilombos" ("Mass of the Runaway Slaves").

17. J. M. Vigil, "La Buena Nueva de la salvación de las religiones indígenas," *Diakonía* 61 (1992), pp. 23-40.

18. L. Boff, *A New Evangelization: Good News to the Poor* (Maryknoll, N.Y., 1992; *Good News to the Poor*: Tunbridge Wells, 1992), p. 23.

19. The same distinction is made by J. Sobrino, "Spirituality and the Following of Jesus," in *Mysterium Liberationis*, pp. 677-701.

PART ONE: THE SPIRIT OF LIBERATION

Passion for Reality

1. J. Sobrino, in *Liberación con espíritu* (Santander, 1985), pp. 24ff. Eng. trans. *Spirituality of Liberation* (Maryknoll, N.Y., 1988); "Spiritualidad and the Following of Jesus" (n. 19 above).

2. R. Oliveros, *Liberación y teología*, (Mexico City, 1977), pp. 80-81. R. Muñoz, *Nueva conciencia de la Iglesia en América Latina* (Salamanca, 1974), studies the major Latin American church documents of 1965-70 and concludes that most of them are organized on this principle.

3. C. Boff, *Teología de lo político* (Salamanca, 1980), p. 44.

4. See P. Casaldáliga, "Los rasgos del hombre nuevo," in Various, *Espiritualidad y liberación en América Latina* (San José, 1982), p. 179.

Ethical Indignation

1. R. Muñoz has given a moving account of this "basic spiritual experience" in *The God of Christians* (Tunbridge Wells and Maryknoll, N.Y., 1991), pp. 24-7. We follow his exposition closely here.

2. Vatican II speaks of "a new humanism" (GS 55), which is unifying the world more and more; see also GS 56, 57, 33, 82, 85, 88, 89; NAe 1; PO 7; DH 15; AA 8; LG 28.

3. "People are divided into whether they have or have not made an act of presence in the face of the misery of the world of today": E. Mounier, cited by J. Lois, *Teología de la liberación: Opción por los pobres* (Madrid, 1986), p. 95.

4. I. Ellacuría, *Conversión de la Iglesia al Reino de Dios* (Santander, 1984), p. 105.

5. G. Girardi, "Aspectos geopolíticos de la opción por los pobres," in J. M. Vigil, *Sobre la opción por los pobres* (Managua, 1991), pp. 67-77.

6. J. Pixley and C. Boff, *The Bible, the Church and the Poor* (Tunbridge Wells and Maryknoll, N.Y., 1989), p. 114.

7. L. and C. Boff, *Introducing Liberation Theology* (Maryknoll, N.Y. and Tunbridge Wells, 1987), pp. 10ff.

8. M. Merleau-Ponty, *Humanisme et terreur* (Paris, 1956), p. 13. E. Durkheim's thesis is well known: at the origin of socialism lies a passion: the passion for justice and the redemption of the oppressed—an ethical indignation; the methodology comes second, in support of the initial choice: *Le socialisme. Sa définition. Ses débuts. La doctrine saint-simonienne* (Paris, 1928).

9. See the fine pages by A. Nolan in *Jesus Before Christianity* (London and Maryknoll, N.Y., 1979), pp. 34-6.

10. J.-M. Diez-Alegría defines two types of religion or religiosity: the ontological-cultural and the ethical-prophetic. See *Yo creo en la esperanza* (Bilbao, 1975), pp. 60ff.

Joy and Festival

1. C. Boff, "The Culture of Freedom," in Pixley and Boff, *The Bible, the Church and the Poor*, pp. 215-8.

2. S. Morley, *La civilización maya* (Mexico City, 1987), p. 48. For examples expressed in song, see M. Salinas, "The Church in the Southern Cone," in E. Dussel (ed.), *The Church in Latin America: 1492-1992* (Tunbridge Wells and Maryknoll, N.Y., 1992), pp. 295-309 (TRANS.).

3. See the text in *Agenda Latinoamericana '92*, p. 57.

4. S. Ziegler, *La victoria de los vencidos*, cited in T. Cabestrero, *En Lucha por la paz* (Santander, 1991), p. 46.

An Option for the People

1. Medellín, "Document on the Poverty of the Church," in A. T. Hennelly (ed.), *Liberation Theology: A Documentary History* (Maryknoll, N.Y., 1990), p. 114 (where the phrase is mistranslated—TRANS.). For the Puebla Final Document see J. Eagelson and P. Scharper (eds), *Puebla and Beyond* (Maryknoll, N.Y., 1979; also *Puebla: Evangelization at Present and in the Future of Latin America: Conclusions* (Washington D.C., Slough and London, 1980).

2. V. Codina, "La irrupción de los pobres en la teología contemporánea," in *De la modernidad a la solidaridad* (Lima, 1984); G. Gutiérrez, *The Power of the Poor in History* (Maryknoll, N.Y., 1985); Muñoz, *The God of Christians*, pp. 31ff. See also the "Documento Kairós Centroamericano," nn. 45ff.

3. I. Ellacuría, "Utopia and Prophecy in Latin America," in *Mysterium Liberationis*, pp. 289-328.

4. Medellín, "Justice," 1, in Hennelly, *Liberation Theology*, p. 97. On the political concept of "people," see Various, *Pueblo revolucionario. Pueblo de Dios* (Managua, 1987), pp. 16ff; G. Girardi, *Sandinismo, marxismo, cristianismo* (Managua, 1987), pp. 138-41. Eng. trans. *Faith and Revolution in Nicaragua* (Maryknoll, N.Y., 1989).

5. See Ellacuría, "El auténtico lugar de la Iglesia," in Various, *Desafíos cristianos* (Madrid, 1988), p. 78.

6. H. Assmann, *Practical Theology of Liberation* (London; *Theology for a Nomad Church*: Maryknoll, N.Y., 1975), p. 54.

7. G. Girardi, *La conquista de América, ¿con qué derecho?* (San José, 1988), pp. 12-13; *La conquista permanente* (Managua, 1992).

8. Girardi in J. M. Vigil, *Nicaragua y los teólogos* (Mexico City, 1987), p. 51. This different "viewpoint" of the poor justifies a re-reading of history, which is being undertaken, mainly by all those connected with CEHILA (Commission for the Study of Church History in Latin America) at its various levels.

9. Cf. P. Freire, "Tercer Mundo y Teología," *Perspectivas del Diálogo* 50 (1970), p. 305. 10. Girardi, *La conquista de América*, p. 13.

Solidarity

1. Cf. J. M. Vigil, "Solidaridad, nuevo nombre de la caridad," in *Entre lagos y volcanes* (San José/Managua, 1991), pp. 173-81.

2. M. Jorda, *Juan Alsina, un mártir de hoy* (Santiago, Chile, 1991), p. 232.

3. P. Casaldáliga, "A solidariedade da Libertaçao na América Latina," in Various, *A Solidariedade nas práticas de libertação na América Latina* (São Paulo, 1987), p. 45.

Radical Faithfulness

1. Interview with *Excelsior* of Mexico City, just two weeks before his death. In *Romero, Martyr for Liberation* (London, 1982), p. 76.

Everyday Faithfulness

1. M. de Barrios Souza and J. Caravias, *Teologia da Terra* (Petrópolis, 1987), p. 416.

2. P. Casaldáliga, *El vuelo del Quetzal* (Panama, 1988), pp. 127ff.

3. Casaldáliga, "Los rasgos del hombre nuevo," in Various, *Espiritualidad y liberación* (San José, 1982).

4. P. Evdokimov, cited by Y. Congar, *Entretiens d'automne* (Paris, 1987).

PART TWO: THE LIBERATING SPIRIT OF JESUS CHRIST

Going Back to the Historical Jesus

1. P. Hilgert, *Jesus histórico: ponto da partida da cristologia latinoamericana* (Petrópolis, 1987), p. 62. Describes the evolution of the theme in modern times. Cf also J. Meier, "The Historical Jesus: Rethinking Some Concepts," *Theological Studies* 51 (1992), pp. 222-32.

2. J. Sobrino, *Jesús en América Latina* (San Salvador, 1982), p. 119. Eng. trans. *Jesus in Latin America* (Maryknoll, N.Y., 1987), pp. 55ff.

3. In this attempt to retrieve the true humanity of Jesus, two works by K. Rahner stand out: "Present-day Problems of Christology, in *Theological Writings, I* (London and Baltimore, Md., 1961); "Towards a Theology of the Incarnation," in *Theological Writings, II* (London and Baltimore, Md., 1962).

4. L. Boff, in *La fe en la periferia del mundo* (Santander, 1981), p. 32. Eng. trans. *Faith on the Edge* (San Francisco and London, 1980); J. Sobrino, in *Ibid.*, pp. 121-2; *idem, Cristología desde América Latina* (Mexico City, 1977), p. 9. Eng. trans. *Christology at the Crossroads* (Maryknoll, N.Y., 1978).

5. Sobrino, *Jesús*, p. 102; cf. 122.

6. On the decisive significance of what Jesus did for our Christian life, see K. Rahner, "Bemerkungen zur Bedeutung der Geschichte Jesu für die Katholische Dogmatik," in *Festschrift für H. Schlier* (Freiburg, 1970), pp. 273-83; also Hilgert, *Jesús historico*, p. 62.

7. Hilgert, p. 206.

8. *Ibid.*

9. On these "suspicions," see Sobrino, *Christology*, pp. xi-xiii; also Sobrino, *Jesus the Liberator* (Maryknoll, N.Y. and Tunbridge Wells, 1994), pp. 67-70.

10. A. Nolan, *Jesus Before Christianity* (London and Maryknoll, N.Y., 1979), p. 5.

11. Sobrino, *Jesús*, pp. 100-02.

12. *Ibid.*

13. *Ibid.*, pp. 112-3.

14. *Ibid.*, p. 115.

15. *Ibid.*, p. 116.

16. L. Boff, *Jesucristo el liberador* (Santander, 1980), p. 90. Eng. trans. *Jesus Christ Liberator* (Maryknoll, N.Y., 1982).

17. Cf. Sobrino, *Jesus in Latin America*, pp. 148-58.

The Christian God

1. R. Muñoz, *The God of Christians*; P. Richard *et al.*, *La lucha de los dioses* (San José, 1980). Eng. trans. *The Idols of Death and the God*

of Life (Maryknoll, N.Y., 1983); V. Araya, *El Dios de los pobres* (San José, 2d ed. 1983); "Documento Kairós Centroamericano," nn. 55-60; international "Kairos" document, *The Road to Damascus* (Washington, D.C. and London, 1980), chs. 2, 3.

2. Muñoz, *The God*, pp. 11-14; J. L. Segundo, *Nuestra idea de Dios* (Buenos Aires, 1970). Eng. trans. *Our Idea of God* (Maryknoll, N.Y., 1973); G. Gutiérrez, *El Dios de la Vida* (Lima, 1981); J. Sobrino, "Reflexiones sobre el significado del ateísmo y la idolatría," RLT (1986), pp. 45-81.

3. P. Trigo, "Vida consagrada al Dios de la vida," (Conf. doc. *Enfoque*, La Paz, Jan. 1992), p. 25.

4. Sobrino, *Jesus in Latin America* (Maryknoll, N.Y., 1987), pp. 98-128.

5. *The Road to Damascus*, pp. 11-13.

The Trinity

1. See L. Boff, *Trinity and Society* (Tunbridge Wells and Maryknoll, N.Y., 1988).

2. Cf. B. Forte, *La Trinidad como historia* (Salamanca, 1988).

3. L. Boff, "Trinity," in *Mysterium Liberationis* (Maryknoll, N.Y., 1993), pp. 389-404.

Reign-Focus

1. J. Sobrino, "Central Position of the Reign of God in Liberation Theology," in *Mysterium Liberationis*, pp. 350-88; *idem.*, "Jesus and the Kingdom of God," *Jesus the Liberator*, ch. 4.

2. Sobrino, *Jesus the Liberator*, p. 66.

3. *Ibid.*, pp. 67-8.

4. L. Boff, *Jesucristo el liberador* (Santander, 1980), p. 66n; see also K. Rahner and W. Thüsing, *A New Christology* (London and New York, 1980); J. I. González Faus, *La humanidad nueva. Ensayo teológico* (Barcelona, 1981); E. Schillebeeckx, *Jesus: An Experiment in Christology* (London and New York, 1979).

5. Boff, *La Fe en la perifería del mundo* (Santander, 1981), p. 45. Eng. trans. *Faith on the Edge* (San Francisco and London, 1989), p. 144.

6. Boff, *Testigos de Dios en el corazón del mundo* (Madrid, 1977), p. 281. Eng. trans. *Witnesses to God in the Heart of the World* (Chicago, 1981).

7. Boff, *Jesucristo liberador*, p. 67.

8. A. Nolan, *Jesus Before Christianity* (London and Maryknoll, N.Y., 1979), p. 101.

9. Boff, *Testigos de Dios*, pp. 280ff.

10. A. Pérez, "El Reino de Dios como nombre de un deseo. Ensayo de exégesis ética," *Sal Terrae* 66 (1978), pp. 391-408.

Incarnation

1. G. Gutiérrez, "God's Revelation and Proclamation in History," in *The Power of the Poor in History* (Maryknoll, N.Y. and London, 1983), pp. 3–22.

2. L. Boff, *A New Evangelization* (Maryknoll, N.Y.; *Good News to the Poor*: Tunbridge Wells, 1992), pp. 72-3.

3. Boff, *Pasión de Cristo, Pasión del mundo* (Bogotá, 1978), pp. 117ff. Eng. trans, *Passion of Christ, Passion of the World* (Maryknoll, N.Y., 1987).

4. C. Escudero Freire, *Devolver el evangelio a los pobres. A propósito de Lc 1-2* (Salamanca, 1978).

5. Cf. CLAR, *Experiencia latinoamericana de vida religiosa* (Bogotá, 1979).

6. V. Codina and N. Zevallos, *Vida religiosa. Historia y teología* (Madrid, 1987), pp. 187, 192.

7. P. Seuss (ed.), *Culturas e Evangelização* (São Paulo, 1991); *idem, Queimada e semadura* (Petrópolis, 1982); Various, *La inculturación del evangelio* (Caracas, 1988); J. Comblin, *Teología de la misión* (Buenos Aires), 1974.

8. "Unfaithful to the gospel of the Incarnate Word, we gave you alien culture as a message": Penitential service of the *Missa da Terra sem males. Gaudium et spes* claims that what the church ought to do is what it has done: "For, from the beginning of her history, she has learned to express the message of Christ with the help of the ideas and terminology of various peoples, and has tried to clarify it with the wisdom of philosophers, too" (44).

9. P. Casaldáliga, *Al acecho del Reino* (Mexico City, 1990), pp. 18-19. Eng. trans. *In Pursuit of the Kingdom: Writings 1968-1988* (Maryknoll, N.Y., 1990).

Contemplatives in Liberation

1. L. Boff, "Contemplativus in liberatione," in *Faith on the Edge* (San Francisco and London, 1989), pp. 80-88.

2. Boff, *ibid.*, gives a brief historical survey of the historical evolution of Christian contemplation. On the Platonic-Oriental mystic influence on Christian contemplation, see S. Galilea, "Espiritualidad de la liberación," in *Religiosidad popular y pastoral* (Madrid, 1980), pp. 148ff. On the Catholic-Protestant polemics of the mid-century around the hellenization of Christian mysticism, see L. Bouyer, *Introduction à la vie spirituelle. Manuel de théologie ascétique et mystique* (Paris, 1962).

3. V. Codina, "Aprender a orar desde los pobres," in *De la modernidad a la solidaridad* (Lima, 1984), pp. 221-30.

4. G. Gutiérrez, "Prassi di liberazione e fede cristiana," in R.

Gibellini (ed.), *La nuova frontiera de la teologia in America Latina* (Brescia, 1975), p. 35. Eng. trans. *Frontiers of Theology in Latin America* (Maryknoll, N.Y., 1979).

5. Casaldáliga, *El vuelo del Quetzal*, p. 128.

6. Boff, *La fe en la periferia*, p. 225.

7. H. de Lubac, *Esegesi medievale, I quattro sensi della Scritta* (Rome, 1952), pp. 220-21.

8. *Culturas oprimidas e a evangelização na America Latina.* Working document for 8th inter-church meeting of CEB's (Santa Maria, Brazil, 1991), p. 90.

9. Hilgert, *Jesús histórico*, p. 39. See also J. M. Castillo, *El discernimiento cristiano* (Salamanca, 1984); J. Sobrino, "Following Jesus as Discernment," *Concilium* 114 (1978).

10. St John of the Cross, *The Ascent of Mount Carmel* (various editions), Prologue, 1.

11. Cf. G. Girardi, *La conquista, ¿con qué derecho?* (San José/ Managua, 1988), p. 14.

12. Cf. P. Freire, "Tercer mundo y teología," *Perspectivas del diálogo* 50 (1970), p. 305.

13. Cf. ST 2-2, q. 180, a. 1, 6; A. Tanquerey, *Synopse de théologie ascétique et mystique* (Paris, 1932), p. 885. St Francis of Sales gives a similar definition: "a loving, simple and permanent fixing of the mind on divine things," *Treatise on the Love of God*, I, iv, c. 3.

14. J. Arintero, *La evolución mística* (Madrid, 1952), pp. 112-31.

15. St Teresa of Avila, *The Interior Castle*, fourth dwelling, chs. II and III. Pseudo-Dionysius, *Mystical Theology*, ch. 1, 3.

16. Cf. Bl. Henry Suso, *Little Book of Eternal Wisdom* (London. 1982).

17. L. and C. Boff, *Introducing Liberation Theology*, pp. 55-6.

18. Boff, *La fe en la periferia*, p. 44.

19. Medellín, "Introduction," 6, in A. T. Hennelly (ed.), *Liberation Theology: A Documentary History* (Maryknoll, N.Y., 1990), p. 96, see note 10.

20. Casaldáliga, *El vuelo*, pp. 19-20.

21. P. Teilhard de Chardin, *Le Milieu Divin* (London, 1964), p. 61.

22. L. Boff, *La vida más allá de la muerte* (Bogotá, 1983), p. 67; idem, *Hablemos de la otra vida* (Santander, 1978), p. 78.

23. On the theme of *contemptus mundi*, see R. Bultot, *Doctrine du mépris du monde, en Occident, de S. Ambroise à Innocent III* (Louvain, n.d.).

24. For the current view of the relation between salvation and liberation, see C. and L. Boff, *Libertad y liberación* (Salamanca, 1982), pp. 84-98.

25. L. Boff, *Jesucristo el liberador*, p. 67.

26. E. Mounier, *Sélections de théologie* 50 (1974), p. 177.

Prayer Life

1. H.-M. Enomiya-Lassalle, *Adónde va el hombre?* (Santander, 1982), p. 75.

2. On the differences between Christian prayer and other models of prayer, see Card. J. Ratzinger, *Letter to the Bishops of the Catholic Church on Some Aspects of Christian Meditation*, 15 October 1989.

3. P. Casaldáliga, *El vuelo del Quetzal*, p. 55.

4. Casaldáliga, *Quetzal*, p. 54

5. St Thomas Aquinas defined it as a "simple and affectionate vision of the truth" (*simplex intuitus veritatis*), cf. ST 2-2, q. 180, ad 1 and 6. K. Rahner and H. Vorgrimler describe it as "The tranquil lingering in the presence of God," (*Concise Theological Dictionary*, London & New York, 1965, p. 99).

6. J. Jeremias, *Teología del Nuevo Testamento* (Salamanca, 4th ed., 1990, p. 146. Eng. trans. *New Testament Theology: Proclamation of Jesus* (London and New York, 1977).

7. Cf. C. and L. Boff, *Introducing Liberation Theology*, pp. 2-3.

8. M. J. Ribet, in his *Mystique divine* (Paris, 1879), vol. I, Chap. X, lists the main classifications. Alvárez de Paz lists fifteen; Scaramelli, in his *Direttorio mistico*, distinguishes twelve steps.

9. A. Tanquerey, *Précis de théologie ascétique et mystique* (Paris, 1932), pp. 900-03, sets out the reasons for thinking that there are so few contemplatives, basing himself on the opinions of St John of the Cross and St Teresa of Avila.

10. While on our part we shall not try to stem the tide or set limits to growth in the spirit, we refer readers to the classic work of R. Garrigou-Lagrange, *The Three Ages of the Interior Life*, 2 vols (London, 1947, 1948).

11. Casaldáliga, *Quetzal*, p. 56.

12. G. Gutiérrez, *Teología de la Liberación* (Salamanca, 10th ed., 1984), p. 270; Eng. trans. *A Theology of Liberation* (Maryknoll, N.Y., and London, revised ed., 1988), p. 119.

13. Casaldáliga, *op. cit.*, p. 51.

14. On the misuse of the term "poor," see Casaldáliga, *op. cit.*, p. 51; see also J. Lois, *La opción por los pobres* (Madrid, 1991), pp. 13-16.

15. P. Casaldáliga, "Vivir en estado de Oración. Vivir en estado de Alegría, de Poesía, de Ecología," in E. Bonin (ed.), *Espiritualidad y liberación en América Latina* (San José, 1982), p. 179.

Prophecy

1. Gustavo Gutiérrez gave his book, *We Drink from Our Own Wells* (Maryknoll, N.Y., and Melbourne, 1984) the subtitle "The Spiritual Journey of a People."

2. See the section "Passion for Reality."

3. Produced as a film and video by Verbo Films (São Paulo, 1987) and translated into various languages. The Spanish version is called *Pueblo de Dios en marcha.*

4. See N. Agostini, *Nova evangelização e opção comunitária. Conscientização e movimentos populares* (Petrópolis, 1990).

5. As Karl Rahner called it: cf. P. Imhof and H. Biallowons, *La fe en tiempo de invierno* (Bilbao, 1989), p. 44.

Putting Love into Practice

1. I. Ellacuría, "The Historicity of Christian salvation," *Mysterium Liberationis*, pp. 251-89.

2. L. Boff, "De la espiritualidad de la liberación a la práctica de la liberación," in Various, *Espiritualidad y liberación* (San José, 1982), pp. 49-58; "¿Liberación como teoría o como acción práctica?," *Teología de la liberación. Documentos sobre una polémica* (San José, 3d ed. 1986), pp. 51-4.

3. *Vida Nueva* 1787 (27 Apr. 1991), p. 35.

4. J. Sobrino, *La resurrección de la verdadera Iglesia* (Santander, 1982), pp. 115-6. Eng. trans. *The True Church and the Poor* (Maryknoll, N.Y., and London, 1985). On the introduction of action (praxis) into the concept of evangelization, see Sobrino, pp. 294ff.

Option for the Poor

1. See the anthology produced by J. I. González Faus, *Vicarios de Cristo* (Madrid, 1991).

2. V. Codina, "La irrupción de los pobres en la teología contemporánea: de la teología espiritual a la teología de los pobres," *Misión Abierta* 74 (1981), pp. 683-92, also in *De la modernidad a la solidaridad* (Lima, 1984), pp. 17-33; G. Gutiérrez, *The Power of the Poor in History,* (Maryknoll, N.Y., and London, 1983); "The Irruption of the Poor in Latin America and the Christian Communities of the Common People," in S. Torres and J. Eagleson (eds), *The Challenge of Basic Christian Communities* (Maryknoll, N.Y., 1981), pp. 107-23; L. Boff, *Faith on the Edge* (San Francisco and London, 1989); DEI, *La irrupción de los pobres en la Iglesia* (San José, 1980). This new position of the poor has made a permanent impact on the Latin American church, and the teaching of Medellín was echoed by Puebla (esp. paras 87-90) and Santo Domingo (esp. paras 178-81).

3. G. Gutiérrez, *We Drink from Our Own Wells* (Maryknoll, N.Y., and London, 1984), p. 28.

4. We discussed the relationship between the "merely human" ethical or political inspiration of the option for the poor at the end of the Introduction. See also J. Lois, *Teología de la liberación: opción por los pobres* (Madrid, 1986), pp. 201ff.

5. On the "theologal basis" of the option for the poor see G.

Gutiérrez' beautiful account in *The God of Life* (Maryknoll, N.Y., and London, 1991), esp. pp. 20-32; and L. Boff, *Faith on the Edge*, pp. 80ff.

6. See Pixley and Boff, *The Bible, the Church and the Poor*, p. 113.

7. *Ibid.*, p. 114.

8. L. and C. Boff, *Introducing Liberation Theology*, pp. 55-6.

9. Pixley and Boff, *op. cit.*, pp. 1-13.

10. Cf. J. M. Vigil, "Opción por los pobres, ¿preferencial y no excluyente?", in *Sobre la opción por los pobres* (Managua, 1991), pp. 55-65.

11. Muñoz, *The God of Christians*, pp. 19-23; L. Boff, *Y la Iglesia se hizo pueblo* (Santander, 1986); G. Gutiérrez, *We Drink from Our Own Wells*, pp. 29-32; C. Boff, "The Poor and their Liberative Practices," in *The Bible, The Church and the Poor*, pp. 202-18.

12. I. Ellacuría, "El auténtico lugar social de la Iglesia," in Various, *Desafíos cristianos* (Madrid, 1988), pp. 77-85; "Los pobres, 'lugar teológico' en América Latina," in *Conversión de la Iglesia al Reino de Dios* (Santander, 1984).

13. On the relationship between the option for the poor and a class option and class struggle, cf. G. Girardi, *Amor cristiano y lucha de clases* (Salamanca, 1971); J. Lois, *Teología de la liberación: opción por los pobres* (Madrid, 1986), pp. 267-81, a summary of the views of L. Boff, G. Gutiérrez, J. Sobrino and I. Ellacuría.

14. I. Ellacuría, "Utopia and Prophecy in Latin America," in *Mysterium Liberationis*, pp. 289-328.

15. Casaldáliga, *Quetzal*, pp. 25-6. On this new element, see also Pixley and Boff, *op. cit.*, pp. 117ff.

16. L. Boff, *Passion of Christ, Passion of the World* (Maryknoll, N.Y., 1987), chs VIII, IX.

17. G. Gutiérrez, *We Drink from Our Own Wells*, pp. 44-7. See also A. Nolan, *Spiritual Growth and the Option for the Poor* (London, 1985).

18. J. Sobrino, *Jesus in Latin America* (Maryknoll, N.Y., 1987), p. 64.

19. CLAR, *Experiencia latinoamericana de vida religiosa* (Bogotá, 2d ed. 1979), pp. 81-2.

Cross/Conflict/Martyrdom

1. G. Gutiérrez, *On Job: God-talk and the Suffering of the Innocent* (Maryknoll, N.Y., and London, 1987).

2. J. Jiménez Limón, "Suffering, Death, Cross, and Martyrdom," in *Mysterium Liberationis*, pp. 702-15.

3. On ministry and its spiritual significance, see P. Casaldáliga, *Quetzal*, pp. 165-94. See also the section "Prayer Life."

4. On religious life from a Latin American perspective, see all CLAR's publications, and V. Codina and N. Zevallos, *Vida religiosa:*

historia y teología (Petrópolis, 1987).

5. See C. Bravo, *Jesús, hombre en conflicto* (Santander, 1986). Shortly before his death, in an assessment of his 80-year life, Karl Rahner said, "I would have liked to have had more love and more boldness in my life, especially as regards those who exercise authority in the church," Imhof-Biallowons, *La fe en tiempo de invierno* (Bilbao, 1989), p. 44.

6. J. Comblin, *Retrieving the Human: A Christian Anthropology* (Maryknoll, N.Y.; *Being Human: A Christian Anthropology*, Tunbridge Wells, 1990), pp. 160-92.

7. Homily, 17 February 1980.

8. Homily, 15 June 1979.

9. Homily, 24 June 1979.

10. On conflict in the church, see J. Sobrino, "Unity and Conflict in the Church," in *The True Church and the Poor* (Maryknoll, N.Y., 1984, and London, 1985), pp. 194-227.

11. O. Romero, *A Shepherd's Diary* (Cincinnati, Montreal and London, 1993).

12. On martyrdom, Various, *Praxis de martírio ayer y hoy* (Lima and Bogotá, 1977); Various, *Morir y despertar en Guatemala* (Lima, 1981); CEP, *Signos de vida y fidelidad. Testimonios de la Iglesia en América Latina, 1978-1982* (Lima, 1983); *Concilium* 163 (1983); G. Gutiérrez, *We Drink from Our Own Wells*, pp. 115ff; M. López Fernández, *Mártires del Reino en América Latina,* thesis at the Instituto Superior de Pastoral (Madrid, 1992).

13. Instituto Histórico Centroamericano, *La sangre por el Pueblo* (Managua, 1983). In the absence of an updated edition, many journals and publications give lists, though they are always incomplete. One of the most comprehensive is that in the *Agenda Latinoamericana* for 1992 and 1993, published in nine countries on the continent.

Penance and Liberation

1. Comblin, *Retrieving the Human*, p. 202. Cf. also R. Vidales, *Cristianismo antiburgués* (San José, 1978); J. B. Metz, *Más allá de la religión burguesa* (Salamanca, 1982), p. 71.

2. ST II-II, q. 44, ad 6.

3. L. Boff, *Jesus Christ Liberator*, pp. 67-79.

4. An excellent discussion of the communal celebration of reconciliation with collective absolution is to be found in D. Fernández, *Dios ama y perdona sin condiciones* (Bilbao, 1989).

5. L. Boff, "Spirituality and Politics," in *Faith on the Edge*, pp. 59-107, quotation from p. 90. See also "Political Holiness," above.

6. Teilhard de Chardin, *Le Milieu Divin*, pp. 83-4. Cf. also GS 34.

7. L. Boff, "How to preach the Cross of Jesus Christ Today," in *Passion of Christ, Passion of the World* (Maryknoll, N.Y., 1987), pp. 129-33.

8. P. Casaldáliga, "Maldita sea la cruz" (poem), in *Todavía estas palabras* (Estella, 1989), p. 53.

Macro-Ecumenism

1. L. Boff, *A New Evangelization* (Maryknoll, N.Y.; *Good News to the Poor*: Tunbridge Wells, 1992), pp. 69-70.
2. Y. Congar, "Ecclesia ab Abel," in M. Reding (ed.), *Abhandlungen über Theologie und Kirche* (Düsseldorf, 1952), pp. 79ff; L. Boff, *Testigos de Dios en el corazón del mundo* (Madrid, 1977), p. 34. Eng. trans. *Witnesses of God in the Heart of the World* (Chicago, 1981).
3. P. Casaldáliga, *El vuelo del Quetzal*, pp. 91-2.
4. Boff, *A New Evangelization*, pp. 80-81.
5. L. Boros, *The Moment of Truth* (London and New York, 1968).
6. *Concilio Vaticano II* (Madrid, 1965), p. 816.
7. J. M. Vigil, "Los 'paganos' . . . ¿al infierno? Valor salvífico de las religiones indígenas," *Diakonía* 61 (March 1992), pp. 23-40.

Political Holiness

1. L. Boff, "Spirituality and Politics," *Faith on the Edge*, pp. 59-107, quotation from p. 90.
2. On the need to break out of a version of Christianity that had become the political religion of the bourgeoisie, see J. B. Metz, *The Emergent Church: The Future of Christianity in a Postbourgeois World* (New York and London, 1981) pp. 67-81.
3. "You deal fairly with us, you don't pull fast ones on us," as the Nicaraguan Mass correctly says. See CIIR, *The Nicaraguan Mass* (London, 1986).
4. Cf. L. Boff, "Contemplativus in liberatione," in *Faith on the Edge* (San Francisco and London, 1980), pp. 80-88. See also the section "Contemplatives in Liberation," above.
5. When we use the term "liberation" we use it in a total sense, just as when we say "redemption" we do not use it in a sense reduced to a socio-economic or psycho-social aspect.
6. J. M. Vigil, *La política de la Iglesia apolítica. Una aportación a la teología política desde la historia* (Valencia, 1975).
7. P. Delooz, "The Social Function of the Canonization of Saints," *Concilium* 129 (1979), pp. 14-24.
8. On the "spirit of working with the people," cf. C. Boff, *Como trabalhar com o povo* (Petrópolis, 1986), pp. 39-50.

A New Way of Being Church

1. I. Ellacuría, *Conversión de la Iglesia al Reino de Dios* (Santander, 1984).
2. On the distinctive features of church life in Latin America, cf.

J. M. Vigil, "Descubrir la originalidad cristiana de la Iglesia latinoamericana," *Sal Terrae* 79 (1991), pp. 629-40.

3. Paul VI, closing speech of the council, in *Concilio Vaticano II* (Madrid, 3d ed. 1966), p. 1028.

4. Y. Congar, "Iglesia y mundo en la perspectiva del Vaticano II," in Congar & Peuchmaurd (eds), *La Iglesia del mundo de hoy, III. Reflexiones y Perspectivas* (Madrid, 1970), p. 40.

5. See J. Sobrino, *The True Church and the Poor*, pp. 253ff; L. Boff, "El Jesús histórico y la Iglesia. ¿Quiso el Jesús prepascal una Iglesia?", *Servir* 63-4 (1976), pp. 263-84.

6. See A. Torres Queiruga, *El diálogo de las religiones* (Santander, 1991).

7. See L. Boff, *A New Evangelization*, pp. 14-19.

8. Boff, *ibid.*, pp. 69-70

9. *Concilio Vaticano II*, pp. 1026-7.

10. *Ibid.*, p. 1027.

11. R. Velasco, *La Iglesia de base* (Madrid, 1991), p. 15; *La Iglesia de Jesús* (Estella, 1992), pp. 239ff.

12. L. Boff, *Ecclesiogenesis. The Base Communities Reinvent the Church* (Maryknoll, N.Y., and London 1986); F. Teixeira, *A gênese das cebs no Brasil. Elementos explicativos* (São Paulo, 1988); A. Parra, *Os ministérios na igreja dos pobres* (Petrópolis, 1991).

13. P. Casaldáliga, *El vuelo del Quetzal*, p. 184.

14. I. Gebara and M. C. Bingemer, *Mary, Mother of God and Mother of the Poor* (Maryknoll, N.Y. and Tunbridge Wells, 1989); J. Pixley, "The Poor Woman Mary Lives Her Life in the Hope of the Poor," Pixley and Boff, *The Bible, the Church and the Poor*, pp. 84-7.

15. Syncretism, the parallels and identification made between Mary and figures from indigenous or Afro-American religions, is a separate subject. See P. Iwashita, *Maria e Iemanjá. Análise de um sincretismo* (São Paulo, 1991).

16. A. Ruiz de Montoya, *Conquista espiritual hecha por los religiosos de la compañía de Jesús en las Provincias de Paraguay, Uruguay y Tape* (Bilbao, 1892), ch. 58; R. Vargas Ugarte, *Historia del culto de María en Iberoamérica y de sus imágenes y sanctuarios más celebrados* (Madrid, 1986).

17. A. González Dorado, *De María conquistadora a María liberadora* (Santander, 1988). On Guadalupe see V. Elizondo, "Maria e os pobres: um modelo de ecumenismo evangelizador," in CEHILA, *A mulher pobre na historia da Igreja latinoamericana* (São Paulo, 1984); E. Hoornaert, *Guadelupe. Evangelización e dominación* (Lima, 1975); J. Lafaye, *Quetzalcoatl y Guadalupe. La formación de la conciencia nacional en México* (Mexico City, 1983); S. Carrillo, *El mensaje teológico de Guadelupe* (Mexico City, 1982); C. Siller, "El método de la evangelización en el Nican Mopohua," *Estudios indígenas* 2 (1981), pp. 275-309.

18. J. Sobrino, "The Church of the Poor: Resurrection of the True Church," *The True Church and the Poor*, pp. 84-124.

19. J. Sobrino, "The 'Doctrinal Authority' of the People of God in Latin America," *Concilium* 176 (1985).

20. L. Boff, *Faith on the Edge; Y la Iglesia se hizo pueblo*.

21. Cf. Human Rights Internet Reporter, *Directory of Human Rights Organizations for Latin America and the Caribbean* (Cambridge, MA, 1990), which lists over a thousand organizations.

22. In the retrieval of the history of the continent from the point of view of the poor, a vital role has been played by CEHILA, the Commission for the Study of the History of the Church in Latin America. See *The Church in Latin America, 1492-1992* (Tunbridge Wells and Maryknoll, N.Y., 1992) - TRANS.

23. Notable scholars include Carlos Mesters, Milton Schwantes, Jorge Pixley, Gilberto Gorgulho, Elsa Tamez, José Severino Croatto, Marcelo Barros, Pablo Richard and Javier Saravia. There are journals such as *Estudos bíblicos* and RIBLA, and collections of popular biblical booklets produced and distributed in various Latin American countries. The *Bibliografia bíblica latinoamericana*, produced annually in São Paulo since 1988, gives the best overview of the vast popular biblical movement in Latin America.

Everyday Faithfulness

1. P. Casaldáliga, *Todavía estas palabras* (Estella, 1989).

2. W. Gruen, *Um tempo chamado hoje* (São Paulo, 6th ed. 1965).

3. P. Casaldáliga, *De una tierra que mana leche y sangre*, forthcoming.

Select Bibliography

Betto, Frei. "La oración, una exigencia también política." Various. *Espiritualidad de la liberación.* (*Cuadernos de Noticias Obreras*, Madrid, Sept. 1985), pp. 47-50.

Boff, Leonardo. "Contemplativus in liberatione." *Christus* 529 (1979), pp. 64-8.

———. "Contemplatives in Liberation." *Faith on the Edge.* San Francisco: Harper; London: SPCK, 1989.

———. *La experiencis de Dios.* Bogotá: Indo-American Press Service, 1977.

———. *Vida segundo o Espíritu.* Petrópolis: Vozes, 4th ed. 1987.

———. *Y la Iglesia se hizo pueblo.* Santander: Sal Terrae, 1986.

Bonnin, E. (ed.). *Espiritualidad y liberación en América Latina.* San José, Costa Rica: DEI, 1982.

Cabarrus, C. *Puestos con el Hijo. Guía para un mes de ejercicios en clave centroamericana.* San Salvador: UCA Editores, 1991.

Cardenal, Ernesto. *Santidad en la revolución.* Salamanca: Sígueme, 1976.

Carrasquilla, F. "Espiritualidad de la evangelización." *Vida Espiritual* (Colombia) 68-9 (1980), pp. 77-89.

Casaldáliga, Pedro. *Al acecho del Reino. Antología de textos 1968-1988.* Madrid: Nueva Utopia and Ediciones Endymión, 1989; Mexico City: Claves Latinoamericanas, 1990. Eng. trans.: *In Pursuit of the Kingdom: Writings 1968-1988.*

Maryknoll, N.Y.: Orbis Books, 1990.

―――. *El vuelo del Quetzal. Espiritualidad en Centroamérica.* Managua: Coordinadora regional Centro-americana O. Romero, 1988, 2d ed. 1989; Bogotá: Maíz Nuestro, 1989; Cuenca (Ecuador): Iglesia de Cuenca, 1989; Mexico City: Centro Ecuménico . . . Mons. Romero, 1989; Caracas: Misioneros Maryknoll/Misioneros Claretianos, 1989.

―――. *Experiencia de Dios y pasión por el pueblo.* Santander: Sal Terrae, 1983.

―――. *Yo creo en la justicia y en la esperanza. El Credo que ha dado sentido a mi vida.* Bilbao: Deslcée de Brouwer, 1976.

Castillo, P. *El seguimiento de Jesús.* Salamanca: Sígueme, 1986.

CLAR. *La vida según el Espíritu de las comunidades religiosas de América Latina.* Bogotá: CLAR, 1973, 4th ed. 1977.

Codina, Victor. "Aprender a orar desde los pobres." Various. *Espiritualidad de la liberación. Cuadernos de Noticias Obreras.* Madrid, Sept. 1985, pp. 42-5.

―――. *Espiritualidad de compromiso con los pobres.* Bogotá: CLAR, 1988.

―――. "La vida según el Espíritu." *Diakonía* 8 (1984), pp. 110-22.

―――. *Seguir a Jesús hoy.* Salamanca: Sígueme, 1986.

Comblin, Jose. *Antropologia cristã.* Petrópolis: Vozes, 1985. Eng. trans.: *Retrieving the Human: A Christian Anthropology.* Maryknoll, N.Y.: Orbis Books; *Being Human: A Christian Anthropology.* Tunbridge Wells: Burns & Oates, 1991.

―――. *A tempo da ação: Ensaio sobre o Espíritu e a história.* Petrópolis: Vozes, 1982.

―――. *La oración de Jesús.* Santander: Sal Terrae, 1977.

―――. *O Espíritu santo e a libertação.* Petrópolis: Vozes, 1987. Eng. trans.: *The Holy Spirit and Liberation.* Tunbridge Wells: Burns & Oates; Maryknoll, N.Y.: Orbis Books, 1989.

Cussianovich, A. *Desde los pobres de la tierra. Perspectivas de vida religiosa.* Lima: CEP, 1975.

David, Bruno. "Espiritualidade e situaçoes políticas." *Grande Sinal* 3 (1989), pp. 261-88; 4 (1989), pp. 413-38.

Diaz Mateos, M. *La vida nueva*. Lima: CEP, 1991.

――――. *El Dios que libera*. Lima: CEP, 1985.

Echegaray, Hugo. "Conocer a Dios es practicar la justicia." *El credo de los pobres*. Lima: CEP, 1982.

Edwards, A. *Seguimiento de Cristo en América Latina*. Lima: CEP, 1987.

Ellacuría, Ignacio and Jon Sobrino (eds). *Mysterium Liberationis. Conceptos fundamentales de la Teología de la Liberación*. 2 vols. Madrid: Trotta, 1990. Eng. trans. (abbreviated, 1 vol.): *Mysterium Liberationis. Fundamental Concepts of Liberation Theology*. Maryknoll, N.Y.: Orbis Books, 1993.

Galilea, Segundo. *Aspectos críticos en la espiritualidad actual*. Bogotá: Indo-American Press Service, 1975.

――――. *El camino de la espiritualidad*. Bogotá: Ediciones Paulinas, 1983, 2d ed. 1985.

――――. *El futuro de nuestro pasado. Ensayo sobre los místicos españoles desde América Latina*. Bogotá: CLAR, 1983.

――――. *Espiritualidad de la liberación*. Bogotá: CLAR, 1979; Santiago (Chile): ISPAJ, 1973.

García, José A. "'Contemplativos en la acción.' Vías de acceso a esta experiencia." Various. *Espiritualidad de la liberación. Cuadernos de Noticias Obreras*. Madrid (Sept. 1985), pp. 61-6.

González Buelta, B. *El Dios oprimido. Hacia una espiritualidad de la inserción*. Santo Domingo: Editora Amigo del Hogar, 1988; Santander: Sal Terrae, 1989.

――――. *Bajar al encuentro con Dios. Vida de oración entre los pobres*. Santo Domingo: Editora Amigo del Hogar, 1988.

González, L. J. *Liberación para el amor. Ensayo de teología espiritual*. Mexico City: CEVHAC, 1985.

Guerre, René. *Espiritualidade do sacerdocte diocesano*. São Paulo: Paulinas, 1987.

Gutiérrez, Gustavo. *Beber en su propio pozo*. Lima: CEP, 1983. Eng. trans.: *We Drink from Our Own Wells: The Spiritual Journey of a People*. (Maryknoll, N.Y.: Orbis Books; London: SCM Press, 1984.

――――. *El Dios de la vida*. Lima: CEP, 1990. Eng. trans.: *The*

God of Life. Maryknoll, N.Y.: Orbis Books; London: SCM Press, 1991.

————. *Hablar de Dios desde el sufrimiento del inocente. Una reflexión sobre el libro de Job*. Lima: CEP, 1986. Eng. trans.: *On Job: God-Talk and the Suffering of the Innocent*. Maryknoll, N.Y.: Orbis Books, 1987.

Libanio, J. B. *Discernimiento espiritual: reflexões teológico-espirituais*. São Paulo: Paulinas, 1977.

———— and M. C. Bingemer. *Escatología cristã*. Petrópolis: Vozes, 1985.

Maccise, C. *Espiritualidad bíblica en Puebla*. Bogotá: Paulinas, 1983.

————. *Nueva espiritualidad en la vida religiosa en América Latina*. Bogotá: Indo-American Press Service, 1977.

Magaña, J. *Seguir al Jesús liberador. Ejercicios espirituales desde la opción por los pobres*. Mexico City: CRT, 1979.

Mesters, Carlos. *A espiritualidade que animou São Paulo*. São Paulo: IETB, 1989.

————. *Flor sem defesa: uma explicação da Biblia a partir do povo*. Petrópolis: Vozes, 1983. Eng. trans.: *Defenseless Flower: A New Reading of the Bible*. Maryknoll, N.Y.: Orbis Books; London: CIIR, 1989.

Moreno, Juan Ramón. "Líneas de espiritualidad según el documento de Puebla." *Diakonía* 14 (1980), pp. 62-73.

Paoli, Arturo. *Diálogo de la liberación*. Buenos Aires, 1970.

————. *La contemplación*. Bogotá: Paulinas, 2d ed. 1984.

————. *Ricerca di una spiritualità per l'uomo d'oggi*. Assisi: Cittadella, 1984.

Richard, Pablo. *La Iglesia de los pobres en Centroamérica*. San José, Costa Rica: DEI, 1982.

Romero, Oscar. *Diario*. San Salvador: Archepiscopate, 1990. Eng. trans.: *A Shepherd's Diary*. Cincinatti, CT: St Anthony's Messenger Press; Montreal: Novalis; London: CIIR, 1993.

Sobrino, Jon. "Espiritualidad y seguimiento de Jesús." *Mysterium liberationis*, II. Madrid: Trotta, 1990, pp. 449-76. Eng. trans. "Spirituality and the Following of Jesus." *Mysterium Liberationis*. Maryknoll, N.Y.: Orbis Books, 1993, pp. 677-701

————. "La experiencia de Dios en la Iglesia de los pobres."

Resurreción de la verdadera Iglesia. Santander: Sal Terrae, 1984, pp. 143-76.

————. "Profile of a Political Holiness." *Concilium* 163 (1983), pp. 18-23.

————. *Liberación con espíritu. Apuntes para una nueva espiritualidad*. Santander: Sal Terrae, 1985. Eng. trans.: *Spirituality of Liberation: Toward Political Holiness*. Maryknoll, N.Y: Orbis Books, 1988.

Seuss, Paulo (ed.). *Queimada e semeadura*. Petrópolis: Vozes, 1988.

Taborda, Francisco. *Sacramentos: praxis y fiesta*. Madrid: Paulinas, 1987.

Various. *Concilium*. Vols. 9 (vol. 9, no. 1, 1965); 19 (vol. 9, no. 2, 1966); 69 (1971); 149 (1979).

————. *Oración cristiana y liberación*. Bilbao: Desclée de Brouwer, 1980.

Vigil, José María (ed.). *El Kairós en Centroamérica*. Managua: Nicarao, 1990.

————. *Entre lagos y volcanes. Práctica teológica en Nicaragua*. San José, Costa Rica: DEI, 1990.

————. "Espiritualidad popular de la revolución." Various. *Pueblo revolucionario, Pueblo de Dios*. Managua: CAV, 1989.

————. "Opción por los pobres, síntesis de espiritualidad." Various. *La opción por los pobres*. Managua: Nicarao; Santander: Sal Terrae, 1990, pp. 129-37.

Zevallos, Noë. *Contemplación y política*. Lima: CEP, 1975.

————. *Espiritualidad del desierto. Espiritualidad de la inserción*. Bogotá: Indo-American Press Service, 1981.

Index

239